FOCUS ON THE FAMILY®

HOUSE OF CARDS

Hope for Gamblers and Their Families

By Tom Raabe
Foreword By Dr. James Dobson

HOUSE OF CARDS

Library of Congress Cataloging-in-Publication Data

Raabe, Tom.
    House of cards : hope for gamblers and their families / Tom Raabe.
        p. cm.
Includes bibliographical references.
    ISBN-10: 1-56179-923-8
    ISBN-13: 978-1-56179-923-7
1. Gambling–United States. 2. Gambling–Religious aspects–Christianity.
      3. Compulsive gamblers–Rehabilitation–United States. I. Title.
    HV6715 .R33 2001
    362.2'5–dc21

                                   2001002597

Cover design: Dale Gehris
Cover photos: PhotoDisc and The Stock Market

Printed in the United States of America

Contents

117501

Acknowledgments

This book would not have been possible without the help of authorities in the field of compulsive gambling, counselors, and financial advisers whose clientele includes those with gambling problems. I want to thank officially those who generously allowed me to interview them for this book. They are: Christopher W. Anderson, Dr. Linda Chamberlain, Tom Coates, Dr. John M. Eades, Eileen Fox, Chaplain Trennis Killian, Rev. John Landrum, Lee LeFebre, Larry Loser, and Randall E. Smith.

Also due thanks are those with gambling problems in their past who permitted me to interview them. Their identities are masked in the book, to protect their anonymity. If their poignant stories influence any readers currently fighting gambling addiction, I hope they'll agree that revisiting the "bad old days" for an hour or so with me was worth any temporary discomfort they may have experienced.

Particular appreciation goes to Ronald A. Reno, of the Focus on the Family staff. Without Ron's exhaustive research into all aspects of the current gambling debate in this country; without his insightful comments on earlier drafts of the manuscript; and without his genial and instant accessibility, writing this book would have been immeasurably more difficult.

Foreword

Gambling destroys. That is the bottom-line conclusion I came to after serving for two years on the National Gambling Impact Study Commission in the late 1990s.

Gambling destroys individuals. It destroys families. It destroys the poor, the young and the old. It destroys the work ethic. And it destroys the fabric and morals of entire communities. Gambling is a cancer eating away at America's soul.

I first became acquainted with the ravages of gambling several years ago when our ministry began receiving dozens—and then hundreds—of phone calls, letters, and e-mails from individuals whose families had been devastated by gambling addiction. I heard from distraught parents in Montana after their son, a college freshman, got hooked on video gambling machines, and wound up in prison for committing crimes to feed his addiction. A South Carolina woman described how she loads her children in the car every Friday afternoon, then drives hundreds of miles to visit her husband who is serving a 10-year sentence for another gambling-inspired crime.

A mother of six wrote to say that her husband was contemplating suicide as a means of escaping monumental gambling debt. I heard also from a woman whose gambling-addicted husband died of a heart attack on a casino floor, leaving her in bankruptcy ... from a Connecticut man separated from his wife of 22 years due to her gambling addiction ... from a 29-year-old church youth worker in California who stole $25,000 from his employer, gambled it away, then found himself in prison ... from a widow in Memphis who went bankrupt after losing tens of thousands at casinos.

At Focus on the Family, we've had the privilege of reaching out to many of these individuals and helping them in some small way. Still, the need is overwhelming. In fact our commission reported that more than 15 million Americans struggle with a gambling problem. Yet, research tells us that only a tiny fraction of these people will ever seek help. This book is for those individuals, but it is also for the spouses, children, parents, friends, neighbors and co-workers touched by a gambling addiction.

Time after time we have heard from these hurting people that they feel alone, that they don't know where to turn for help. This book is an excellent first step. If you have opened these pages because of a loved one's gambling problem, you will quickly discover that you are not alone. You will learn that there is help, and there is hope. Gambling addiction is a powerful adversary, but it can—by God's grace—be overcome.

For those who have not experienced the devastation of gambling personally, this book will be an eye-opener. It describes how this insidious industry entices its victims, and what happens as a result. After reading *House of Cards*, you will thoroughly understand why the $60-billion-a-year gambling racket is such a potent toxin to our national health.

Though gambling continues to ride a tidal wave of popularity, more and more Americans are gradually awakening to its dangers. In many places, churches are leading the way in sounding the alarm. We have seen pastors and other Christians organize successful efforts to keep the scourge of gambling out of their communities. In addition, a number of churches now minister to those decimated by gambling.

Twice before in our history this greed-driven industry has gained a toehold in the United States, and twice before Americans have risen up and resoundingly rejected legalized gambling as a threat to our common welfare. I am convinced that this third wave of gambling will be turned back only if and when the body of Christ unites against this voracious predator.

Sometimes combating this formidable adversary seems an insurmountable challenge. The gambling industry has nearly limitless financial resources and unsurpassed political clout. High-powered casino and lottery marketing campaigns have deceived many into believing that "gaming" is merely "harmless entertainment." Gambling kingpins have bought favor in virtually every state legislature. Their influence in Congress—where they dump multi-millions in campaign contributions each year — is even more staggering.

But we have an even more powerful weapon on our side— the truth. My prayer is that this book will help expose the dark lies of the gambling industry, and bring comfort and help to many of its victims.

—James C. Dobson, Ph.D.

Introduction

It's been called everything from the new national pastime to a "fever" upon the land, from an entity more American than apple pie to a vice that destroys lives. It has been recipient of such malevolent descriptors as "evil," "predatory," and "odious," as well as such uplifting identifiers as "economic savior" and "commercial juggernaut."[1]

It is legalized gambling, and it is more popular and more widespread today than ever before in our nation's 225-year history.

In 1976 Americans toted a relatively minuscule $17.3 billion to gambling venues,[2] but now, a few short decades later, we haul over $700 billion to gambling sites and leave a large chunk of it, $60 billion at least, there.[3] Revenue figures indicate that gamblers lost double the amount of Coca-Cola's sales in 1996.[4] People gamble away more than they spend on books, movies, amusements, and music combined every year—and five times more than they spend on toys[5]—and casinos alone were visited more times than the stadiums and arenas of all four major professional sport leagues combined in 1994.[6] Clearly, gambling has become an extremely popular activity among Americans.

As for its ubiquity—well, where isn't it? Only a few short decades ago, legalized gambling was relegated to one state and the horse and dog tracks of only a handful of others. Now all states but three—Utah, Hawaii, and Tennessee—allow legalized gambling of some sort within their borders. Thirty-seven states plus the District of Columbia offer lotteries; casinos legally operate in twenty-eight states; and you can bet on the horses or the dogs in forty-three. It is now possible to pull slot machine handles or punch electronic video poker machines in restaurants, bars, truck stops, or convenience stores not only while driving through Nevada, but in a host of other states as well. So much has gambling been de-stigmatized that "Monte Carlo nights" are a staple for many charitable fund-raisers and even for after-prom gatherings of high school kids. In short, when the itch to "test your luck" comes over you in twenty-first-century America, you don't have to travel far to scratch it.

At some point, we Americans are going to have to sit up and take notice of this new national obsession and determine what it means for our health, both corporate and individual. We will have to learn "more rather than less, sooner rather than later," to quote a popular presidential saying of the late 1990s, about our nation's gambling "problem." And we will have to deal with its many attendant issues.

But there is a larger issue than merely what gambling does to us as a nation. And that is what it does to us as individuals and as families. For the sad truth of "gambling fever" is that many who catch it end up ruining their lives. Like alcohol or drugs, gambling can become addictive, and many who succumb to its lures put at risk their families, marriages, and financial solvency.

Not a few gamblers, in addition to squandering their finances and destroying their families, end up forfeiting even their lives—indeed, two of every ten gambling addicts attempt suicide.

And some, tragically, are successful. An Oregon man became addicted to that state's lottery and video-poker industry and committed suicide. His mother requested that his death certificate include the phrase "suicide due to the Oregon state lottery." "This is wrong," she said. "It is shameful what our state is doing."[7]

Even more dramatic: a policeman, despondent over gambling losses—he dropped $20,000 into casino coffers earlier in the day—pulled out his service revolver and killed himself at a blackjack table in a Detroit area casino. The casino itself did not shut down in the aftermath, even temporarily, and after a couple hours' cleanup, gamblers were placing bets in the very area the suicide occurred, blood-stained carpet notwithstanding.[8] Countless stories, equally heartbreaking, could be added to these two.

Compulsive gambling is the dark underbelly of our national infatuation with games of chance. It's the side people don't notice when standing on the sidewalk gawking at the fire and smoke spewing from a forty-foot exploding volcano on the Las Vegas Strip, the part they don't think about while waiting in line for their daily Powerball "fix," when popping an extra buck or two into the one-armed bandit on their way to or from the $4.99 buffet—and the element the gambling industry wishes you didn't know about. The fact is, this "harmless pastime," so promoted by the potentates of gaming, is not so harmless after all for millions of Americans. Accompanying our headlong plunge into sanctifying gambling activities across our land is an attendant—and shocking—rise in the rate of problem and compulsive gambling.

This book is written to address these issues, especially this latter one, compulsive and problem gambling. We will devote the brunt of the book to those with gambling problems and their loved ones.

Chapters 1, 2, and 3 will define terms and identify problem and compulsive gambling. They will also explore, among other topics, the two basic types of this disorder: action-seeking gamblers and relief-and-escape gamblers. Chapter 4, then, will lay out the steps one given over to gambling problems will tread on his downward slide into compulsivity. Pathological gambling is an addiction, and like all addictions, it follows a definable and recognizable course. Chapter 5 will deal with recognizing gambling problems, with practical tips spouses and family members can look for in the behavior and emotions of the one they suspect of gambling too much. Chapters 6, 7, and 8 will lay out treatment options, for, as severe as the difficulties problem gamblers encounter, many are able, usually with help, to pull themselves out of this morass. Chapters 9 and 10 will concentrate on two groups experts consider quite vulnerable to gambling problems: youth and elderly. Chapters 11, 12, and 13 discuss the morality and scope of legalized gambling in the United States.

The last chapter will offer rebuttals to the arguments pro-gambling forces use to perpetuate legalized wagering in our land, and will also look at what common American citizens are doing to rebuff this incursion.

One

Compulsive Gamblers: Who They Are, What They Do

Gamblers who can't quit while they're ahead have been with us from time immemorial—since even before the early Romans tipped a chariot wheel on its side to fashion an ersatz game of roulette.[1] Indeed, written three hundred years before Christ, the *Makabharata* details the story of one warrior-prince who, playing a dice game, lost everything from his pearls to his bags of gold to his cattle to his land to his entire kingdom, and still unable to quit, finally put his wife and himself on the betting line, losing that too.[2] Other ancient societies also bear witness to compulsive gamblers within their midst: ancient Egyptians who came under gambling's sway worked in quarries to offset their debts, and the ancient Romans, particularly some of their more infamous emperors—Caligula, Claudius, and Nero—were bitten by the bug,

Nero regularly laying down the equivalent of $50,000 on one dice roll.[3]

Fast-forwarding ahead a millennium or so, soldiers in the Middle Ages were prohibited from purchasing weapons because of their problems with gambling. A 1619 manuscript proclaims that most gamblers begin with small stakes but gradually "rise to great sums; some have played first all their money, then their rings, coach and horses, ... and then such a farm; and at last perhaps a lordship."[4]

The fourth earl of Sandwich, an eighteenth-century English nobleman, was so enamored of gambling that his servants invented a portable meal so he wouldn't have to break away from the gaming table to eat.[5] Fyodor Dostoyevsky wrote some of the best works in Russian literature while mired in the living hell of compulsive gambling. We today are undoubtedly better served by the gambling obsession of these two than they were—the former giving us the sandwich; the latter *Crime and Punishment, The Idiot,* and *The Possessed,* all written to pay off gambling debts,[6] and *The Gambler,* a novella largely regarded yet today as the best case history of the condition, albeit fictionally related.

Some modern victims of gambling are no less famous. Baseball great Pete Rose, pop singer Gladys Knight, TV producer Chet Forte, former pro football owner Leonard Tose, and college football star Art Schlichter are only some of the luminaries that have sacrificed their names—and their bankrolls—at the altar of Lady Luck.

Schlichter's case is very poignant, but sadly, apart from his high profile, not atypical. An all-American quarterback at Ohio State, the fourth overall pick in the 1982 NFL draft, Schlichter was such a straight shooter—no drink, no drugs, no tobacco—that his biography bore the title *Straight Arrow.* He did gamble, though—catastrophically so. He blew a $350,000 signing bonus on sports betting, was suspended by the league for his gambling activities, and eventually ended up in an Indiana jail cell, having stolen $800,000 to sustain his gambling habit.[7]

Lesser-knowns offer stories no less tragic:

* ✤ A Michigan man, home after an unsuccessful trip to Las Vegas, smothered his three small children, shot his pregnant wife, and then killed himself. He was over $500,000 in debt. A suicide note read: "There is nothing more destructive to life than gambling. I wonder why there are government agencies to fight drugs and not gambling. A drug addict destroys his life, a gambler destroys his life and the lives of those he cares about and care about him."[8]

* ✤ A sixty-year-old grandmother, trying to numb the pain of her husband's death, began visiting riverboat casinos in Kansas City. On the one-year anniversary of her husband's passing, she decided to put in some serious time in front of a slot machine. She hit it big several times that night, including one jackpot for $28,000. From that night on, though, her wins only disguised her numerous losses—so many that she blew her husband's life insurance, his $50,000 pension, and her own social security payments. After that she piled up $85,000 in debt on fourteen credit cards and eventually filed for bankruptcy.[9]

* ✤ A successful South Dakota health-care executive lost his career, his savings and retirement, his self-esteem and reputation—and almost his life—to gambling. He also embezzled $670,000 from his company. He sat in his car in a casino parking lot awaiting delivery of a gun he had purchased. "My life was ruined by gambling," he said later. "I didn't see any way out except suicide." The gun never arrived, though, and

the man had a religious experience right there in the car—he believes God spoke to him and assured him of His presence no matter how bad things got. The next day he confessed to his employer, then to his family, and has decided, if he goes to prison, to help other addicts serving time for gambling-related crimes.[10]

If these were mere isolated incidents, it would be tragic enough. But they are not. In fact, they represent a trend. Many, many Americans can tell stories like these, some less dramatic, some equally so. The question now becomes: How many?

PUTTING NUMBERS TO AN OBSESSION

So great is the allure of winning something for nothing that millions of Americans have succumbed to this debilitating and ultimately destructive obsession. Estimates of the number of persons with severe gambling problems in the United States have for years vacillated between 1 and 5 percent of the adult population, depending on whom you asked and which geographical area of the country you asked about. Some of this uncertainty has been laid to rest, however, with the 1999 publication of the final report of the National Gambling Impact Study Commission (NGISC), a congressionally authorized study of the gambling industry, which commissioned two separate studies on problem gamblers in America.

One of these studies, performed by the National Research Council (NRC) of the National Academy of Sciences, estimates that 5.4 percent of the adult population (approximately 10.8 million people) have exhibited gambling problems during their lifetimes, while 2.9 percent (approximately 5.8 million people) meet the criteria for problem gambling during the past twelve months. In the other study, the National Opinion Research Center (NORC) at the University of Chicago randomly interviewed 2,417 adults and 534 adolescents on the telephone and 530 actual patrons in gambling venues. They found that 2.7 percent (about 5.5 million people) admitted to significant gambling problems during their lifetimes while 1.3 percent (about 2.6 million people) had exhibited serious problems during the past twelve months. In addition, the NORC study estimated that more than 15 million Americans were "at risk" of developing gambling problems, based on the lifetime data (5.8 million based on "past year" criteria). This latter group may never develop serious problems with their gambling, but they did exhibit gambling-related problems, albeit only one or two at a time.

The lifetime numbers are the more accurate of the two. Because pathological gambling is a chronic condition, it often reappears after months or even years of abstinence; the "past year" figures would not reflect these individuals. Other considerations also contribute to the relative reliability of the lifetime numbers. But whatever numbers you prefer, they are probably too low. Posits the NGISC report: "The actual prevalence rates may be significantly higher than those reported."[11]

For one simple reason: People with gambling problems are notorious for their dishonesty—they have a lot to cover up and will often go to any lengths to do so. In fact, one of the ten criteria for diagnosing a gambling problem is whether that individual lies about his gambling. That a random telephone survey conducted by an unknown party will elicit truthful responses from individuals who routinely lie to even their spouses, is exceedingly optimistic thinking at best. Says Christopher W. Anderson, past executive director of the Illinois Council on Problem and Compulsive Gambling and a therapist whose Chicago-based business deals exclusively with gambling-related problems: "How in the world can we make an assumption that we're getting anywhere close to an accurate picture with telephone surveys? The prevalence rate—it's going to be grossly underreported, not the other way around."[12]

Whatever the numbers, this much is clear: A lot of people in our society have a problem with gambling. Even random face-to-face and telephone interviews yield a startlingly high number of Americans with gambling problems—approximately one in twenty-five. This figure compares favorably—or unfavorably, as the case may be—with the 6 percent of adult Americans who reportedly abuse alcohol and the 5 percent beset with serious clinical depression. "Problem gambling is as common as many of the most common psychiatric disorders, affecting more than one out of twenty-five, or about eight million adults in the United States."[13]

AND IT'LL ONLY GET WORSE

The proposition that where there is gambling there will be people with gambling problems seems like the sort of wager even the most stalwart Baptist preacher would gladly take. Indeed, the contention that introducing myriad new legalized gambling opportunities, that plopping down dozens of new casinos in the land, increasing the frequency and payouts of state lotteries, and jamming video poker machines in the corner of convenience stores (right next to the ATM), would result in an increase in problem gambling seems to fit what television talk show host John McLaughlin terms "a keen grasp of the obvious."

Or at least one would think so. The promoters of gambling, however, do not see it that way. Frequently they deny any relationship between the availability of gambling and gambling addiction. Sure, there are casinos, they say, and there are compulsive gamblers—but the one bears no relation what-soever to the other. The cause has no effect on the effect.

But testimony from experts and data from gambling com-munities have joined common sense in saying otherwise. Con-sider Las Vegas, where gambling has been blessed with governmental approval since 1931. Suffice it to say that opportunities to gamble in this man-made desert oasis are, well, available—in spades (and hearts and clubs and dia-monds). Virtually every eating and drinking establishment, every convenience store, many supermarkets and Laundro-mats and other commercial enterprises, and even the airport have banks of one-armed bandits. Those prone to compulsive gambling can hardly turn a corner in this town without being enticed by the sirens of the spinning reel.

And the result is what you would expect it to be. Las Vegas is home to fifty-six Gamblers Anonymous (GA) meetings a week—the same number as held in all of Southern California, which boasts twelve times the Nevada city's population.[14] Pre-liminary studies put the percentage of southern Nevadans with gambling problems way above the national norm—from 6 to 9 percent of the adult population.[15] And those closest to the action seem to suffer most: Dr. Robert Hunter, the pre-mier gambling addiction treatment expert in Las Vegas, has put the number of casino workers with compulsive gambling problems at 15 percent.[16] As if it needed to be spelled out, the NGISC study, citing the NORC on-site survey mentioned above, concluded that "the presence of a gambling facility within 50 miles roughly doubles the prevalence of problem and pathological gamblers."[17]

It is also no coincidence that states in other parts of the country, with their headlong plunge into legalized gambling over the past decade, are beginning to tally Vegas-style num-bers in these shameful categories. The NRC's overview of prevalency studies revealed that "some of the greatest increases

in the number of problem and pathological gamblers . . .
came over periods of expanded gambling opportunities in the
states studied."[18]

Some specific examples:

* Iowa has traditionally enjoyed a reputation of being
  very inhospitable to gambling activities. In 1989 only
  1.7 percent of the state's adult population could be
  categorized with serious gambling problems. By 1995,
  however, after casinos were introduced into the state,
  that number had more than tripled, to 5.4 percent.[19]
* On the Mississippi Coast, the number of Gamblers
  Anonymous (GA) meetings has increased by a factor
  of twenty-six (to thirteen a week) since the gambling
  boats first docked in 1992.[20]
* Five years after video poker machines were introduced
  to Oregon, the number of GA chapters had risen
  from three to thirty.[21]
* From 1992, the date Indian casinos were allowed to
  open in Wisconsin, to 1999, the number of cities in
  the state holding GA meetings has gone from six to
  twenty-nine; half of them are held within thirty miles
  of a casino.[22]
* The number of GA meetings in the Chicago area has
  jumped from thirteen a week in 1990 to almost sixty
  in 2000, according to a GA spokesman.[23]

It seems clear that where there is gambling, there will be
gambling addicts. And it seems equally clear that as gambling
spreads, the number of those addicted to it will increase. Writes
Robert Goodman, director of the U.S. Gambling Research
Institute: "As new gambling ventures proliferate and the
appetites of more people are whetted, the number of problem
gamblers will expand."[24] Corroborates the NGISC report: "As

the opportunities for gambling become more commonplace, it appears likely that the number of people who will develop gambling problems will also increase."[25]

COMPULSIVE GAMBLING: WHAT IS IT?

It's time to clarify some terms. We have been somewhat inexact in our terminology thus far, using a variety of words interchangeably to refer to this particular behavior. Social scientists lean toward words like "abuse" and "dependence" to describe it, while laypeople feel more comfortable with "addiction," "compulsion," "obsession," and their cognates. All will be used synonymously in this book. We have also been using "problem gamblers" to describe those whose lives have been negatively affected by their gambling behavior, and "problem gambling" to denote the behavior itself. Social scientists, however, recognize gradations within those exhibiting gambling problems. Such can be placed into three categories: compulsive, or pathological, gamblers; problem gamblers (used as a specific term); and at-risk gamblers.

The most widely accepted tool for recognizing pathological gambling, the most serious of the three, is given in the fourth edition of the American Psychiatric Association's (APA) *Diagnostic and Statistical Manual of Mental Disorders* (*DSM*-IV), published in 1994. (Other reliable diagnostic instruments include the "Twenty Questions" of Gamblers Anonymous and the South Oaks Gambling Screen.) The *DSM*-IV classifies compulsive gambling as an impulse control disorder and lists ten behaviors to guide psychotherapists in their diagnoses. These behaviors include preoccupation, tolerance, withdrawal, escape, lying, loss of control, and risking significant relationships, among others, due to gambling. Again, an accurate diagnosis is usually dependent on gamblers being forthcoming about their behaviors, for, as noted above, gamblers are prone to misrepresent their activities, motivations, and gambling losses. So, a pathological gambler will exhibit—but not necessarily admit to—at least five of the following ten behaviors:

1. Is preoccupied with gambling (i.e., preoccupied with reliving past gambling experiences, handicapping or planning the next venture, or thinking of ways to get money with which to gamble).
2. Needs to gamble with increasing amounts of money in order to achieve the desired excitement.
3. Is restless or irritable when attempting to cut down or stop gambling.
4. Gambles as a way of escaping from problems or relieving dysphoric mood (e.g., feelings of helplessness, guilt, anxiety, or depression).
5. After losing money gambling, often returns another day in order to get even ("chasing one's losses").
6. Lies to family members, therapists, or others to conceal the extent of involvement with gambling.
7. Has made repeated unsuccessful efforts to control, cut back, or stop gambling.
8. Has committed illegal acts (e.g., forgery, fraud, theft, or embezzlement) in order to finance gambling.
9. Has jeopardized or lost a significant relationship, job, or educational or career opportunity because of gambling.
10. Has relied on others to provide money to relieve a desperate financial situation caused by gambling.[26]

Dr. Robert Custer, considered the trailblazer of modern gambling diagnosis and treatment, offers this concise definition: "Compulsive gambling is an addictive illness in which the subject is driven by an overwhelming uncontrollable impulse to gamble. The impulse progresses in intensity and urgency, consuming more and more of the individual's time, energy, and emotional and material resources. Ultimately, it invades, undermines, and often destroys everything that is meaningful in his life."[27]

A problem gambler, meanwhile, a less severe category than the compulsive, or pathological, gambler, is like a pathological gambler but less so. He will exhibit four or fewer of the *DSM*-IV behaviors. Those designated "at risk" will meet one or two of the criteria. Dr. Linda Chamberlain, a licensed clinical psychologist who treats gamblers and has written on the topic, attributes much of the difference between problem and pathological gamblers to the workings of compulsion, the inner drive to gamble. "Problem gamblers spend more than they intended to; they will incur some problems in their relationships because of their gambling. But it stays within certain limits. They start to lose more than they really want to, but stop it, at least temporarily. And usually they exhibit more of a stop-start pattern, where they won't stop altogether, but it does create some problems for them. There seems to be kind of a crossover that happens when people begin to gamble more pathologically, where it becomes much more of that sense of compulsion, that I need to do this, that if I'm not doing this, or anticipating that I get to do this, or have some sense that I'll be able to continue to do this, then it produces a real sense of desperation, depression, anger, irritability."[28]

Adds Eileen Fox, a certified compulsive gambling counselor in Colorado Springs, Colorado: "I think it's the progression. It's just where you are on the continuum. And some people can go back and some people go forward. You can be a problem gambler, and if you get help, you don't necessarily become a lifelong compulsive gambler."[29] Thus problem gamblers may be either on the road toward pathological gambling, meeting more of the criteria and developing a more severe form of the disorder as they go along, or on the road back from pathological gambling, still exhibiting a substantial number of problem behaviors but gradually recovering; or they may simply be people who have and will retain gambling problems in their milder form.[30]

The distinction is analogous to that between problem drinkers and alcoholics. The bare fact that a person drinks to excess on occasion and/or has been arrested for DUI—both criteria in problem drinking evaluation tools—does not *necessarily* mean he's an alcoholic. But DUI and drinking to excess, even on occasion, certainly are problems, for both the drinker and those close to him, regardless of whether the drinker himself meets sufficient criteria for an alcoholism diagnosis. And a problem is, well, a problem, and problems need to be addressed.

It is also possible that any distinction between problem and pathological gambling is eclipsed by the power of the addiction and the speed with which it takes hold. Dr. John M. Eades, a recovering compulsive gambler who is certified as a therapist in gambling addiction and chemical dependency, says the gambling bug can develop so quickly, "sometimes a person's addicted before he really has what we would call problem gambling." He likens it to cocaine. "Cocaine is so fast that a person's a cocaine addict before he really has any major problems from cocaine. In other words, the problems come along with the addiction at the time. It's almost like in the same real-time framework. By the time you know you've got a problem, you're hooked."[31]

In sum, although the line demarcating problem from pathological gambling is blurred and indistinct, in the end the effective result is the same: problems for the gambler and those near him because of his gambling. If the behavior is not arrested, the problem gambler will become a pathological gambler in many cases.

IN SEARCH OF ROOT CAUSES

While all agree that compulsive gambling is all-consuming in its later stages, taking on a life of its own in the gambler, and that its effects are detrimental and often catastrophic to both the gambler and those near him, there is strong disagreement as to this condition's origin. Is it a moral choice with definite moral consequences, a learned behavior deriving from poor judgment, or is it a disease, a distinct and definable psychiatric disorder that emanates from one's biological or mental make-up? Is it, in short, a moral problem or a medical one?

Everybody seems to know the answer, but nobody seems able to prove it—at least to the satisfaction of those who disagree. "Several theories attempt to explain the compulsion to gamble," writes Andy Hjelmeland, "but for each theory, a counter argument seems to exist. So far, the cause has been elusive."[32]

When the APA designated pathological gambling as an impulse control disorder in its 1980 edition of the *Diagnostic and Statistical Manual* (*DSM*-III), it effectively labeled it a disease and prompted its subsequent treatment on the medical model. Thus has the disease model become the preferred paradigm among professional counselors and researchers, including Gamblers Anonymous and the National Council on Compulsive Gambling. Compulsive gambling's precursor and example for diagnosis is alcoholism, and advocates of the disease model are fond of saying the study of pathological gambling is thirty or forty years behind that of alcoholism. Alcohol abuse was largely seen as the exclusive province of the morally craven for centuries and indeed millennia, until two men, Bill Wilson and Robert Smith, met in 1935 and agreed they were powerless in the face of the bottle. They subsequently formed the Alcoholics Anonymous fellowship, and the public mood on the cause of alcohol abuse began to change from one of moral turpitude, or failure, to one of miswiring on the psychological motherboard.[33] By 1956 the American Medical Association had formally endorsed the disease model of alcoholism.

The cause of compulsive gambling may be attributed to psychological, environmental, sociological, and biological factors, either singly or in concert. Whether a person was a victim of "too much" parenting or "too little" parenting; whether the parents themselves suffered from dependence on alcohol, drugs, or gambling; whether the gambler himself is beset with some other addiction, like alcohol or drug dependency, or a mental illness like schizophrenia or ADD; whether the gambler began gambling early on in his life; whether gambling was accepted or even valued in the family or society the child grew up in; whether gambling opportunities are accessible to the gambler—all these and more have been cited as contributors to the onset of compulsive gambling.

Of major interest—and controversy—has been the contention that a genetic link within the gambler has created this disordered behavior. Researchers have recently discovered that pathological gamblers are more likely than others to carry a certain receptor gene that has been linked to other addictive and impulsive disorders. When this gene is in imbalance in a person's body, "the brain may substitute craving and compulsive behavior for satiation,"[34] and this may lead pathological gamblers to behave in a self-destructive manner. Other researchers have focused on serotonin, which is found in the central nervous system, and a by-product of the brain chemical that controls arousal and excitement, called norepinephrine.[35]

Although the NRC acknowledges the accumulation of evidence for the role biology may play in the cause of pathological gambling, it does call for more research before any conclusions can be reached. It may bear noting that gambling interests favor the biology argument because it partially absolves them of complicity in the field of gambling addiction; indeed, they funnel millions of dollars into research designed to uncover biological "causes."[36]

Some, however, doubt that biology is destiny. Citing that there is "no evidence that compulsive gambling is a disease . . . or uncontrollable," Richard E. Vatz and Lee S. Weinberg contend that the disease model is used as a tool to help manufacture sympathy for those with severe gambling problems and, in turn, to help open the wallets of foundations to underwrite research.[37] The contention that compulsive gamblers have no control over their actions also draws Vatz and Weinberg's fire. "It is time for at least some skepticism regarding the unquestioned need for addicts to admit powerlessness over their own behavior. It is worth considering whether such admissions constitute a self-fulfilling prophecy—that is to say, the belief that a habit is uncontrollable actually may discourage people from trying to stop behaving in a self-destructive manner since it is beyond their control."[38]

Other commentators as diverse as Stanton Peele, Charles Sykes, and Wendy Kaminer, while not addressing gambling addiction specifically, are also troubled by the disease model as applied to behaviors. Peele, whose *Diseasing of America* is a book-length refutation of alcoholism-as-a-disease, maintains that "people are *active agents* in—not passive victims of—their addictions."[39] To contend otherwise can "legitimize, reinforce, and excuse the behaviors in question—convincing people, contrary to all evidence, that their behavior is not their own."[40]

Sykes, who devotes a chapter of his *Nation of Victims* to the topic, claims: "Once the language of disease and addiction could be applied to *behavior* rather than merely to biological disorders, almost any aspect of human life could be redefined in medical terms."[41] One need only observe the panoply of often-dubious isms that have entered our vocabularies in the past twenty years to take his point: workaholism, shopaholism, rageaholism, chocoholism, not to mention disease treatments for those afflicted with overworry, overeating, incompetence, forgetfulness, too much TV watching, too much sex, and for those who love them (that is, the spouses and/or adult children of one subjected to any or all of the above). Kaminer, for her part, takes on the self-help, twelve-step recovery model in an amusing work entitled *I'm Dysfunctional, You're Dysfunctional.*[42]

The issue with the disease model for gambling for some Christian thinkers runs along similar lines: It centers on accountability. If some entity other than one's own self-will governs one's actions, it is thought, one is let off the hook for one's sin. Writes Rex M. Rogers, president of Cornerstone University and Grand Rapids Baptist Seminary: "Physiological imbalances and psychological stresses may weaken people's judgment, but such maladies do not cause people to gamble. That's why it seems inappropriate to call compulsive or pathological gambling a disease. This would also undermine the biblical idea of individual responsibility. Gambling is a moral choice with moral consequences. Gambling is learned behavior. It may become habitual, like many other 'besetting sins,' but the Spirit of God provides the power to break any sin."[43]

It is precisely this power to break gambling addiction, which he has seen frequently in his ministry to casino workers and gamblers as chaplain to Mississippi Beach, that prompts Rev. John Landrum to discount the disease model, which he terms "a fabrication of convenience." "We've seen [gambling addiction] broken so quickly," he says, "that there's no withdrawal period . . . for some people. And it just blows away the disease paradigm." Landrum believes the paradigm was put in place after treatment for compulsive gambling was well under way. "Rather than saying, 'Well, here's the disease, how do we treat the disease?' they have been treating it and they said, 'Well, if we treat it this way, then it must be a disease. So let's call it a disease, because all we're doing is teaching people how to cope with it. It's not going to take their lives necessarily, but they're going to have it the rest of their lives because all we've been able to do is teach people how to cope and none of them ever get free. So it must be a disease that they don't get rid of.' I don't put people down for that. I just personally have found a better way to look at it, and I believe God has given us a handle on how to deal with it. And it's not our way, it's His way, and it's been there all the time."[44]

Other Christians, though, are comfortable demoting the will's importance in the operation. Eades believes the sin must be separated from the sickness. "We used to think that when somebody had cancer, they were sinful. Or if they were struck with a terrible disease, ... they had done something wrong or so forth." He does not believe the will is involved in compulsive gambling. "In fact," he says, "a person gambles against their will. Just like the alcoholic drinks against his will. It is not a willful act. You know, to willfully get drunk is a pretty bad thing. We know that scripturally. But an alcoholic has no choice. Once they have that first drink, it takes over. And the same thing with gambling. Once a person becomes a gambling addict, there's no way they can gamble in moderation." Gambling, Eades believes, is a sin, and sinful behavior emanates from the gambling, but the gambling addiction is not sin—it's sickness. "I think that the gambling addict is more sick than they are sinful, because nobody plans on becoming a gambling addict."

Eades, along with other therapists, also lauds the disease model as a therapeutic tool. "It does not help the gambling addict to point out the fact that you think they're a sinner. It's a lot easier for me to say to them, 'I think you're sick. I know you didn't plan on becoming a gambling addict.' And that's a true statement." People already convicted of their sins don't need to be told they're sinners. "It really doesn't do a whole lot of good to tell that gambling addict, hey, you're a sinful person, because they already are at the bottom of the barrel."[45]

Anderson agrees with the disease model. The clearly defined progression inherent in pathological gambling, the ease with which it's diagnosed, the very predictable consequences—"I've been doing this for so long that I can sit in my office and listen to somebody tell me their story, and I know where they're going with it long before they get there"—and recent genetic studies all convince him of the veracity of the disease model. "To me it fits every criteria for a disease," he says.

He also shares a diminished view of the will's involvement in the process. Once one predisposed either psychologically or biologically toward gambling addiction pulls his first handle or places his first chip on the green felt, he's lost his freedom of choice. Compulsive gambling is "a consequence of the fallen world that we live in. It's not how . . . God designed us, but it certainly is a consequence. . . . There are people who have predispositions to certain things and people who have natural resistances to things. So how do we explain those differences? Well, you know, it's part of the fallen world we live in."[46]

Although contentious and unresolved at present, the debate over the derivation of compulsive gambling is secondary in importance to the urgency of identifying those with gambling problems and helping them help themselves. In the long run, it really does not matter so much where it came from as what is to be done about it. In fact, obsession with the *why* question carries its own set of problems. First, answering it doesn't actually change anything. Speaking to a group of alcoholics, counselor Joe Pieri said: "If you ever figured out why you're a drunk, you'd still be a drunk. You would simply be a drunk who knew why he was a drunk."[47]

And second, finding an answer gives the unrepentant gambler a leg up on continuing his habit in a "smarter" way. Writes Eades: "Over the years I found that individuals seeking the 'why' answer were often trying to figure out a way to return to the chemical or the behavior and this time control it so that it does not cause problems in their lives."[48]

The disease-versus-moral-failing part of the argument may also be less than vital. Science may in fact develop harder and more conclusive evidence that certain people are psychologically or genetically predisposed toward compulsive gambling, and if such evidence is used in successful insanity-type court pleas, there may be cause for concern. But from a theological perspective, whether the acts of a compulsive gambler are a result of sin or sickness may not matter. We are all born into sin, and as a result some of us are born with certain predispositions toward certain kinds of sin. Call it the lingering, and powerful, effects of original sin. Whether one is born genetically wired for alcoholism, or even homosexuality, does not excuse one from giving in to the temptations presented by that activity, difficult as that may be. The will, and the strength to resist, come into the equation after the original difficulty is ascertained. So it may be with gambling. Once one discovers that one is drawn to the activity, is indeed fascinated and captivated by it, then it is up to the person, with God's help, to prevent it from taking over his life.

AN EQUAL OPPORTUNITY ADDICTION

Compulsive gambling is no respecter of race, creed, ethnic origin, or sex. People with gambling problems are anyone and everyone—it is impossible to predict through demographic data who will become one. Youth, college students, the elderly, housewives, businessmen, solid citizens, prison inmates, and all other groups of people are susceptible to the gambling "jones."

But while all are equal in theory, as in various "people's republics" and at Animal Farm, some are more equal than others. The classical composite of a compulsive gambler developed over a decade ago by Dr. Robert Custer goes something like this: the compulsive gambler, in the late states of the condition, is probably a male, aged thirty-five to forty, who has graduated high school (many have graduated college as well; some hold a graduate degree), lives with his spouse, was blessed with a traditional family life, and boasts a history of success in school and at work but no criminal record prior to his gambling problems. Although hailing from all parts of society, most compulsives appear to be lower middle class and middle class.[49]

Further reflection and study, as well as the proliferation of legalized gambling in the country, have added nuance and shading to this composite portrait. For example, the he in the picture is becoming more and more a she. While traditionally compulsive gambling has been a male preserve, many more women are now showing up on the psychiatric couches and in the treatment centers. In 1985, when Custer composed his portrait, the ratio of men to women compulsives had been estimated at everything from 5 to 1 to 20 to 1 (Custer set his mark at 10 to 1).[50] But as values and lifestyles have changed in our society, "women of all ages now have the time, money, and access to legal and illegal gambling,"[51] and that ratio has been cut to 3 to 1, 2 to 1, or even less.[52]

Women generally start gambling later in life than men, and their motivations and choice of games are usually different as well (more on that below), but their numbers have increased, not enough to eliminate the gap but to narrow it. Dr. Linda Chamberlain, a Denver psychologist, believes the ratio between men and women may approach fifty-fifty within the next five years. Nine years ago the Denver area played host to only two GA meetings, "no women in either of them.

Now," Chamberlain says, "GA finally established a women's-only group here, in the Metro area anyway. And there's a lot more women going into GA as a resource to help them."

Also showing up in greater numbers in the research are African Americans and Native Americans. Both studies commissioned by the NGISC found that, although continuing to constitute a minority of compulsive gamblers, more African Americans are pathological, problem, or at-risk gamblers than representatives of other ethnic groups. Native Americans have been less researched than other groups, but the few studies that have been conducted indicate they may be at greater risk for gambling problems.[53]

As for income and education, the NORC study found pathological gambling occurring less often among college graduates, people over sixty-five, and in households exceeding $100,000 in income; however, it also found that "college graduates are more likely to be at-risk gamblers than those at other education levels."[54] The NRC survey reports: "Prevalence rates were . . . somewhat higher for lower-income and less-educated people than for their higher-income and more-educated counterparts."[55]

At highest risk to develop gambling problems appear to be people with other addictions and those with immediate proximity to the games. Many pathological gamblers are addicted to drugs or alcohol, at rates of from 25 to 63 percent, and people "admitted to chemical dependence treatment programs are three to six times more likely to be problem gamblers than are people from the general population."[56] Although the reasons for this association are complex, and may include cultural factors, early family life, and maybe even biology, "Perhaps the most easily understood factor is the presence of alcohol in many gambling locations and the availability of gambling opportunities in many places people go to drink."[57] The two addictions tend to work in concert to dissuade the addict from putting a stop to either. The drinking or drugs may deter the gambler's efforts to quit gambling, while the gambling may have a similar effect on the alcoholic's or drug addict's attempts to kick his habit. "Together, the problems can be doubly difficult to resolve, creating a cycle of relapse and failure."[58]

There is another connection between gambling and alcohol/drugs as well. It seems that many recovering alcoholics and drug addicts get hooked on gambling—indeed, it is estimated that up to half of problem gamblers are former alcoholics or drug abusers.[59] Says Mike Brubaker, a recovering compulsive gambler now counseling the same: "Gambling is a big relapse issue for drug and alcohol patients. One big win or loss and they get loaded."[60] Writes Richard J. Rosenthal, a leading expert on compulsive gambling: "One should always be cautious of the recovering alcoholic who starts to gamble. Whether it is because of the free drinks often served in gambling establishments, the stresses associated with gambling, or the depression and lowering of self-esteem that accompanies losing, gambling may be a potent precipitant in relapse."[61]

The substitution of one addiction for another is understandable when one considers the importance of the addiction to the addict's life. It is, indeed, the centerpiece, the focal point, of his existence. Every waking hour is consumed with the substance or behavior—where and when he will engage in it again, how he can hide it, how he can get money to do it, etc. When what has become his *raison d'etre* is removed—that is, when he stops drinking or drugging—he is left with a not inconsiderable emptiness in his heart, and he seeks to fill that vacuum with something else. In too many cases this substitute is gambling, which may provide many of the same "benefits" that the drinking or drugs did.

Those close in proximity to the games also succumb to their allure in greater numbers than those not. In addition to the study by Hunter mentioned above, another study, this one funded by the gambling industry, put the rate of compulsive gambling among casino workers at nearly twice that of the general population.[62]

But in recent years, two groups on either end of life's chronological continuum have caught the eye—and the concern—of researchers. More youth and more elderly are developing gambling problems. Because of the particular concerns for family, and societal, well-being that these two groups represent, we will devote respective chapters to them later in this book.

However specific the scientific research becomes in singling out various groups or individual character traits as more susceptible to gambling problems than others, keep this in mind: Pathological and problem gambling is not restricted to any one group or personality type. Anyone anywhere in the United States can fall to its allures. Its grasp is eclectic and nondiscriminatory. And its grasp, as you will see in chapter 4, is to be respected and feared.

But before we get there, we must increase our understanding of gambling addicts. And to do that we must comprehend what it is about gambling that is so seductive and entrapping to these individuals.

There are, within the sphere of compulsive gamblers, those who get hooked on the action gambling offers and those who use their gambling as an escape pod to temporarily exit a world of hurt.

In the next chapter we will explore these two basic types of gambling addicts.

TWO

The Games Problem Gamblers Play

All forms of betting draw into their orbit pathological and problem gamblers. Long, long ago the poisons of choice were the horses and illegal bookmaking, with the exception of those who got hooked on casino games in Nevada. (Indeed, *The Chase*, by Dr. Henry R. Lesieur, still regarded as one of the best books on compulsive gambling, was written largely about horse track and sports betting.)

But since the first modern state lottery was instituted in New Hampshire in 1964—and more likely since 1978, when Atlantic City broke Nevada's stranglehold on legalized casino gambling in the United States—the product line of poisons has expanded greatly. To get addicted to gambling these days, you don't have to study the *Racing Form* and squeeze out "sure things" from grooms and horse trainers, nor must you memorize the weekly injury report and know whether the Philadelphia Eagles have beat the spread historically as a double-digit underdog road team playing on natural grass in night games on the West Coast in November. Not by any stretch. Now you need only stop at the local Gulp 'n' Go to pick up lottery tickets, or at its most inconvenient, tool on down the road to a nearby, friendly casino. And casinos are "nearby" almost everybody these days; as for "friendly," you'll likely find no friendlier people in the land than casino employees, as long as you're perched dutifully on your stool feeding the machine tokens or pushing your chips across the felt.

The horses (and the dogs and jai alai and off-track betting) still draw gamblers with problems, but track betting in general has not kept pace with the astronomical upsurge in lottery and casino play during the past two decades, and legalized sports betting is but a tiny sliver of casinos' intake pie. To find the pathological and problem gamblers, we must go to the games gamblers in general play, and that is the lottery and casino games.

Each of these forms of gambling presents its certain charms to the pathological and problem gambler, and the motivations the gambler brings to the table, so to speak, often determine which game he will choose. In addition to wanting to win, of course, an emotion that recedes in importance, sometimes disappearing altogether, as the condition progresses, experts believe problem and pathological gamblers try to satisfy one of two basic desires with their activity. They either seek out and feed upon the "action" of the games, or they want their gambling to afford them relief and escape from their workaday (and perhaps problematic) lives. The games they choose reflect these desires.

WHERE THE ACTION IS

"Action" is what happens when a skydiver exits the airplane, when a hang-glider leaves the cliff, when a firefighter enters a burning building. Action is the surge of adrenaline, the rush, the high that accompanies activities in which winning and losing are both possible—and both in meaningful measure.

And action is calling for the hit at the blackjack table when the dealer is standing on eighteen and you have a four and a king. Action is pushing a $500 line bet onto the felt as the shooter lets the dice fly toward the back wall of the craps table. It's watching your 20 to 1 long shot round the final turn in the lead, knowing that if he holds it you're looking at a $2,000 payout.

"Action. Supposedly the word speaks to the process of betting," writes Frank Trippett. "I suspect it speaks more deeply to what happens within the gambler. He places the bet, juices flow, he feels really alive: action. When the bet is on, his existence is confirmed."[1]

The excitement of the bet is what most compulsive gamblers seek, and they describe the inner tension betting produces "in terms that evoke physiological states of agony and ecstasy. There is a tempest brewing within the event. Each win is described in terms of being a 'high,' and each loss is a 'downer' or 'depressing.'"[2] Writes Timothy L. O'Brien: "Winning money is, of course, the goal, but few gamblers win regularly. Action, on the other hand, is its own reward. It keeps gamblers on the edge, in a certain solitary place where they find purpose. It keeps them involved in the world."[3] When compulsive gamblers talk about the high they receive, says Chamberlain, they say it is "beyond any pleasurable feeling or powerful feeling or rush or whatever that they've ever felt, that it's just the best that they've ever, ever experienced."[4]

Call it action, call it excitement, call it a high or a "euphoric state,"[5] it is under any name a powerful force, so intense that, in its thrall, gamblers care less about winning money than about playing the game. "Early on, you notice that winning and losing are not so different," write Frederick and Steven Barthelme, literature professors at the University of Southern Mississippi who got hooked on gambling on the Gulf Coast. "Both involve this huge buildup of pressure; the higher the stakes, the greater the pressure, the more intense the experience. This is one of the reasons you end up betting two or four thousand dollars at a throw, because whether you win or lose, you still have 85 percent of the experience, you still get 90 percent of the thrill. . . . It is as good to lose as to win. There is only a shadow of difference between them, and that shadow is insignificant. Winning is better than losing, but neither one is the goal of gambling, which is *playing*. Losing never feels like the worst part of gambling. Quitting often does."[6]

So inimical, or loathsome, is quitting that compulsive gamblers are often capable of performing nigh unto superhuman feats of endurance and strength just to stay at the table. It is not uncommon to hear of compulsive gamblers who remain on their stools for twenty-four hours straight; who refuse to interrupt their play for meals or bathroom runs, who indeed sometimes wet their pants; who are infuriated by the inactivity that ensues while the dealer shuffles cards for thirty seconds every half hour or so. One addict now in recovery spent four days in Las Vegas at the height of his addiction, during which he "slept maybe four or five hours out of that four days. I would go twenty-four hours a day." One time he was "at a blackjack table in the morning, and I was at that same blackjack table the next morning. I hadn't left." A dealer who worked that table recognized him from her shift of the previous day and kicked him off the table, telling him to get some sleep. "Of course, I didn't. I just found another table."[7]

And so great is its power that the one under its sway becomes oblivious to everything else. Compulsive gamblers will often neglect their duties to stay in action—failing to keep appointments, to pick up kids from school, even to attend a daughter's wedding, etc. Lesieur cites one compulsive gambler who, while holding three kings in a hand of poker, learned that his car was on fire—and played out the hand.[8]

This desire for action is progressive; that is, the gambler develops tolerance for the activity much like an alcoholic develops tolerance for liquor. While for a drinker this means ever increasing amounts of alcohol to get high, for a gambler it plays out in increased bets and/or increased playing time needed to produce the level of excitement he wants. Once you've played the $250-minimum blackjack table, the $2-maximum table no longer gets the job done.

Some games provide more action than others, however, and these are the games to which the action-seeking compulsives gravitate—blackjack, craps, poker, baccarat, the horses, sports wagering. Such games are termed games of "skill," wagers in which some measure of knowledge and acumen and proficiency allows the gambler to minimize the house's advantage. Compulsive gamblers are often very intelligent people. "I've never met somebody that's dumb that's a compulsive gambler," says therapist Fox, "but really highly intelligent, and a lot of professionals." And that native intelligence serves them poorly in the long run, for they think they can beat the math.

All gambling ventures favor the house (even in poker, in which gamblers play against each other, the house takes a cut of every pot). Certainly the odds on some are better than others—blackjack, for example, sports the best odds for the gambler at a 0.7 percent house advantage, while roulette gives the house a 5.3 percent advantage, and slot machines anywhere from 20 to 3 percent. But action-seeking gamblers believe, erroneously, that by using their intelligence or by devising or utilizing a "system" of play, they can beat the house. This strokes their ego and makes them feel special, or at least lucky. But it is a transient emotion, for while gamblers in some cases do win—there are winners in casinos (just look at the pictures on the walls)—problem and compulsive gamblers, even when they do win, usually lose it all back eventually because they can't leave the table. And the longer they stay, the poorer their odds of winning become.

More and more women are becoming action-seeking gamblers, but this category is still largely comprised of men. In fact, the Arizona Council on Compulsive Gambling provides this curt synopsis: "Action gamblers are usually domineering, controlling, manipulative men with large egos. They see themselves as friendly, sociable, gregarious, and generous. . . . They are energetic, assertive, persuasive, and confident. In spite of all this, they usually have low self-esteem."[9] Men like the excitement, the action, the interaction among the players and dealers; the opportunity to apply their smarts to the task at hand; and the feeling of being respected and lucky and special that winning brings them. Women, on the other hand, have traditionally sought a different "benefit" from their compulsive gambling.

RELIEF-AND-ESCAPE ARTISTS

Escape is a natural human desire. We get into a jam, and rather than facing up to the circumstance immediately and working through it, we run to refuge of some sort. Maybe we take a walk or a drive; maybe we see a movie or get lost in a novel; maybe we seek temporary refuge in the bottom of a glass. Many people bring this same motivation to their gambling; they relieve their stress with an hour or two at the slots, they escape their predicament by going to the track. And most of them, like most of us, realize that their brief escape has no bearing on the problem that instigated it; when they return, it will still be there. The escape was a mere attitude adjustment, temporary relief from a problem that they, provided that succor, will turn to face in due time.

But for some people it becomes far more troublesome. They so much love the comfort the escape offers them that they never return to deal with the problem that precipitated it. Do this once or twice when a crisis arises and it's not a problem. Do this enough times over a long enough period of time—the amount of time differs with individuals—and it becomes a way of life. And if the escape is alcohol or gambling, these folks frequently become alcoholics or people with gambling problems.

Like their fellows on the action side, escape gamblers usually have low self-esteem and become manipulative liars during the progression of their condition.[10]

NUMBING OUT

The gambling world offers no respite quite so comfortable as the slot machine. It is a brainless game for those wanting to be brainless—at least temporarily. Thinking and strategizing are not part of the enterprise—despite books touting titles like *Slot Machine Strategy* and such—nor is any interaction with other players or the house. It's just you and the machine, you and the whirring of the reels and the clinking of the payouts, you and the lights and the colors, you and the fruit and the sevens and the bars—an intimate communion of player with machine that effectively removes the rest of the animate and inanimate world and the problems entailed therein from your mind and thoughts.

These qualities, plus the low-stakes involved (quarter machines are still extremely popular) and the infusion of psychological principles to keep people on their stools, like frequent, small payouts, have made slots the casino world's number-one moneymaker, with up to 60 or 70 percent of the revenue of even high-roller resorts derived from them.

And it is exactly these qualities that draw compulsive

gamblers. They like the idea of zoning out in front of a machine, of numbing their pain or their boredom or their loneliness with the bells and whistles and clinking coins that accompany play. It does have its charms for one seeking refuge from the problems of life.

The Arizona Council, speaking of slots among other mechanical gambling devices, lays out its allure: "It is exciting, it is fun, it does not talk back, it requires her full concentration. She has to pay attention to the results of each roll; keep pushing the button or pulling the arm; [s]he does not have time to think about her problems. After just a brief period of time at the machine an almost hypnotic trance occurs. She realizes she has found a way to completely forget about all problems in her life. She feels comfortable, happy, and free from turmoil. She may later report that, in retrospect, she realizes she was 'hooked' the very first time she played."[11]

One Las Vegas mother of two gambled four hours a night four days a week at a city lounge, a habit that eventually led her to embezzle over $1 million from her employer. She served for eighteen years as a paralegal in the U.S. attorney's office, during which time she fabricated several thousand false witness vouchers and submitted them to the U.S. Marshals Service, which cut checks to these fictitious witnesses for their services, which this woman subsequently cashed. She admitted to having a gambling problem, and her downfall was the slots. Testified an expert witness at her trial: "Just putting those coins in and pulling the lever and doing that was the only peace that she had in her life. It was just anaesthesia."[12]

Traditionally more women than men have gambled for relief and escape. Writing in 1992, Rosenthal said: "[Women] are more apt to be depressed, and gamble less for the action or excitement than for escape. Winning big is less important, as is the need to impress. They typically play less competitive forms of gambling in which luck is more valued than skill, and they play alone."[13] Women, as well as others without table game experience, are also intimidated with blackjack, craps, poker, and such. Says Lenny Frame, who writes video poker guides, "In blackjack, the minute a woman makes a mistake, the men give her all kinds of stares. . . . You can play [video poker] at your own pace and not have to worry about what the person to the left of you is thinking."[14] So they play the slots, where they can numb out, relax, get away from their problems, without the social pressure surrounding the table games.

But men are horning in on the female domain. The Arizona Council notes a recent and substantial increase in calls to its hotline from or about male escape gamblers. In 1998, 38 percent of men calling the hotline were escape gamblers; in 1999 the number had risen to 49 percent. (Of the women callers, about 95 percent were escape gamblers, a rate that has remained steady.) The council attributes the rise to the greater accessibility of casino gambling in Arizona—the number of Indian casinos in the state has grown to nineteen since the early 1990s—which may make the phenomenon more than a local aberration.[15]

Escapists also play video poker, a particularly popular game often called the "crack cocaine of gambling." Explains one woman video poker player featured in Pete Earley's *Super Casino:* "I am not a stupid woman, but when I sit down in front of one of those machines, it's like the entire world gets blocked out. It's just me and my machine and nothing else matters. I ignore my beeper. I forget to eat. I'm not even tired. I could play for days without stopping if I had enough coins."[16]

The speed with which this game can be played, coupled with the absence of distractions, make it a very addictive event. "There are fewer components and less room for the secondary rituals and fantasies associated with horse racing, for example, or poker," says Rosenthal. "For the video machine player, there's an immediate stimulus-response. It is very addictive, and the trend is toward developing faster and faster games."[17] Besides which, says Chamberlain, there is an allusion of control, "some sense of actually playing a game, and some sense of control with it." This, she believes, is the attraction of video poker, especially for women. "They can do it anonymously, and they also have a little bit of that sense of … skill built into it. Minimal, for sure. But it's there."

People playing video poker can lose a lot of money—and they can lose it very quickly indeed. The woman in Earley's book could play a hand every fifteen seconds loading up a quarter machine (inserting five quarters per hand), which meant she could lose $5 a minute, which, extended out, adds up to $300 an hour.[18] Chamberlain and a colleague wanted to see how long they could make a thousand points last at video poker at an online casino that offered neophytes dry runs with imaginary money. It took her fifteen minutes to lose it all; her colleague lasted about thirty minutes because he kept winning. "That's how fast it goes," she says. "Go through fifty dollars in four or five minutes. Easy. Real easy."

Slot players, and especially those who play video poker, can become addicted to gambling much more quickly than the traditional action-seeker. "I see them getting addicted within [a] three-month time span, three to six months," says Eades. "Which is unusual. Like, with table games, it usually takes six to seven years." He compares table games to alcoholism in the speed with which the addiction takes hold. "Video poker and the slot machines are very often . . . like cocaine. It's very fast."[19]

CATCHING LOTTO FEVER

The speed element is one of the things that concern many gambling opponents about developments in state lotteries as well. Those on the pro-lottery side often claim that lotteries don't addict nearly so many as slots or table games—they're slow, after all; you sometimes have to wait upwards of a week to learn that you've lost. And in their traditional form, with reasonably low jackpots and infrequent drawings, perhaps they didn't addict as many.

But they do serve as an entry point for the gambler. "It's a little bit like marijuana—the gateway," says Tom Coates, director of Consumer Credit of Des Moines, whose office sees close to five hundred new clients per month, of whom nearly 15 percent are gambling addicts. "It desensitized the individual mentality, and it allowed them to move from one form to another. They might start out playing the lottery, but then they're much less concerned about going out and spending a day and a night at the slot parlor or at the casino."[20] Charles T. Clotfelter and Philip J. Cook, lottery researchers, call the lottery "a powerful recruiting device, which in 1974 was responsible for inducing about one-quarter of the adult population who would not otherwise have done so to participate in commercial gambling."[21]

As for the slowness of the traditional lottery form, well, the gambling industry, which includes state governments these days, has been working on it for a while now. Beginning in the 1970s, state lottery agencies discovered instant games, scratch-off tickets that eliminated the time lag between drawings; this variety of game accounted for 42 percent of lottery sales in 1997.[22]

Recently the speed element has been ratcheted up via a new innovation: video lottery games (VLTs). VLTs propound a variety of games, including video poker, and are tantamount to slot machines, offering immediate payouts and rapid play. In fact, while traditional lottery sales have stagnated in recent years, VLT revenues are soaring. It is precisely the addictive qualities of VLTs that have prompted legislatures around the country to ponder long and hard about their introduction into their states. "If anyone thinks that putting lotteries and video terminals on every block won't lead to addictive and criminal behavior, they're in outer space," says Valerie Lorenz, a compulsive gambling expert in Maryland. "We saw keno addicts within two weeks after it was introduced in Maryland."[23]

The other "problems" of the traditional passive drawings have been solved in turn. Jackpots have seen an exponential increase in size to lure more players. The instant scratch-off tickets come now in a myriad of attractive themes. An element of "control" has been added via keno, lotto, and the numbers—where one can putatively court Lady Luck by picking one's favorite numbers. And as a result, lottery activity in the United States has boomed: from 1973 to 1997 the number of states with some form of lottery increased from seven to thirty-seven, plus the District of Columbia; state lottery sales grew from $2 billion to $34 billion; and per capita sales from $35 to $150.[24]

If people play it in such volume, it stands to reason that some will get addicted to it. Fifty-two percent of the forty thousand calls to the Council on Compulsive Gambling of New Jersey in 1994 were about the lottery.[25] The largest outpatient treatment center for problem gamblers in Massachusetts reports that 40 percent of its patients are lottery players.[26] The National Council on Compulsive Gambling puts the percentage of lottery players who are addicted at 10 percent.[27] The fact that the top 5 percent of lottery players account for 54 percent of lottery sales, the top 10 percent account for 68 percent, and the top 20 percent for fully 82 percent,[28] suggests that the largest-volume players might have a problem.

This has not escaped the notice of the states, for some of their advertising plays directly to the weaknesses of the problem gambler. The button lottery ads push unrelentingly is the same one that impels inveterate slot players to remain on a stool even when the machine is not spitting: that is, it's ready to hit; if you leave, it'll hit for the next guy; you must keep playing until you are no longer physically able or you run out of money (whichever happens first). With the lottery the message is slightly different—it's that your numbers will come up on the day you don't play. One Pennsylvania lottery ad says: "Don't forget to play every day." The theme song of a Tri-State Megabucks ad (in New Hampshire, Maine, and Vermont) says, "It could have been you. ... / But what can I say? / You just didn't play."[29] Add to this the constant barrage of ads lauding the magical transformation to an idyllic life of riches and wealth that winning the lottery will bring, and the temptation widespread lottery advertising presents to a recovering gambling addict, and the lottery plays no insignificant role in the world of compulsive gambling.

Studies show that lottery playing is slightly more prominent among men than women, that blacks and Hispanics spend much more on average than other groups, that married or divorced people buy more tickets than never marrieds, that per capita expenditure is highest among people ages forty-five to sixty-four, that those who have not completed high school spend the most and those with college degrees the least, and that lower-income people spend the most per capita. The top 20 percent of lottery players—that is, those who will more likely accede to problem gambling habits—is heavily overrepresented by "males, blacks, high-school dropouts, and people in the lowest-income category."[30]

But whoever they are, and whatever "advantages" they pursue in their gambling—whether it's the juice of the blackjack table or the mind-numbing repetition of the spinning reels—once they get hooked, they will find that the losses they incur extend far beyond their ever-thinning billfold.

Oh, they'll lose money all right. But all other aspects of their lives will probably be devastated as well. It is to the costs the gambling addict pays for his obsession that we next turn.

THREE

A Cost Too High

Pain and suffering are nigh unto impossible to quantify. We hear reports of a tornado or a flood doing x billion or x hundred million dollars' worth of damage, and unless we are on the ground scratching through the rubble of a flattened three-bedroom house or slogging through two feet of mud in a living room, the numbers don't mean a whole lot. They are an abstraction, beyond our comprehension.

So it is with pathological gambling. How do you put a dollar figure on a broken family? on an abused child? on a beaten wife? on a broken trust? on lost job or educational opportunities?

How do you quantify the damage done to the family of a single mother who allegedly robbed two banks on her way to a casino? She had raised four children, one of whom she was supporting in college, and held an airline job for thirteen years, but told authorities she was a regular at a Detroit casino. Now this woman, with no prior criminal record, could go to jail for twenty years.[1]

How do you assess in money terms the heartbreak of a

Montana family whose son succumbed to video poker? Away from home for an extended period for the first time in his life, this college freshman blotted out his loneliness with the frantic activity of video poker. He was immediately hooked. Within months he was living out of his car. He forged checks from his parents' checking account and ripped them off of rifles, skis, and other items, which he pawned for gambling funds.

His parents called the authorities—going the "tough love" route—who arrested the boy, put him in jail, then placed him in a pre-release program, during which he was allowed to work. Sentence completed, he walked out with $2,500 in earnings and gambled it away in a few days. Then he ripped off a VCR from his employer, which he pawned. He went back to jail for that—for seven months this time.[2]

How do you calculate the emotional damage incurred on a Massachusetts community where a grade-school principal stole $20,000 she had ostensibly collected from students for field trips, science projects, workbooks, and school plays, only to feed her gambling problem by dumping the money into lottery tickets and slot machines?[3]

How do you compute the spiritual damage wreaked in their flocks by pastors who succumb to the gambling bug? Two Kansas City–area preachers resigned their pastorates because of gambling problems. One stole $60,000 from his congregation and blew it at the casinos; the other donned a wig and glasses to mask his identity while gambling.[4] A Colorado pastor resigned his charge after admitting to embezzling $10,000 from his church over an eighteen-month period. He paid back the money and agreed to undergo treatment for gambling addiction.[5]

Tragedy and heartbreak do not easily convert into monetary figures. So, rather than trying to affix dollar amounts to personal and interpersonal calamities, perhaps the easiest way to determine the effect, or cost, of compulsive gambling is to focus on how many compulsive gamblers experience negative consequences for their behavior, and how negative those consequences are.

IT'S ABOUT THE MONEY—BUT THEN AGAIN …

When assessing the individual damage incurred by compulsive gambling, one statistic is more telling than all the others combined: nearly one out of every five, two out of every ten, compulsive gamblers attempt suicide.[6] This number is higher than that of any other addictive disorder. In another study, two-thirds of the almost four hundred GA members surveyed had thought about suicide, 47 percent had fashioned a distinct plan to carry it through, and a full 77 percent didn't want to continue living.[7] Says Randall E. Smith, a counselor in Englewood, Colorado: "This is a very lethal group of individuals who, when their fantasy crashes, have this overwhelming sense of hopelessness and guilt and shame, and so they commit suicide."[8]

This is sobering—and startling—information. And it begs the question: What is it about compulsive gambling that prompts one in its grip to want to end it all rather than face and work through his problems?

A big part of the answer deals with money. Says one recovering gambling addict: "We can lose our family, our friends, our house, our jobs—doesn't matter. But once we've lost all our money—that's what matters for us. We cannot gamble if we don't have the money. We can gamble if we don't have all those other things. They don't matter to us."

Getting that money is where the problems start, because, as the compulsion progresses, the amount of money needed to satisfy the gambler, to give him his high, is always increasing. To get this money he will beg, borrow, and ultimately even steal, and he will do it in very innovative ways. He will max out credit cards. He will establish new lines of credit unbeknownst to his spouse and max those out. He will get home improve-ment loans and use the money for gambling. He will tap out all the joint accounts he shares with his spouse—for the kids' college education, for retirement, for anything held in a joint arrangement—going so far as to forge his spouse's signature or obtain the services of a coworker or friend to impersonate his spouse when necessary. If he can swing it, he'll rip off his boss or his company for a thou here, a thou there. He'll bounce checks. He'll wheedle relatives out of their money; he'll hit up his friends, his spouse's friends, his parents' friends—anyone in his social circles—for all the funds he can.

And when he finally hits bottom; when the realization that his problem will not in the near future be solved; when he at long last recognizes that even if the big win he's been chasing to solve his financial problems does come his way, he won't put it against his outstanding debts but he'll simply sit there, be it at a blackjack table or a slot machine, and give it all right back to the casino—when that moment comes, everything falls apart.

"There's no hope," says one spouse of a gambling addict. "They're looking at a debt so high, it's unreachable. And they're looking at possibly having engaged in white-collar crime to support their habit. They're looking at the loss of everything—everything. So for them, the idea of death is pretty welcome." One compulsive gambler now in recovery com-pares the gambling addict to a person trying to outrun a tidal wave. "And as long as they gamble, they can really stay one step ahead of it. But finally they have to stop. And once they stop this whole thing hits them … hits them and their family." Smith uses a different analogy: "It's like swimming up a water-fall, because they've got so many things coming at them at this time. Issues with their family. Oftentimes legal issues. Cases where they have maxed out credit card accounts. Maybe they've been kiting checks. All of these consequences are rolling at them, and they feel overwhelmed by the process."

The bottom, when they do hit it, can be a lot lower than that for other addictions. Although some seek counsel early on for their out-of-control gambling, "the more common scenario is that people are in the hole six figures, one hundred fifty, two hundred, three hundred thousand dollars, and they finally hit bottom," says Smith. "And at that point they think about things like their insurance policy, if they still have one and haven't cashed it in, and have the idea that they're worth more dead than alive."

Or they think about things like rigging a fatal car "accident." One recovering addict who relapsed, after considering the life insurance option, began on occasion to drive on the wrong side of two-lane highways and hope a truck would come around the corner and hit him. "What's interesting is that I didn't think about . . . the family in the station wagon coming around the corner there. Had they hit me, I would have killed them. You don't think that way, with a gambler." Says Fox, who counsels in Colorado Springs: "So many people I've talked to: When they're coming down the mountain, they just want to drive off the mountain."[9]

One reason might be because they think driving off a mountain is preferable to facing the mountain of debt confronting them when they get down. This latter mountain was quantified by the Council on Compulsive Gambling of New Jersey at an average of $43,150 per gambling addict when he finally sought help.[10] Gambling-attributed debt in a Wisconsin study was put at $39,000 per gambler, while an Illinois study set the number at $114,000.[11] Some of Tom Coates's clients drag $60,000 in debt into his Des Moines office, which he says is not unusually high.[12] And of course, the debt of some compulsives is out of sight: Brian Molony, a loan officer in a Canadian bank, was about $10.2 million in the red when the police finally picked him up.[13]

So substantial is their debt that many compulsive gamblers

flee to bankruptcy courts for relief. One of the few studies addressing bankruptcy revealed that "28 percent of the 60 pathological gamblers attending Gamblers Anonymous reported either that they had filed for bankruptcy or reported debts of $75,000 to $150,000."[14]

And in municipalities where gambling is permitted, the rates of bankruptcy filings, not surprisingly, have skyrocketed. The rate in Iowa counties with a racetrack or casino exceeds the state average by 21 percent.[15] Six of the sixteen counties with the highest bankruptcy rates in the country were near Tunica, Mississippi.[16] And within a year and a half of the opening of Windsor Castle, a casino in Ontario across the river from Detroit, bankruptcy attorneys in metro Detroit reported that gambling-related bankruptcies jumped by as much as forty times.[17] Concluded SMR Research Corporation, after studying the personal bankruptcy crisis in 1997: "It now appears that gambling may be the single fastest-growing driver of bankruptcy."[18]

Gambling addicts also experience problems only tangentially related to money. For example, their performance on the job suffers, and many lose their jobs because of their gambling. One recent survey indicates that from 69 to 76 percent of gambling addicts had missed work to gamble at some time in their lives.[19] One recovering addict spent many work-hours writing computer simulations of blackjack and craps games, he said, trying to better his chances when he got to the tables; he also nicked out of the office to pursue his obsession. "I would come in for a couple hours in the morning; leave early for an early lunch and actually go to the casino, and then generally be gone for the rest of the day—at the casino." Calling in sick in order to gamble is also common among compulsive gamblers.

Not surprisingly, their need for ever more financial resources leads many gambling addicts astray of the law. Two recent studies of GA members indicate that 46 and 56 percent of them admit to having stolen money or valuables to finance their gambling. About one-third of problem and pathological gamblers interviewed in another study had been arrested, compared to 10 and 4 percent of low-risk gamblers and no-gamblers, respectively.[20] Over 20 percent of pathological gamblers had been imprisoned, as opposed to an expected rate of approximately 6 percent, based on the study's simulation.[21] This same survey revealed that problem and pathological gamblers who had ever been arrested, had heard their Miranda rights 3.3 and 1.6 times in their lives, respectively.[22]

Some of these cases are as sad as they are eye-opening, and testify to the power of this addiction.

♣ In a ten-month period in the late 1990s, a man allegedly pummeled and stabbed to death six rich, mostly elderly Louisiana people, and wounded two others, stealing a total of about $101,120 from their safes and their pockets. Investigators say he was after cash to support his near-daily forays to casinos and video-gambling halls. Sometimes he headed for the games immediately after his crimes. In fact, as the victims of his final attack struggled for their lives in a Baton Rouge hospital—they miraculously lived through close-range shotgun blasts—he was smiling for a casino photographer with a cardboard check for $18,000, reflecting his fortune at the slot machines. In less than a year, he dumped nearly $280,000 into the riverboat casinos alone, according to authorities.[23]

♣ A sixty-four-year-old grandmother of fourteen, the manager and sole employee at a Wisconsin credit union, stole about $275,000 over a ten-year period to feed her slot machine habit. She created fifty-one fraudulent loans to ex-members, writing the original loan checks payable to herself and the duplicate checks payable to the former members. She cashed the originals and then destroyed the canceled checks when they showed up in the mail. The woman was "extremely remorseful," her lawyer said. She "violated her own code, not only the criminal code of the United States, but her own personal code of honor and morality." She got four years.[24]

✤ A North Carolina man who fantasized and dreamed about gambling, and who could push chips onto the felt of a craps table for twenty-six hours without resting, bilked his life insurance clients out of at least $1.6 million to feed his gambling addiction. Many of his clients were relatives, close friends, and people he had sold insurance to for years. Some of his victims, owed as much as $340,000, have not gotten their money. He faces from five to six years in jail.[25]

✤ A former city councilman and longtime bank president in an Oklahoma town admitted in court to embezzling at least $1.9 million to feed his gambling habit. "I got very addicted to gambling, your honor," the sixty-year-old man, a regular churchgoer, told the judge. "I got in way too deep … and I used money that was not mine." Part of the $1.9 million— $190,000 of it—was stolen from a trust established to support charities. He could get from five to seven years and a fine of $3.8 million.[26]

FAMILY MATTERS

As for the effect all this has on the pathological gambler's spouse, consider this: *One in ten spouses attempts suicide.*[27] Why is that?

First, the pathological gambler's financial perils are almost always shared, either emotionally or monetarily, by the spouse.

Lifestyles are necessarily curtailed, luxuries are forgone, extras are out of the question—and the resulting privations make tension often unavoidable. This is not even to mention the hassles the spouse must undergo from creditors wanting repayment or relatives seeking explanations.

In addition to which, even the spouse suffers physically from the ordeal. One survey of spouses at Gam-Anon, an organization like GA but for the spouses of the gamblers, "found that most of them had serious emotional problems and had resorted to drinking, smoking, overeating, and impulse spending." Another found headaches, both chronic and severe, as well as "stomach problems, dizziness, and breathing difficulties" among the spouses.[28]

The physical damage, though, pales in comparison to the emotional devastation. In order to get his money "fixes," the pathological gambler will have lied continually to his spouse, he will have probably betrayed the spouse's trust almost as much, and he will have most likely retreated into a cocoon of secrecy and suspicion to protect his financial machinations.

Because the gambler has to cover up his time spent gambling as well as his finances, most spouses think he has been having an affair. After all, where in the world is he for hours at a time? Why isn't he where he said he was going to be—at work, at the bowling alley, at a friend's, wherever the cover story he had spun to explain his prolonged absences had put him? An affair answers those and similar questions.

But when the gambler finally does fess up, the relief the spouse feels over not being married to an adulterer is replaced by the anger, the shame, the disillusionment, the sadness, the depression over looking at a mountain of family debt and having to apologize to nearly everybody in her acquaintance—as well as rebuild the trust between spouses that has been decimated.

Sadly, the spouse probably doesn't know the half of it at that time. Most pathological gamblers, when they feel forced to "come clean," will come only partially clean—so great is the embarrassment, the shame, the humiliation of their behavior, or, on the other hand, the desire to continue their gambling. They will divulge only what they think they need to, or what they think the spouse will find out on her own. "And usually," says Smith, "what you think you know about the depth of the loss at the beginning, is just the tip of the iceberg." The more the spouse looks, the more problems the spouse will find. "And [the gambling addict] will usually tell you that this is it, this is it, there's nothing else, absolutely nothing else out there. . . . And next month, here comes another bill from some other direction. . . . It's just devastating blow upon devastating blow upon devastating blow. And the spouses can just be so deeply overwhelmed."

These marriages frequently end in divorce. One recent study found that between 26 and 30 percent of GA members were divorced or separated because of their gambling.[29] According to another source, gambling addicts are five times as likely as the rest of the population to have married three or more times.[30] Economically the effects are dire: The average cost for a divorce is $20,000 in legal fees alone. Women who are divorced, and their children if they get them, fare inestimably poorer than do their husbands, whose economic health actually increases in the aftermath.[31] It goes without saying, though, that any dollar figure put on divorce is inconsequential when compared to the incalculable and long-lasting damage done to the emotional, familial, and spiritual well-being of the parties involved.

And divorce is only part of the sad story. One study indicates that fully half the spouses of gambling addicts had been physically abused; another said 23 percent had been verbally or physically abused.[32] And in or near communities where casino gambling had recently been inaugurated, domestic violence rates rose accordingly—in six of ten communities surveyed in one study.[33] One shelter in Harrison County, Mississippi, reported a 300 percent increase in domestic violence intervention calls, a substantial percentage of which were gambling related, after the casinos arrived.[34] Other areas around casinos reported similar rises.[35]

As for the children, they can be devastated emotionally by the erratic behavior of the addict—sometimes he's cuddly and demonstrative; sometimes he's angry and irritable; sometimes (in fact, most of the time in the disorder's later stages) he's off in his own world, distant, uncommunicative, withdrawn. And in far too many cases the children are abused as well. One study indicated that 17 percent had been physically or verbally abused; another put the number at 10 percent for physical abuse.[36]

Or, even more frightening, children are locked in the car in the casino parking lot while the parents are inside fighting their internal demons. At least two of these children have died,[37] one of whom was under the supposed care of a baby-sitter who was gambling.[38] Rev. Tom Grey, a visible gambling opponent, says, "I've got over twenty 'kids in the car' stories."[39] It got so bad at the Foxwoods casino in Connecticut that casino management posted signs informing patrons that police would be called in for kids-in-cars situations.[40]

Being reared by a gambling addict also bodes ill for the child's future: Children from households in which a compulsive gambler lives are more likely to become compulsive gamblers themselves.

Suicide, divorce, bankruptcy, spousal and child abuse, arrest, and imprisonment—when it runs its full course, compulsive gambling lays waste not only the lives of the addicts themselves but also those of their families and all who are near them. But something producing such baleful results does not happen all at once. The dedicated family man with a wife and two kids does not wake up one morning as—presto-chango!—a compulsive gambler with a dozen maxed-out credit cards who beats his wife and is bent on ending it all. Compulsive gambling is a journey, a progression, and it is only very late in this slide into disgrace that these repelling events occur.

How spouses and families can prevent this slide is one of the reasons this book was written. But to deal with it, they must recognize it as it progresses.

It is to that progression that we now turn.

FOUR

The Decline and Fall of the Gambling Addict

G ambling is pervasive in our society. The 1999 report of the National Gambling Impact Study Commission (NGISC) found that 86 percent of all Americans had gambled at some time in their lives.[1] Looked at from a different angle, that means 14 percent of the American population, should they remain gambling-free, have absolutely no chance of developing gambling problems—if you don't gamble, you don't have to worry about giving your fortune to a casino (you only have to worry about your son or daughter, father or mother doing it if that person becomes a gambling addict).

Of that 86 percent that have gambled, many will engage in the activity without severe consequences. These are the so-called social, or recreational, gamblers that the gambling industry is so fond of talking about. They will probably lose

55

money—maybe significantly so—and they will likely bow to the god of greed and will be indirectly subverting the Christian work ethic, but they will not be turning their futures over to the gods of chance.

They are engaging in entertainment, true, but it is a form of entertainment fraught with peril. Four or five percent of moviegoers do not end up ruining their lives because of movies; 20 percent of inveterate bowlers or miniature golfers do not end up trying to kill themselves because they keep leaving a 7-10 split or keep hitting the windmill blades.

For a tragic minority, the risks are too great to overcome, and gambling becomes much more than one pastime among many. It becomes an addiction. Dr. John M. Eades explains addictions with what he calls the three *Cs*: all addictions entail (1) a "*craving and a compulsion* to continue the activity"; (2) a "*loss of control*"—"after all, if an individual could control the substance or the behavior, then there would be no problems arising from the activity"; and (3) "*continuing the activity despite negative consequences.*"[2]

Like all addictions, a gambling addiction becomes its own animal, an independent unit within a person making demands and requiring obedience. "Like other addictions," write Linda Berman and Mary-Ellen Siegel, "gambling addiction takes on a life of its own. From the initial attraction to the discovery that the substance or activity can provide an escape from unpleasant feelings or situations, a psychological dependency commences and escape is sought whenever the person feels 'uncomfortable.'" Soon the person will brook no feelings of discomfort whatever—all are met with gambling expeditions—and "the addiction becomes the person's best friend and confidante, and soon healthy and normal relationships with other people and other activities become less important."[3]

Addictions have a history, a life course, a beginning and an end, and compulsive gambling is no exception. Dr. Robert

Custer, considered the grandfather of diagnosis and treatment of compulsive gambling, divides the progression into three phases: a winning phase, a losing phase, and a desperation phase.[4] Mary Heineman also lists three: early, middle, final.[5] Eades delineates five: winning, losing, chasing, bailout, and desperation.[6] Richard J. Rosenthal and the Arizona Council on Compulsive Gambling describe four: winning, losing, desperation, hopelessness.[7] All are talking about the same thing, and all chart similar courses of decline.

The lines dividing the phases are somewhat fuzzy, however, with activities assigned to one phase popping up in other phases in greater or lesser intensity, and the occasional period of abstinence appearing somewhere along the line before the gambler relaunches himself full-bore back into his addiction. Escape gamblers also seem to embark upon a slightly different, and more abbreviated, decline than action seekers. Custer himself wrote: "Compulsive gambling has not been studied for long enough to permit the charting of a precise 'life history' of this disorder."[8] Other experts approach the condition with less linear, more topical analyses.

We will briefly lay out an amalgam of these different approaches, with three stages: winning, losing and chasing, and desperation.[9] Keep in mind, it is a scenario steeped in generalities, and specific cases may deviate from it.

WIN EARLY, WIN OFTEN

"Casinos Love a Winner"—whether it's on a billboard or in a newspaper advertisement, no truer words have ever been written. Oh, casinos love losers too. In fact, they love losers *a whole lot more* than they love winners. But very few of the losers they love will ever become losers if they are not winners first. So it's very good for business to push some chips in your direction or peel off some fifties and hundreds at the cage when you cash out every once in a while. Casinos know that it is a mere short-term loss for them, that the more you play and the longer you play the better their odds become, and that if you win once you'll think you'll win again. And you might. But in the long term you won't. To quote another true phrase: "If you want to make money in a casino, own one."

Action-seeking compulsive gamblers win more than they lose—or at least think they do—early on in their careers (as opposed to escape gamblers, who often don't and will be discussed below). This is an enjoyable time for them, lasting from one to five years, during which they gradually bet more money and gamble more often, often with positive results. They frequently find they have some gambling "skills" and develop those skills by educating themselves about the games they play. Many develop a system which "turn[s] out to be quite dependable" and they "[resist] sharing it with others."[10]

The winning feeds their ego, bolsters their self-esteem, and manifests itself in gregarious, generous behavior. They're proud of their good luck and don't mind talking about it. Says one recovering gambling addict: "I remember the slot machine where I won my first thousand-dollar jackpot. It was up in Las Vegas. How thrilled I was. You know, I came home and I showed my wife a thousand dollars in cash, and had it in my pocket and felt like a big man. This was neat. I remember showing my kids: Look what I did. See this money I won."[11] Says another, who put a twenty into a video poker machine and walked out moments later with $220: "I go back to the office. I'm kind of bragging to all the guys in the office and telling everyone how great this was and called my wife and told her, 'Hey, we'll go out for a big dinner this weekend. It'll be great.'" Neither do they mind sharing the wealth, grabbing for the tab at dinner, tipping big, and buying presents, some quite expensive, for their spouses and children.

But then something bad happens: They hit "the big one."

This win equals a month's or even six-months' or a full year's salary, and it is a *major* reinforcement for further gambling. Writes Eades, who did not experience an early big win in his gambling career but understands the psychology: "If the mouse gets cheese at door 'A' instead of door 'B,' he usually changes his address to door 'A.' If he gets a really big block of cheese at door 'A,' he often will move in and use the laboratory telephone to summon an interior decorator."[12]

This big win serves a number of purposes for the gambler: It shoots his self-esteem into the stratosphere. "Remember how that felt?" Heineman asks. "Nothing you had ever experienced before equaled it. You felt special, loved, successful, powerful, and your sense of self-esteem shot sky high."[13] And it only confirms what these gamblers knew all along—that they were smarter and better gamblers than everybody else; they had savvy, skills, talent. And it proves something they could only heretofore suspect: that they had the magic touch. Many gamblers, after hitting the big one, even fantasize about making gambling a career—going pro.

Because if it happened once, it will happen again. One recovering gambler recalls winning two jackpots in one night, one for twenty-five hundred and the other for three thousand. "And then you start thinking every time you go you're going to win. That's what really started setting it off. It deteriorated from there."

Writes Custer: "The big win is the booster on the rocket that tears him loose from the gravitational forces of reason and reality and sends him flying into a weight-free flight of illusion and fantasy where there are no limits to what he can do and become."[14] Tom Coates, director of Iowa's largest nonprofit credit counseling agency whose clientele includes many with gambling problems, employs a different analogy: "That first big win that hooks them gives them such a high that they're always trying to go back and achieve that. And they can't. The highs get lower and the lows get lower. It's a roller coaster ride, but it's only heading downhill."[15]

In short, the early big win changes the action gambler's thinking; it puts new contours on his world; it alters his life.

A different pattern seems to apply to escape gamblers, however. They may have gambled recreationally with no problems during their lives, or not gambled all, but when predisposing factors enter their lives—unwelcome emotions or circumstances, including everything from boredom to stress to grief to loneliness to chronic pain or any number of other conditions—they escape to gambling. They may win at the machine for a short while, or they may not, but there is no winning phase per se—the real win has nothing to do with money: it is the "emotional escape from life's problems experienced while in the act of gambling."[16] Many claim to have known they were "hooked" from their very first episode following the appearance of the predisposing factors.

In addition to temporarily anesthetizing their emotional pain, other "benefits" of escape gambling include: a false sense of empowerment from being in a world free from outside control that boosts their self-esteem; independence, especially if they are married to an abusive, controlling spouse or if they are handicapped or sick and thus prevented from living a "normal" life; the thrill of "stepping over the line"; and camaraderie with others at the casinos.

While intense, this phase is also relatively short-lived. Whereas it typically takes action gamblers from ten to thirty years before they seek help, escapists reach the devastating later phases of the addiction in a mere two to three years.

THE CHASE IS ON

As the action gambler continues to win (or at least think he's winning), his confidence rises along with the amounts he wagers. He's winning, after all. Of course he's winning—he's been winning for *years;* why would he stop winning now? And if he's going to win anyway, he might as well walk away with two thousand rather than a paltry two hundred. But there's something else: The action phenomenon has kicked into gear. More betting and bigger bets mean bigger thrills, bigger surges of adrenaline, bigger "rushes." The twenty-dollar maximum blackjack table once a week no longer tickles his synapses; now it's the hundred-dollar, the two-hundred-dollar table four nights a week.

But eventually things begin to change. Maybe the math starts to assert itself. Maybe his sense of omnipotence—winning will do a number on one's head—leads to stupid bets. At any rate, he starts to lose, not just once or twice, but consistently.

Losing affects him on a number of levels. It is a brutal blow to his self-esteem and the image he had manufactured for himself as the buoyant and outrageously successful gambler. Maybe, he thinks briefly, he's not so smart, or so lucky, as he thought he was. Oftentimes his gambling behavior will change as well. No longer does he want his spouse or a friend sitting in the next chair at the blackjack table or nestled up close to him at the craps table; he gambles alone now to hide the fact that he's losing, and how much he's losing. And it hurts his bankroll big time, for by this time he has ratcheted up the frequency and dollar amounts of his betting substantially. This losing stuff, he thinks, *cannot stand.*

And then he crosses another line. No longer is he gambling to win; now he is gambling to recapture the losses. He doesn't go to the casino to win money but to get even. And because the losses are bigger because he's betting bigger, recouping them will require bigger bets as well. He has entered what experts call "the chase."

Chasing is insidious, for, to the gambler, the only solution to his problems is to continue the activity that produced them in the first place. Writes Edward C. Devereux, Jr.: "He sees himself getting in deeper and deeper; yet if he quits now, all this is irretrievably lost. The only way to get it back is to keep on playing."[17] Dr. Linda Chamberlain illustrates the chase to her Regis University students by employing an old bar trick: she auctions off a ten-dollar bill. The catch is: While the highest bidder gets the ten spot, the second-highest bidder also has to pony up. "I've never failed on a ten-dollar bill to make less than fifty dollars," she says. "Usually I stop them at about two hundred." She starts the bidding at a dollar, and people start dropping out at six dollars, eight dollars, until there are two left. One of the two bids nine dollars, which is a good price— he still makes a dollar, after all. But when the other bids nine-fifty, the nine-dollar bid doesn't look so good. If that bidder drops out at that point, he's out nine dollars. So he stays in. "And that's what happens in gambling," Chamberlain says. "People get locked into that spiral, and that's how it begins to go. . . . That whole sense of the chase in gambling is what really begins to hook people."[18]

To quit gambling after losing substantial dollars, to leave the table after a big loss, is to choose the greater of two evils in the gambler's mind. It is to face reality, and it is to face a large debt that can be paid off using only traditional means, over a long period of time. "When you stop gambling," Christopher W. Anderson says, "what you do is, you give up the fantasy of solving your problem. . . . When we invite somebody to stop gambling, we're inviting them to lock in their losses." Most compulsive gamblers are unwilling to do this, however, at least at this stage, for the reality—and the insidiousness of this addiction—is that the very next pull of the slot machine handle, that the very next lotto ticket they buy, that putting everything they have on the 20 to 1 shot in the ninth race at the track, *might* solve the problem. "That element in and of itself is what makes this so incredibly seductive," Anderson says.[19]

Chasers gamble more often and wager larger amounts of money, and the gambling smarts they so pride themselves in take a backseat to the urgency of getting that big win that will put things right. Says one recovering gambling addict, "When you're chasing money you gamble very poorly, because you finally get to the point where you have to win so much money that you have to bet large amounts of money. Or you have to gamble at things that have very low odds. For example, there were times when I would chase money playing slot machines that had very low odds of winning, but I'd look at that $100,000 or million-dollar prize and say, 'That's what I need.'"

During the chase, gamblers start doubling up on bets and staying in hands where folding would be a more prudent play, or they take fliers on long shots where the odds are low but the payout large. One gambler, while chasing a high five-figure loss, would stop by the keno game on his way to bed at the casino, after gambling seriously at blackjack for hours, for what could be called a nightcap: He would "buy five hundred dollars worth of keno numbers or keno games or whatever, thinking, oh, maybe I'd win a hundred grand that way, or fifty grand."

Throwing Good Money After Bad

Once the chase is on, it dominates the compulsive gambler's activities until the fantasy crashes sometime after the onset of the last phase. During this time, which can last for as many as five years, or even longer, the gambling produces innumerable difficulties in his and his family's life.

One such difficulty is money, or to be more precise, getting money to gamble with, to chase the loss. What one would consider friendly sources are tapped first: family members and friends, whom he always presents with a convenient and usually plausible sob story that does not allude to or mention gambling as the reason the money is needed. Because they know him and like him, they almost always accede to his request. Also tapped are impersonal, third-party sources.

Attitudes about money in our credit-laden society shoulder much of the blame here, thinks Coates. A little more than a decade ago, he says, the average person had five credit cards at his disposal, with an average line of credit on a bank card of about two thousand dollars. Today the average person's wallet is lined with ten of them, with the average line approaching four thousand dollars. "In our society, where you get so many cards offering you a new line of credit at a reduced rate, you take out a new line and you transfer [the] balance of one to another, and you start revolving that around." When the pressure from creditors begins to mount, compulsive gamblers often take out a bank loan—a home equity loan or home improvement loan—and use that to pay down the credit cards, which allows them to start tapping the cards once again. The cycle continues until any and every legal source of money is drained.

Feeding his ever-growing appetite for gambling—and for gambling money—requires secrecy from the gambler, and lying becomes an integral part of his life. He lies to his spouse about where he's going and where he's been. He calls in sick to work and hits the casino. He misses important business meetings, and has a ready excuse. He lies about how much he wins and how much he loses, still concerned as he is to maintain his reputation as a premier gambler. He lies about what he's doing with the weekly paycheck. He lies to money sources. He lies to his spouse, his family, his relatives, his friends, his boss, his creditors. His life is taken over by mendacity, so much so in some cases that he becomes habitual about it, lying even when he doesn't have to. Sometimes the lying begins shortly after the serious gambling begins, sometimes it is installed into his "game plan" incrementally, as needed.

And the lies *work*. Write Linda Berman and Mary-Ellen

Siegel: "These deceptions usually take the form of lies of omission or commission. The lies may be believable, so many times you're frustrated because you just don't know whether the gambler is telling the truth. Other times the lies may defy all credibility. If you challenge gamblers, they will persist in their lies, seldom backing down. They can be so convincing that you begin to think *you're* crazy."[20] This latter phenomenon the authors call "gaslighting," after the movie *Gaslight*, in which a husband relentlessly attacks his wife's sense of reality.

As for secrecy, if he is not already in charge of the family's finances, he puts himself in charge. He begins to play what one recovering gambler calls "mailbox tag"—making sure he is first to see the mail at home or having creditors send statements to his office. Or he'll arrange for a separate post office box, either clandestinely or under false pretenses—he says the family must be losing mail out of the mailbox, or the kids are running off with the mail, and so forth.

Social and family relationships suffer commensurately. Gambling takes such a large part of his everyday life that he makes himself unavailable for family outings and get-togethers, for trips to the relatives, for events that used to be occasions for familial togetherness and bonding. The family wants to hike in the hills; he wants to hit the blackjack table. He reneges on his family responsibilities, both physically and emotionally, because of his gambling. Even when he's not gambling in body, he's doing so in spirit, thinking about the next bet, his next stint at the table. The emotional distance he requires to obsess on his gambling—it is a constant in his thoughts—wreaks havoc in the home. Communication lines break down, marital intimacy becomes but a memory, the kids start acting out or going into a shell. Many spouses complain that he's changed; he's not the man I married, they say.

What has happened is what happens with any addiction: this one, gambling, has supplanted the family's place in his hierarchy of priorities. Spouse and children soon become second-class citizens in their own home.

His spouse, at long last, stiffens her back and becomes unwilling to accept the usual rationalizations. The dog cannot eat his homework forever, she says. She's gotten wise to the source of the family's continual financial dilemma: The computer down at the bank can't *always* be screwing up. Perhaps she waves a sheaf of unpaid bills as evidence. It's his gambling that's the problem, she says. He denies it—nah, we're just having hard times. Maybe it's her spending that is the problem. In fact, if she would just get off his back, quit nagging him about the gambling, things would work a lot smoother around here. As for the gambling itself, it's a mere losing streak, a small spate of bad luck that will soon be overturned. He's won before (a long time ago); he'll get them out of their financial pit by winning again. The gambler's denial system is very strong, and his denials are ever so inventive, but this time they don't work. This time his spouse stays resolute: In addition to all the rubber checks she's been writing, the scavenging for a dollar here and a dollar there just to make it from day to day, and the tough decisions of what to go without while making her tri-weekly grocery runs, there's also the emotional unavailability, the way he's totally capitulated his parenting role, his never "being there" for anybody.

A day of reckoning has arrived. So long has he been robbing Peter to pay Paul and Paul to pay Peter that one day both Peter *and* Paul show up on his doorstep wanting to balance the ledger. The little financial hole he has dug for himself has grown to a cavern of Carlsbad proportions that could cave in at any time were he to make a false step or forget what lies he told to whom. So great has the pressure built at work that he fears losing his job. And so great has the heat become at home that, in order to save the marriage, he feels a need to mollify, or appease, his spouse and give himself some relief. The problems both financial and familial have grown to such scope that he can't rectify them by himself. He needs help.

He needs to be bailed out. He's been bailed out before, of course—every loan, every new credit line was a bailout of sorts—but this bailout is different. It's bigger for one thing, substantial enough to clear him of all the other debts he's accumulated over the years. Second, it may involve the spouse herself (or another family member). Up to this point he had employed every weapon in his arsenal to keep his family in the dark, but drastic times require drastic measures. He approaches his spouse on bended knee and confesses (almost) all. He begs forgiveness and pleads for help. She's angry, true, but she's relieved as well—now, at least, she knows what she's dealing with (she probably thought there was another woman). And in return for his promise to quit, or at the very least cut down, the gambling, she rescues him. How? "She went to her family to raise money, or she agreed to sign a consolidation loan, or she signed the bank papers for a second mortgage. She did what [he] asked because she wanted the debts, the financial troubles, and the gambling to end,"[21] writes Heineman. And she believed his promise to stop or cut back.

And he might fulfill his promise too—for a little while at any rate. Maybe he even shows his face at Gamblers Anonymous meetings to fulfill his end of the deal, laying low until the heat has died down some. "More likely, there is an upsurge of omnipotence," Richard J. Rosenthal writes. "Believing they can get away with anything, they bet more heavily and lose control altogether."[22] This is the third aspect that makes this bailout different from the others: It marks the beginning of his serious final decline into desperation. For many gambling addicts respond to this bailout with the euphoria that accompanies a big win. The pressure on the home and money front is temporarily off, and although absent for a good number of years now, the lady named Luck has once again assumed her rightful place on his arm. He's pulled himself away from the dark precipice; he's managed to get through another crisis.

The chase grows in strength; the gambling becomes feverish. The "big win" still awaits him. And it hasn't gone anywhere. It's still where it always has been and always will be—right around the corner.

The Escapist's Chase

Although the above scenario applies to action gamblers, much of it pertains to escape gamblers as well.[23] They quickly learn their friends don't gamble with the same intensity or longevity as they, and they take to visiting casinos alone. Their time and money expenditures increase, and they will win some, lose some (or more accurately, lose *more*), and break even some, just as their action counterparts do.

But their wins are qualitatively different, for they don't provide them money to set right some of their financial arrears so much as they offer them more time at their machine. Time is not money for them; money is time. And as such, it loses its reality and becomes play money; it becomes nothing more than time spent at the machine. Write Frederick and Steven Barthelme: "Many times we walked around the casino with five, eight, even ten thousand dollars in hundreds stuffed in our pockets. When we had the money in our hands it wasn't ten thousand dollars, it was just playing time, time at the table or in front of the slots. You don't care about it as you would at home. You don't feed and nurture it."[24]

And no win is ever enough, for to leave their machine is to reenter the world of pain and suffering they're fleeing in the first place. The machine is their true refuge. "While at the machine, she does not have to worry about anything except how to stay longer and play more often. No one is telling her what to do, no phone calls, no one wanting this or wanting that, no demands, just freedom."[25]

Many form real relationships with a machine—it becomes "her" machine—and may talk to it, cajole it, threaten it, swear at it, thank it when it spits. Some get jealous when another person happens to play it and accuse their machine of infidelity if the other player hits a jackpot. But all is forgiven once she returns to communion with it.

And while an escapist exerts control over her gambling at the beginning, vowing to leave when her money and/or time is depleted, "as soon as she sits down at the machine a trance-like hypnotic effect takes place. She pulls the handle or pushes the button and all plans are abandoned. She will stay at the machine, often not even getting up to use the bathroom or eat, only leaving her machine to go to the ATM or to write a check, asking an employee or another gambler to watch her machine while she is gone."[26] The result is, she does not leave when she promised she would, but stays until she has fed the machine the last dollar she had available for that visit.

On her way home she feels the same deprivation the action gambler feels when removed from action, and may vow never to return. But once home amidst the problems she had fled, and the problems she is creating with her gambling, her mind changes. She will indeed return, and she will need money.

Bailouts will follow as needed, from the same sources as come the action seeker's financial help, and escapists will also become secretive and dishonest about their financial situation, lying to their spouse to cover their activities and losses. They may lose time from work to gamble, making excuses just as the action gambler does. They may neglect familial responsibilities and get irate when confronted about their gambling. They will probably get into the same kinds of troubles the action seekers do.

But the good news is that they get there a lot quicker (they're already at the desperation phase from one to three years after they start gambling), and when there, they are more likely than action seekers to get help, and for a number of reasons, more likely to successfully recover.

THE PERSONAL TOUCH

Before we progress to the bottom of the gambler's journey, the desperation phase, a few words about how casinos in particular exploit the gambling addict's weaknesses. The gambling industry is quick to officially distance itself from people with gambling problems, to assert that problem and pathological gamblers are a mere necessary evil to their business. Indeed, some elements of the industry posture themselves as helping problem gamblers. Lottery tickets in some states contain a warning, much like that on cigarette packs, that compulsive gambling is a disease and can be treated. Casinos themselves contribute funds for specific treatment options or preventative campaigns, and post discreet signs on their premises with phone numbers for problem gambling hotlines and pithy sayings like "Bet with Your Head, Not over It."[27] Their executives stroke their chins with deep concern that some people happen to develop this addiction and hand over to them their hard-earned fortunes.

Compulsive gambling may be a nuisance to the gambling industry—but it is an exceedingly profitable nuisance. Recent studies indicate that problem and pathological gamblers account for an extraordinary percentage of the approximately $60 billion in annual gambling revenues. One Illinois study found that 52 percent of casino revenues come from people with gambling problems.[28] Another in Connecticut, based on interviews with 900 gamblers at casinos and pari-mutuel betting houses, found that 47 percent of gambling patrons in the state had gambling problems, while a telephone survey of the general population revealed that only 1.2 percent qualified as problem and pathological gamblers.[29] The National Opinion

Research Center, in its on-site survey, found that fully 31 percent of casino patrons displayed gambling problems.[30] Other reports have corroborated the general sense that casinos and other forms of gambling profit handsomely from people with gambling problems.

It is unlikely casinos will change their ways voluntarily. "There's too much money at stake," Tom Coates says. "They give lip service to wanting to do something about problem gambling, but when anywhere from a third to a half of their revenues come from these kinds of gamblers, the reality is they're not going to do anything until they've drained that individual dry and he poses the kind of potential threat that the detective in Detroit did recently, that stood up in the middle of the casino and blew his brains out. That kind of thing they don't want. Just short of that, that's fine."

Dr. John Eades confirms Coates's opinion. "They love gambling addicts," he says, speaking of casinos. "The public policy statement of the casinos is, 'Oh, we don't want anybody to have problems, and we try to be on the lookout for problem people, and they're really bad for business.' Well, all told, probably between $250,000 and $300,000 I gave them, and no one ever said a word to me about it. So, I think they know what they're doing. It's a science. And it's the most cold, calculating thing I've ever seen."[31]

Having a sense of how casinos entice people to leave their money inside may help problem and pathological gamblers, either in recovery or on the way to recovery, as well as people with potential gambling problems to resist their lures.

We start at the beginning. Getting people inside the doors—and then keeping them there—is integral to a casino's bottom line. And casinos do this as well as any business in the world. Hotel rates are often quite cheap—in fact, getting you to stay at the hotel in the first place ups your "trip worth," as casino personnel term it.[32] Meals are also cheap (the Las Vegas $4.99

buffets are world famous). One casino placed a bank of quarter slot machines around a snazzy new Jaguar XJ8 (which could be won on the machines) just inside the front entrance. Quarter slots attract players, as do cars as prizes, and the enthusiastic players near the doorway project an atmosphere of excitement and activity deeper inside the bowels of the casino even on slow nights, which draws people in. Nickel slot machines also attract players—so many that they often line up to play—and are used in the same way.[33] On a slightly different but amusing tack, Caesars Palace in Las Vegas offers a moving sidewalk from the Strip into the casino, but none from the casino back to the Strip.[34] Makes sense. You're going to be a lot lighter coming out of there than you were going in, right?

Once inside a big casino, there is absolutely no reason to leave, for everything is at one's fingertips—beds, restaurants, bars, shops, fitness rooms, you name it. And all roads lead to the casino floor—from the lobby to the restaurant, from the bathrooms to the lobby, etc. Many are the folks whose sandwich in the snack bar inadvertently cost them $150.

Fresh air is circulated frequently to keep you stimulated for your task, and some casinos reportedly pumped a special fragrance into their slot areas to prompt players to wager more. One casino has been experimenting with lighting only the felt on the blackjack tables, thus keeping the draining rays off the players' foreheads and sapping them of their strength.[35]

Slot machines get a lot of attention from the casino psychologists. The colors of the machines themselves are tested to see which will elicit the most playing time, as are the symbols on the reels. The machines are equipped with bill changers, thus precluding those inconvenient, and costly (to the casino) trips to the change cage. The frequent, small payouts serve as an enticement to keep playing. And spreading a few more generous slots around the banks sends patrons into a frenzy looking for the ones that spit.

Blackjack dealers are often "encouraged" to deal seventy-five or eighty hands an hour, and to shuffle six decks in eighty seconds—time is money, after all, lots of money as it turns out. (The Aladdin estimated it would reap $1.2 million more in profit in a year's time if its dealers never had to shuffle.)[36] When big-denomination chips are changed at the tables, they are changed into lowest-possible-denomination chips for the same reason the waitress at a restaurant bringing you change from your twenty on your $13.99 meal will give you six singles rather than a one and a five.

It is in the area of time management that casinos best ply their trade. Time is so important to a casino's success that it employs every trick in the book to make you forget about it. You will notice no clocks, for example; nor will you be peering out of any picture windows. Casinos do not want to "remind players that there was a world outside where day and night came and went and schedules had to be met."[37] They want a world where time ceases to be an issue. This is for a reason, as the science of probability dictates that the longer you play a given game, the more money you will lose. Says Randall E. Smith: "I've heard people say, 'You know, I thought I was there for maybe three, four, five hours,' and it's twenty-two."[38]

All the above are interesting ploys from a psychological perspective, and to be forewarned is to be forearmed. But the tactics used to exploit the weaknesses of those with gambling problems are more insidious.

One is offering the easiest possible access to money. Casinos know that before they can separate you from your money, you have to have money from which to be separated. Ergo the ATMs on casino floors, some of which do not have preset limits on withdrawals. The gambling industry is fully aware of the potential for easy credit in twenty-first-century America, Coates says, "and that's why they make it as easy as possible and they fight like a cornered rat every time you talk about trying to do something to remove the credit card machines from the midst of the casinos, because they realize that a lot of their dollars are tied in to the problem gamblers that are reaching increasingly fast for their credit cards." Eades knows of casinos that make it even easier to get their customers' cash. "You can go into a casino and mortgage your home—right there in the casino. . . . You got the bill of sale for your car, you can sell your car right there. There's somebody to go out and take a look at it."[39]

The effects of this easy money are sometimes disastrous. Coates tells of one Iowa man who, by all accounts, had no serious addictions or problems before casinos came to the Hawkeye State. He plunged himself into a $60,000 gambling debt, took a gun to an out-of-town motel, checked in, and then killed himself. But he left behind an indictment of casinos' easy-credit policies, an eloquent statement from the grave. His suicide note read, in part: "I never thought of gambling prior to two or three years ago. I really can't blame anyone but myself. But I sincerely hope restrictions are placed upon credit card cash availability at casinos. The money is too easy to access and goes in no time. My situation is now one of complete despair, isolation, and constant anxiety."

Making ready money a little more unready on the casino premises, or at least giving problem gamblers more hoops to jump through to get it, would be a good place for casinos to begin to make good their assurances that they take the compulsive gambling problem seriously.

But where casinos really speak to the needs of gambling addicts is in their treatment of them. It used to be only the high rollers who received special treatment, but now, in many casinos, every grind player sitting at her slot machine is likely to own a casino "preferred customer" card that she runs through the machine before she inaugurates play. This allows casinos to track her play—how long she pulls the handle, how much she spends—and to reward her commensurately with free food, meals, lodging, or other perks. The information the gambler provides the casino to get her card tells the casino when her birthday is, when her kids' birthdays are, and any number of other personal facts. And casino personnel are quick with a congratulatory comment or a personal remark, or even to send a gift or a card in the mail, all intended to make the slot player feel special. It works remarkably well, especially with escape players who may not get civil, much less special, treatment at home.

If all that works for regular slot players, think how much better the personal touch and "comping," as the practice of offering freebies is called, must separate the often narcissistic action gambler from his bankroll. "Casino executives are part bloodhound, part monitor, part schmooze," writes Gary Ross, who chronicled the decline of Canadian loan officer Brian Molony. "The idea is to sniff out money and establish a 'personal relationship' with those who have it. The idea is to look after them so they won't take their action next door. The idea is to get the money—every dollar." This personal relationship is established with glad-hand artificiality on the casino floor— "How's the wife? the kids? How 'bout them Broncos/Packers/Browns, etc.?"—and with a desire to meet the gambler's every need. "The warmth is that of a sunning snake," Ross writes, "the smile is purely transactional—hypocrisy of the first order. Crazy thing is, it works."[40]

Comps are based on average playing time and average amount bet and comprise free rooms in the hotel, free meals, rides to and from the airport, etc. For those who provide heavy action, these comps are on an order usually reserved for the glitterati: expensive suites, fancy meals and bottles of champagne in the room, a limo to snatch you from the airport and deliver you back, paid airfare to and from your hometown, show tickets. Comps of this latter sort are also by definition free, but in reality a gambler must blow a lot of money in a casino to receive these "free" benefits. Says Rev. John Landrum, who ministers to casino workers and gamblers on the Mississippi Coast: "We have met some high rollers, . . . the kinds that are wined and dined and are given the suites and the use of the limo and all this kind of stuff on a regular basis. They spend so much money for the treatment that they get, that they could buy the treatment in the Bahamas or somewhere at hotels. They could buy the treatment and spend way less. But they get caught up in the glamor."[41]

Another crazy thing is, this works too. It plays to the gambler's ego, massages his self-esteem, makes him feel very important, and it is inordinately seductive. Says one recovering addict: "I got wrapped up in that whole thing of getting treated like a king, like a big shot. I used to tip huge dollars just because I wanted everyone down there to love me. And I thought it was great that all the casino managers knew my first name and they treated me like a king." He loved the attention, "betting big bets and having people around. And I always went down at the high-volume times when there were a lot of people."

He received all the usual perks—the suites, the meals, the limo rides—but he also enjoyed the little things. "You know, you're playing blackjack, and it's a crowded Saturday night at the high-limit table, and I would have one of the casino hosts come over and tell him, 'Hey, I want to get some dinner.' And they just wait on your every need. 'Do you want it sent up to your room, or do you want to go sit in the restaurant?' 'Hmmm, send it up to my room.' You know, leave five, ten thousand dollars in chips sitting there, and I'd leave for a couple hours and come back, you know, just because I thought it was cool." Occasionally, based strictly on his word, the casino would comp his friends. "I would call them up sometimes and tell them, 'I've got a friend coming into town. He's a young professional. Can you treat him right?' And they would comp the room based off of me telling them." All of which can go straight to the head of a compulsive action gambler. "It's the biggest power trip. It totally is."

The gambling industry, for their part, claim to be powerless to identify problem and pathological gamblers, much less evict them from their casinos. The reality, however, is that they track a regular gambler's activity quite closely—his gambling behavior, after all, is the basis for the comps they bestow on him. "They will deny that they can spot a problem gambler on their computer system," says Eades, "but you don't have to be a whizbang to see you're there for two hours and then you're there for four and eight hours a day, and you're going from two hundred dollars a week to two thousand dollars a week. That's a progression. And you can see it and notify the person of it, but they swear they just can't do that. It's beyond the capabilities of their computers. Which is a lie."[42]

As a final point, the gambling industry also promotes the notion of luck, that an unsuccessful gambler merely had the capricious lady against him on one visit and will successfully court her on the next. Serious gamblers dearly wish to believe in luck, but in a casino there is no such thing. A casino operates only on probability, on mathematics. Every spin of a slot machine, every drop of a roulette ball, regardless of the previous spins and drops, has the same likelihood of hitting a jackpot or landing on the chosen color as all those that preceded it. If the ball lands five times straight in a red slot on a roulette wheel, the odds that it will on the next spin land on a red slot is the same as it is for every spin. There is no self-correction in games of chance. The money the casino makes derives from the odds, and the odds, favorable to the casino in all cases, are built into the game itself. Luck has nothing to do with it. And yet, tapping into the gambler's sense that he is due, that his luck will change, as casino employees are wont to do, serves its purpose: it brings the gambler back. "Casino personnel are well aware that a gambler faces the same disadvantage each time he plays and that luck is merely a euphemism for short-term fluctuations in the inevitable long term," writes Ross. "Their livelihoods are staked on the certainty that if a gambler stays long enough, or returns often enough, he'll lose everything. A dealer at Caesars, asked if he could spot a losing gambler, replied, 'Sure. Anybody you see more than twice.'"[43]

Losing gamblers are not unlucky. They just think they can beat the math.

"FEELING THE DEVIL'S BREATH"

Hope springs eternal, and it is hope that has brought the gambler to the point of desperation. But while this hope is unrealistic and delusionary, it is also severe in its intensity and not easily extinguished.

The hope is, of course, that he will get the "big win," that hitting one big jackpot or having one amazing streak of fortune at the tables will extricate him from the quicksand of problems that's swallowing his life and vault him back to normalcy.

The "big bailout" has breathed into his gambling new life—and new funds—and he pursues that redemptive and ever elusive big win with unflagging passion. Even if he would win big—and gamblers do win, throughout the course of the addiction—it really doesn't matter, for by this time he cannot leave well enough alone, he cannot walk away with the money and apply it against his outstanding debts. After a gambler with problems gets a big win, say $10,000, "rarely do we ever hear of anybody saying, 'Well, now I can pay those back bills with this money,'" says Landrum. "It's 'Well, here's ten thousand dollars to go win a hundred thousand dollars.' So they spend that."

One recovering gambler who was chasing a $90,000 debt got up by $15,000 at a blackjack table in about an hour one slow Sunday night. Then he lost a couple hands and decided he'd had enough for the evening. "I went upstairs and had food brought up, and I remember sitting in my room thinking, You know what? Tonight's the night. Tonight's the night I win $100,000 playing blackjack." At about 2 A.M. he returned to a nearly empty casino floor and announced his grandiose vision to a casino manager he knew. "Tonight's the night," he told him. "'Tonight's the night I take you.' And [the casino manager] sat down on the next chair over just to watch. And I played a thousand dollars a hand, and I had two hands going, and in fifteen minutes I lost $10,000."

Whether or not some stray wins offer periodic upturns to his downward course during this phase, in the end he blows the totality of the big bailout chasing the win. As the math doesn't change, this continual losing can be attributed to, as mentioned above, the gambler's impetuosity. "When the compulsive gambler starts to lose he becomes frightened and bets less carefully and intelligently than he did before, giving up the only real advantage he ever had," Custer writes. He also starts betting on hunches and superstitions, as well as laying his money on outrageous long shots. His sophisticated approach to these games of chance is but a memory. "By the time he arrives at the end of the Losing Phase and the beginning of the Desperation Phase," writes Custer, "all that is lost. He is desperate and his betting is desperate. He no longer has the composure and control to reflect, to weigh, to choose. His betting behavior is now frenetic, spastic, unreasoned, panicky."[44]

As a result, he sinks ever deeper into a morass of desperation and depression. Gambling now dominates his thoughts continually; it is his first thought in the morning and his last thought in the evening. His gambling has brought him all the pain he is experiencing, and yet the gambling is the only relief available to him. The depression during this stage is of such puissance, or intensity, that action gamblers take on the characteristics of their counterparts on the escape-and-relief side. It was never the money that mattered for escapists, and now it isn't for action gamblers either. Only the action itself could lift them out of their world of hurt and pain. "By then, your gambling had only to do with ACTION," writes Mary Heineman, addressing the gambler, "because ACTION was what you craved. Every cell in your body cried out for it whenever it wasn't at hand. It was your 'drug of choice'—your stimulator, your tranquilizer, and your faithful painkiller. It removed you from a reality you could not face and took you to nirvana."[45]

But action is a pricey tranquilizer at this stage of the addiction, and there is no prescription drug plan for the compulsive gambler. He needs money now more than he ever did. But no longer do the pity stories work with friends and family; no longer do legitimate money sources entertain his loan applications. At some point during this stage he crosses another calamitous boundary: He starts doing things that were inconceivable to him previously. Perhaps he sells big-ticket possessions. Eades sold a boat, an outboard motor, a van, and a motorcycle to finance his gambling.[46]

Or maybe he turns to crime. These may be white-collar transgressions, running the gamut from forgery of checks, to get-rich-quick scams foisted on the general public, to insurance fraud involving staged break-ins at home or the business, to kiting checks, to "borrowing" the spouse's credit cards and hitting a cash machine, to pawning the wife's jewelry.

But some gamblers stride purposefully into violent crime. No act, however egregious, seems beyond them at this stage. One woman, whose attorney said she was "addicted to gambling," over $100,000 in debt, tried to rob a Kansas bank on New Year's Eve 1999. Although no one was injured, she prompted an eight-hour hostage drama before being disarmed by one of her captives early the next morning. She faced charges of attempting to rob a bank, taking hostages, and employing a firearm in a violent crime. Said her attorney: "Her gambling addiction ruined her and her husband financially."[47]

Another woman, a thirty-nine-year-old wife and mother of three, with no prior felonies, got hooked on gambling in Minnesota. Accompanying her to a local gambling hall, her husband noticed nothing more than that she was hard to pry from the slots and tables when it was time to leave. Over time, though, her problems grew. Falling into debt, she gambled away the family's earnings, then pawned her wedding ring, the VCR, the TV, borrowed money from her mother, and even got her to take out loans for her. One day she swallowed forty Tylenol tablets, trying to end her losing the hard way.

A month later, after blowing another paycheck at the casino, she drove home to get a ski mask and some duct tape. She drove up to a convenience store, pulled the ski mask over her head, tried to bind the clerk's hands and feet with the duct tape, and walked out with $233. She drove around for a while, then headed for the casino. Later that day she was arrested at her home.[48]

Even upstanding citizens, when deep within the gambling obsession, will step over the line into criminal acts.

"Think about it," says Christopher W. Anderson. "What's my situation to get me to that point? I'm going to cross that line. Why? Because the reward . . . it's a risk-reward. I mean, by the time I'm at that point, I've already lost so much I'm at that place of saying it doesn't matter anymore. I'll take a long shot. I'm dead anyway. It doesn't matter. Or I've already stolen money away. They're going to catch me anyway, so, you know, why not take another shot?"

Once the first offense is committed, the others are much more easily dispatched. "The offense is initially rationalized as a short-term loan with the intention to repay it just as soon as they win," writes Rosenthal. "They believe they are just one winning streak away from solving all problems."[49]

It is an ugly place for the gambler to be. Forlorn and in self-imposed isolation, unable and unwilling to share his dilemma with those nearest him, his daily life is a living hell. "I'll tell you what it's like to be a gambling addict in this stage," one gambler says. "It's feeling the Devil's breath on your neck as you sit there gambling until everything you have is gone."[50]

The end is near. The bottom is at hand. And the gambler knows it. Some even seem to welcome it. One gambler who had bilked his employer of $90,000 for gambling arranged for the closure of his own addiction. He tallied up his debts one day and thought, "This is getting out of hand. This needs to stop. But how's it going to stop? I actually scheduled an audit. . . . My reasoning was, either I'll have won the money back or it'll be a stopping point for me."

Some experts tag on another phase to the process, one of hopelessness, and they say not all compulsive gamblers will go through it. Gamblers mired in this phase have given up. "They believe nothing can help; they don't care if they live or die. In fact, for many the latter is the preference. They will all consider suicide during this phase. Most will commit actions which could place them in jail or prison. Clinical depression is a given. In their minds, no one cares, no hope is available."[51]

When the compulsive gambler finally hits bottom, he hits it hard. The fantasy he has been nurturing for years has finally been destroyed; the hope he has harbored has finally evaporated. "What creates the bottom is when that fantasy world comes tumbling down and you cannot rebuild it," says Anderson, who himself gambled pathologically in securities. "For me it was the day that I realized I needed the equivalent of three big wins to get even. And I said to myself, 'And I can't even get one.' It was as if at that point that veil of delusion and denial comes crashing down and you begin to see things as they really are. That even if I did win, it wouldn't matter. I would just give it all back, and then some."

The choices while on the bottom become very stark for the gambler. "When reality invades and we cannot manufacture that next fantasy to solve the current problem or whatever we define as being the current problem, then we either kill ourselves or we get well. It's really kind of either/or."

Obviously the "or" is far preferable to the "either" in this case, but when on the bottom, the "either" looks tragically appealing to the compulsive gambler. While the "or" entails an arduous and painful and tedious ascent back to normal life, the "either" offers, as the saying goes, "permanent relief for a temporary problem."

It is a decision those close to the gambling addict want to prevent at all costs, and in many cases the spouse and family can have an influence. If they can detect the symptoms of problem gambling, if they can take appropriate measures to nip it before it grows to monster size, they can either raise the bottom for him or deter him from entering this self-destructive cycle of despair.

FIVE

Identifying the Problem

It is bad enough that a compulsive gambler harms himself, sometimes fatally, by the time he reaches the end of his long downhill slide into desperation. But that gambler also impacts directly the lives of others, sometimes for a long time afterward. Chief among these are, of course, the gambler's spouse and children.

The cost paid by the immediate family, and even the extended family and friends of the gambler, is severe and has been treated in an earlier chapter; it includes financial, emotional, marital, and even legal consequences of often staggering scope. In too many cases these consequences make their initial appearance very late in the play. In fact, it frequently happens that only when spouses are confronted with an avalanche of unpaid bills or a cavalcade of demanding creditors, or even worse, the long, unforgiving arm of the law do they become apprised of the problem. For some, the actual or threatened suicide by the compulsive gambler is the first scent they get that a problem is even in the air.

One of the purposes of this book is to arm spouses and family members with strategies that will help them curtail the scope—and the eventual tragic endgame—of gambling problems in the one they love. But unfortunately, among the addictions, the compulsion to gamble is one of the most difficult to detect, much less arrest. The addict does not sport telltale needle tracks on his arm, nor can you smell gambling on his breath—there are no throwing-up or falling-down-drunk episodes, nor any physical "blackouts." And gamblers make other addicts look like mere dilettantes in the science of secrecy and deception. They do not leave their "poker face" with their money at the table. They can lose thousands at the casino and walk into the house as though nothing happened, sphinxlike in their demeanor. Says Chaplain Trennis Killian of the Riverboat Casinos Ministry, who ministers to casino workers and counsels problem gamblers: "Anyone who is trained can pretty well pick an alcoholic or a drug addict out of a crowd. But there's no way you can pick a problem gambler out of a crowd unless that crowd is in the casino. . . . I could walk into a room of ten people. Nine of them [might] be compulsive gamblers, and I wouldn't know it."[1]

Certainly, late in the progression the spouse will recognize it. In the desperation phase everything about the gambler says—no, screams—to the family that he has been overtaken by a severe problem. He looks terrible and eats very poorly, is given to fitful sleep and nightmares, and has let his health and even personal hygiene slide. He is anxious and depressed, may think he is going to die, and breaks down into weeping spells. His behavior swings between volcanic anger and near catatonic listlessness. Even prior to all-out desperation, late in the losing phase, the compulsive gambler can be identified, primarily because his every thought and word and action center on gambling or gambling-related concerns. If he isn't absenting himself physically and emotionally from his family, to gamble and to think about gambling, he's off obtaining money with which to gamble.[2] To the family this may seem better than dealing with the guy face-to-face, though, for he is virtually an impossible case—short-fused, imperious, demanding.

Early on it is the stealth addiction. It is difficult even to tag the label "abnormal" to the initial signs, for they largely involve temperament and personality, and do not point to gambling any more than to other general emotional problems. A specialist might identify later, intermediate symptoms, but to the unschooled they fall within the range of normalcy—a little excessive and unusual, true, but still tolerable and easily rationalized.[3]

On the upside, though, at no time in their careers are compulsive gamblers more candid about their behavior than right at the beginning. Gambling is still an enjoyable, exciting diversion for them, and they feel no need to lie about where they go or how much they spend. Indeed, many compulsives brag about their winnings at the beginning.[4]

This presents a unique opportunity for the spouse and family members. If they know something about how the gambling addiction progresses, they may be able to ferret out potential problems through simple observation and tactful interrogation of the gambler. Here are some activities to look for and ask about:[5]

- ✤ *Is the gambling increasing?* Does the gambler go gambling more often, play more money, increase his bets, spend more time at the gambling venue?
- ✤ *Does he lose control?* Does he change his plans while gambling, playing longer than he had agreed to or losing more than he planned to?

✤ *Does he chase?* Chasing is an attitude as much as anything else, and does not necessarily entail large amounts of money. It can be short term and involve as little as a few dollars. "The fact that they lost, that they are 'down' so much money, becomes the reason to gamble further."[6]

✤ *Is he able to quit while he's ahead?* People with gambling problems find this difficult.

✤ *Is the gambling an escape from other problems or concerns?* If the gambler is depressed, on edge, bored, or frustrated before he goes gambling and somewhat down and tense afterward, but excited, relaxed, sure of himself, or ostensibly unaware of his problems while he's gambling, this may bode trouble. The gambling may be his escape from his worries.

✤ *Does the gambling excite him?* Gambling excites a lot of people, but the person on the road to trouble is more excited more often than people who will not develop problems.

One very simple and often effective recognition tactic is to simply ask the gambler straight out to quit his gambling. Eileen Fox, a certified compulsive gambling counselor in Colorado Springs, advises spouses of gamblers in the early stages to simply ask the gambler to stop his activity. "Just ask them to not gamble," she says. "Tell them they're affecting the marriage." If the person goes into denial mode—"I can control it. It's not a problem"—Fox advises saying to him, "If our marriage is really important to you, this is something I'd like you to do. If it's just a preference or an activity, would you give it up for the sake of our marriage?"[7]

What happens next will go a long way in determining whether you're dealing with problem gambling or not. If the gambler is able to cease and desist without any uncomfortable side effects—he does not obsess about the gambling, he does not sneak off to sate his desires—the problem may be solved. Conversely, if he is unable to get gambling out of his mind or starts gambling behind your back, you may have a problem on your hands.

And as the problem increases, so, unfortunately, does the gambler's need for deception and secrecy, and recognition of the problem becomes ever more difficult.

A DIFFERENT KIND OF TIP SHEET

The gambler himself can easily ascertain if he has a problem by honestly—key word here—completing a reputable screening device like the Gamblers Anonymous "Twenty Questions." This questionnaire cuts right to the heart of the gambling addiction—and to the heart of the gambler too (again, if he's honest)—and has set many potential pathological gamblers on the road to help.

For the family, though, it's a little more complicated—and a lot more inexact. They may not even know if the person is gambling. Or if they suspect he is, they may be unsure of their conjecture or whether his activity has metastasized to problem levels.[8] After all, with the proliferation of legalized gambling in our country, how would you know how often he bought lottery tickets or how many he bought, whether he drops in on a nearby casino more times than he tells you about, whether those business trips to the West Coast involve a lengthy layover in Las Vegas or Reno, whether he takes lunch at the off-track betting parlor, whether five hundred or even a thousand dollars is in his pocket when he leaves for the "friendly" poker game with the guys? You could ask him, true. But some gamblers who have enjoyed candid, transparent, completely guileless relationships with their spouses for many years admitted that, once the gambling bug bit, lying to cover up their gambling—even to their spouses—became habitual. Gamblers also typically destroy or hide any "evidence" of their activity. They don't come home from work waving two hundred losing lottery tickets for all to see; they don't put their bookie's number on the kitchen phone's speed-dial. Their gambling is a very hush-hush operation.

Because the gambler's problems quickly become their own, the family is thus left in a very precarious place. But if they know where to look and what to look for, they may be able to identify the problem and subsequently settle upon a course of action.

Basically, a gambler needs two things to gamble: He needs money with which to gamble, and he needs time in which to gamble. Gamblers know this as well, which is one of the reasons, when their gambling becomes problematic, they become very reticent and evasive about these topics. A spouse or family that can identify changes in these two areas may be on to something.

Follow the Money

Money is a lot of things to a lot of people, but it is definitely the engine that makes the gambler's world go round. Fully six of the twenty questions in the Gam-Anon survey for those who think they might be living with a compulsive gambler deal with money, and range from whether the spouse is hounded by bill collectors to whether she feels she cannot trust the gambler with money to whether she has to hide money to cover normal, daily living expenses for the family.[9]

Action may be the end purpose of the gambling addiction, but where there's no money, there's no action. Money is clearly the lifeblood, and the gambler needs to be pumped with ever increasing units to keep his compulsion healthy. First he will tap his own resources—his spending money, ancillary funds, etc. But when these discretionary monies are depleted, he will begin to look elsewhere, which is when things start to get complicated. Everything from bank books to credit cards to stock certificates to bank loans to friends' and relatives' financial resources become the reservoir from which he must quench his financial thirst, and the more sources he taps the more complex his money life becomes. He grows into a circus-quality juggler, moving funds from one account to another and back again to keep all his financial balls in the air. "Without this juggling act," write Linda Berman and Mary-Ellen Siegel, "he can't lead any kind of normal life *and* also be in on the gambling action!"[10]

As mentioned above, he becomes exceedingly secretive about his or the family's financial situation. Although it doesn't have to—finances are something to be kept to oneself in many cultures and families, and in our society many males feel it their familial responsibility to handle money matters exclusively—overprotectiveness and furtiveness about financial matters can in itself offer a clue that gambling is a problem. A gambler with problems will often be reticent to share financial information with a spouse when asked; indeed, he may grow irate at the mere broaching of the topic, or at the least, offer equivocal and convoluted explanations to questions about income, assets, or expenditures.

Many gamblers are able to elevate the "blame game" to levels of deceit usually seen only in Washington, D.C. The gambler is the one who loses the money, yet he is able to shift the blame onto the spouse, and in some cases, even make her feel guilty for the family's financial straits. "His only goal is to blame her for anything that might get him off the hook so he can continue to gamble," Heineman writes.[11] Running up the utility bills, talking too much on the phone, buying clothes that are too expensive, "pampering" the children with school supplies, being a mean shrew and denying him one of the few joys he has remaining in this life, etc.—the gambler will employ these reasons and many more to deflect attention from and cover his losses. Gamblers are without peer in verbal manipulation.

The net effect of the gambler's reticence, equivocation, rage, and/or blaming tactics is this: The spouse backs off. Either she will only very warily broach money matters to the gambler in the future, or she will forgo the topic completely. Peace in the marriage and in the family is more important to her than her curiosity and concern.[12]

Other money problems are thankfully more easily noticed. What follows is a list of mostly visible financial markers (with a few subjective ones thrown in also) that the gambler leaves on the money trail. Bear in mind that not all gamblers will exhibit all these traits, and some might display only a few. Many of the criteria are not exclusive to gambling behavior but might apply to other problems as well. The money trail is faint and hard to follow, obscured by stealth and duplicity. But following the money may lead you to someone with gambling problems.[13]

❧ *Problems with bills.* Unpaid bills may fly beneath your radar if the family's financial matters are the gambler's exclusive province, but if you have access to the invoices and notice irregularities—or a change from how he normally discharges monthly finances—in the payment schedule, this may indicate a problem. A gambler has cash-flow considerations too, you know. He might have to let one month's bill slide and then pay off two months' worth the next time. He may pay bills only in part. He may also pay one or more months' charges in advance, in effect setting that money aside so he can't gamble with it. As an illustration of this latter principle, one recovering gambler took great pains to fill his car with gas *before* he arrived at the casino, certain that he would have no money for it when he left.[14]

✤ *Loans.* If you discover the gambler borrowing money simply to pay normal bills when his income and the family's financial situation have not changed; if by accident you come across loans he has taken out that you don't know about; if you have ever been urgently implored to cosign a loan for him; or if creditors phone inquiring not so gently about repayment schedules, this could indicate gambling problems.

✤ *Changes in assets.* Gamblers often tap into savings accounts, pension accounts, and other money funds to get their gambling money. If you notice a deviation from the normal pattern in contributions to these funds—or in charity contributions, as well—this may be a pointer. Health and life insurance policies may also be allowed to lapse. Also, look for large, unexplained withdrawals from, say, a savings account followed quickly thereafter by an equally large deposit; the gambler often attempts to cover his tracks.

✤ *Credit cards.* We live in a credit-happy society. The average Joe or Jane—indeed, 90 percent of the population[15]—has access to credit and can pull any one of ten pieces of plastic from his wallet or her purse, with a credit line averaging $2,000 for each. This runaway credit situation is like dying and going to heaven for gamblers with problems. It is not unusual to hear of addicts with a dozen or more maxed-out credit cards when they finally come in for treatment. If the gambler in your life frequently changes cards or seems to be acquiring a lot of new ones, this may be a tip-off.

✤ *Tax returns.* Shortly after the sirens and bells of a slot machine announce another "lucky" winner in a casino, somebody appears over the gambler's shoulder with a W-2G form for him to sign. Any substantial winnings

is regarded as income, and Uncle Sam wants his cut.
Alas, for many gamblers that money goes right back
into the machine, often within hours, and unless he
can document his losses, he faces a double whammy
come national Invest in America Day, April 15. Says
Tom Coates of Consumer Credit of Des Moines:
"Not only are you losing your dollars net, the feds are
going to come after you for a tax bite on winnings
that you had for a little while." A magnetic-stripped
casino slot-club card, which the gambler slides
through a slot machine prior to play, catologs the
losses and takes care of that problem. But many gamblers still try to hide winnings from the IRS and file
inaccurate returns. Some forgo the whole unpleasant
business of tax returns entirely. Those filing jointly
with you may ask for your signature prior to completing the form.

❖ *Possessions.* Gamblers will often pawn items from the
house for wagering money. If a big-ticket possession
of some sort—jewelry, VCRs, TVs, stereos, etc.—dis-
appears, this may have happened. If it reappears in
equally mysterious fashion a few days later, this may
still have happened (he bought the item back). If the
gambler tries to persuade you to sell something to
cover some outstanding bills, he may have blown the
money allocated to pay those bills. Or if you feel com-
pelled to pawn household items to cover bill payments, this can sound a similar warning.

❖ *Subjective observations.* Changes in the gambler's recent
behavior regarding money may point to gambling
problems. For example, does he avoid family gatherings or get-togethers with friends? He may be avoiding
a face-to-face with people who have loaned him money
or "know too much" about his gambling habits. Is the

gambler working a lot of overtime, or even taking on a second job, for no particular reason? Has he become particularly cost-conscious in areas like transportation, clothes, or home repairs? If the gambler is all of a sudden riding his bicycle to work instead of driving, if he seems to be wearing that old blue suit to death, and if the homeplace is going to seed, gambling problems may be at the root of this behavior. Alternately, one recovering gambler bought many expensive garments with gambling winnings, which he reported to his wife as getting on sale to cover himself. If the family always seems to be short of money and you can't put your finger on why, or if you find yourself resorting to trickery of your own to ensure enough money to cover your own expenses—overestimating your monetary needs, underreporting your income, and so forth—gambling may be the reason.

It's About Time

More than an alcoholic needs time to drink, more than a drug addict needs time to ingest forbidden substances, the gambler needs time to gamble. While drinkers and drug users can only take so much of their craved-for substance before biology steps in to stop the madness—they drink or drug themselves into sleep, oblivion, a near-comatose state, or even death—no such phenomenon occurs with gamblers. It is not uncommon to hear of gambling addicts plying their obsession for unthinkable periods of time at one sitting.

As the addiction deepens and the gambler becomes ever increasingly ensnared in its web, he will gamble more and think about gambling more, until his entire life is centered around the activity. To do that takes time—and toward the end, lots of it. Indeed, time is of the essence in gambling. And because it is so crucial, it can offer the spouse and family clues that they have a gambling problem in their midst. In fact, says Coates, time may be easier to track than the money trail with its many labyrinthine passages and cul-de-sacs.

Obviously, if time spent gambling increases, this may indicate a problem. A spouse may gamble too much for your liking—indeed, any gambling at all may be problem gambling from your point of view. But when attempting to determine if there is a problem, try to set aside your personal standards. Ask yourself how his gambling compares to that of your friends and acquaintances. As far as you can see, does he spend about as much time gambling as they do, or does he spend significantly more time? [16]

Following are some other possible tip-offs concerning time, with another caveat: Any single behavior should be evaluated as part of a whole; a spouse or family member should not jump to conclusions based upon the gambler meeting a single or even a few of the following criteria. His activities must be judged on the whole.[17]

* *Absences from work.* As more time is needed for gambling, many gamblers will tap into their normal working hours to supply it. Calling in sick is popular, and the excuses run the gamut from the mundane—a sick child, a doctor's visit—to, when those are exhausted, the spectacular—a wholly fictitious but dying aunt, etc. This also has the advantage of being reasonably safe, for the spouse or family learns of it only if the gambler's boss or fellow employee makes a solicitous inquiry.[18] A gambler may also take his vacation days one at a time rather than in big blocks; this allows him to get away for a day to a nearby casino or track.[19] He may also start working at odd times of the day. One recovering addict, after discovering his lunch hour did not provide him enough "juice," started

"getting up very early in the morning and telling my wife I was going in to work." He would go to the casino at 3:00 A.M., gamble until 7 or 7:30, and then "rush back to work and get to my office in time for my wife to call me and say good morning." Gamblers working on flexible time schedules, or who are not tied down to a specific location—people who travel a lot or have occupations that offer free time during working hours—can easily mask their gambling.

✤ *Withdrawal from social and family life.* Time spent at a casino is time spent away from the family (in most cases). To get this time the gambler must curtail certain family responsibilities and activities. A heretofore loving, caring spouse may gradually omit himself from family outings, begging off for some reason or refusing outright to participate. He may suddenly not want to go to the spouse's mother's for Sunday dinner, or to a child's school activities. Maybe he shows up late; maybe he wants to leave early. His formerly eager acceptance of social invitations may now take on an I'll-have-to-get-back-to-you tone—he has to see if it will fit into his gambling schedule.

He may start neglecting some of the chores so omnipresent and necessary to continue a high level of existence in a civilized country—getting an emissions test for his car, visiting the dentist, etc.—because the time spent on these trivial matters is time *not* spent at a blackjack table or slot machine or thinking about blackjack or slot machines.

Perhaps he was once an avid golfer or hiker or jogger or bird-watcher, what have you, but now time formerly reserved for his avocation is forgone, given over to gambling-related action or thinking. Maybe the activities that he once shared with you are less frequent—the drives in the country, the evenings at the theater—or quit altogether. Sexual intimacy between husband and wife may suffer as well—when he wins he doesn't need it, when he loses he doesn't want it. On the other hand, the gambler might be very gung-ho about family outings where gambling is available. He may suggest or insist on family vacations or romantic getaways to a destination like Atlantic City or Las Vegas, or he may organize group outings to casinos and such.

✤ *Where exactly* is *he?* Big blocks of time are preferable, if not absolutely necessary, for problem and pathological gamblers. Obviously, one hooked on the lottery can temporarily sate his addiction with a five-minute stop at a 7-Eleven, and sports bettors are as close to the action as they are to their phones or televisions. But to travel to a casino, even a nearby one, and to play in quantity enough to get their "fix," gamblers need a few hours. If he cannot account for big blocks of time when you don't know where he is, this may signal a gambling problem (it may also signal an affair, a mistaken conclusion many spouses make).

The gambler may simply sneak away and worry about the consequences—and explaining his absence—later. More likely the gambler will "spring" himself with an excuse beforehand. These alibis, like those used to get off work, range from the commonplace to the bizarre, and if they seem over the top, or seem to have holes in them, it might be cause for worry. You can check out his story if you want, but be prepared to be disappointed. It is not uncommon for the spouse's on-site inspection of his stated whereabouts—at the bowling alley, at the office, visiting a sick colleague, etc.—to come up empty. One gambler told his spouse he had an appointment at his office at 9:00 P.M. one night. Says the spouse: "I just decided to ... drive down there. And I knew where he would park. And of course, his truck was nowhere to be found." Or he may simply come home at ridiculous hours. "What really got my attention," one gambler's spouse says, "was him not coming home till about three-thirty in the morning four nights a week."

The gambler will throw off any number of indicators other than those concerned primarily with money or time. You may notice subtle or even overt changes in his personality, from outgoing effervescence to inward brooding to obvious agitation to seismic and inexplicable sarcasm and rage. You may also notice him emotionally detaching from the family. One recovering addict who was losing enormous bets at the blackjack table while chasing a considerable debt, spent nearly every waking non-gambling hour thinking about card-playing techniques, placing between himself and his family a barrier his wife noticed. "I mean, at one point she confronted me and asked me if I was having an affair, because just mentally I was so focused on this and not on our family. She didn't know what was going on." It may happen that the gambler is content and calm only when engaged in the act or thinking about it. One recovering gambler admits to being irritable when he wasn't gambling. "If I wasn't gambling, I wasn't happy basically. And that's all you think about: ... when [is] the next time you can gamble and how you're going to get money and how you're going to get time to go over there."

And if you accompany him to a gambling venue, you may see what the gambling does to him up-close and personal. Although many gamblers pride themselves in maintaining an expressionless visage when actively in play, they do have chinks in their emotional armor. One spouse went with her gambling husband to a casino when he was already deep within the cavern of his addiction, and she watched him without his knowledge. A bell was rung to indicate the casino was about to close, "and he had this glazed look over his eyes, like he had taken a drug, and a look of panic. And he was running to the ATM" to get a final hit of money. He acted, she says, "like life is over because they're kicking us out. And I think he had gotten, like, forty or sixty dollars and dumped it all in that period, and didn't get any back."

Another indication of possible gambling problems is his reaction to his losses. If he is remorseful or upset after a bad day and announces "never again," but then goes right back to it soon thereafter, this may indicate a problem. As might his reaction to discussions about gambling and wins and losses. However, this can cut both ways. Many gamblers enjoy reliving the glories and lamenting the failures. This stokes the internal gambling fires and is a substitute, albeit an inferior one, for action itself. Others want to steer clear of the topic altogether. They may be worried about being discovered, or embarrassed or feeling guilty about losing so much, or afraid they will be required to confront their denial, and thus may be on edge during the discussion or try to quickly change the subject.[20]

A spouse can find other pointers by merely looking within. If she is constantly on edge; if she wonders why her life seems out of control; if she is ashamed of the gambler's debts; if she finds herself trying to change his behavior; if she feels somehow responsible for his obsession; if she lies to cover it up or tries to conceal the financial effects of the gambling—these emotions in the spouse may in and of themselves indicate gambling problems in her loved one.[21]

You've seen what the problem is and you've learned how to recognize it. The question now becomes: What can you do about it?

SIX

Dealing with the Problem

There are myriad ways you can react to a person with gambling problems, some good, some bad, some productive, some unproductive, and some even counterproductive. We begin with the antithesis: *what you should not do.*

DENYING THE OBVIOUS

"Denial," like its peer in pop psychology, "codependency," has been worked to death in the last couple decades and can now be applied to nearly any situation, however remote from actual psychological contexts, without drawing the least little notice. But it is a true phenomenon, a psychological concept that is more than real for those living with gambling problems. Writes Custer: "In the psychiatric context, denial means refusing to acknowledge something to oneself, getting oneself to actually believe that there is no danger at all."[1]

Obviously, the gambler himself can exhibit it, and in fact probably luxuriates in it for many years—it is, after all, a mental framework that allows him to continue gambling while the structures of what was once a happy personal and family life burn merrily on. He lives amidst the smoldering rubble created by his own gambling, and yet refuses to see the problem for what it is. Open confrontations are met with rationalizations—"Oh, sure, honey, I gamble. But *85 percent* of all Americans gamble"—and dissimulation—"It's not the gambling that's the problem, dear. It's *these bills!*"

Tom Coates, at his credit counseling agency, sees many clients who come to him seeking financial solutions to what is a behavioral problem. One couple he counseled, both compulsive gamblers, put themselves into six-figure debt by borrowing against their pension, their cars, and their home; maxing out as many credit cards as they could; securing a couple of home equity loans; and borrowing all they could on signature loans, and then revolving that money around—all to support their gambling habits. They faced, they said, not a gambling problem but a *debt* problem. "That's a window into the mind-set of the addicted gambler who's in denial," he says. "They are denying that they've got a real problem. They may have a lot of manifested problems around them because of it, but they don't recognize, at least in their conscious mind, ... that [gambling's] the real issue, and so they're wanting to deal with the manifestations and not this core issue."[2]

Unfortunately, it is not only the gambler who often flounders in denial, but the spouse and family too. Denial is a chameleon, capable of frequently changing its appearance, and as such is sometimes difficult to identify. But in all its many forms it is a technique used to explain away, minimize, justify, and rationalize the problem gambling. The spouse may remain in this state of denial for years, until some incident related to the gambler, often quite dramatic, throws her back into reality.

The simplest form of denial is to insist that the gambling per se is not happening. Sometimes this is done despite clear evidence or firm testimony to the contrary from friends and relatives.

More complex is the rationalization that admits that he gambles but discounts the severity of the gambling: "Sure, he plays blackjack, but he goes only on weekends." "He only buys lottery tickets." Or the spouse decides to look on the bright side—it could be a lot worse, after all. "The kids have school supplies and clothes." "He's not running around with other women, anyway." "After he stopped drinking, I didn't want to take from him all his joys in life."

Another fruitful area of deception is explaining why he gambles, under the false pretense that to know is to understand: "He gambles because of the way he was raised." "If he didn't have such an overbearing boss, he wouldn't need to blow off steam at the casino every once in a while." "If people in her church treated her better, she wouldn't be so lonely, and wouldn't feel the need to go to bingo so often." Or the spouse can get philosophical: "If gambling weren't so readily accessible in our society, he wouldn't gamble at all"—which may be true, but doesn't change anything.[3] Some spouses treat the problem as an intellectual dilemma, "an interesting social phenomenon affecting everyone but [themselves]."[4]

As the gambling increases, so does the strength of the denials. Denial, like gambling itself, grows incrementally, so that an excuse raised early on in the process prepares the spouse's reasoning for further, and gradually greater, deceptions. The result is that, later in the process, the spouse is "no longer dealing with reality as reality," Custer writes. So great is the spouse's fear of reality, of the truth that she in fact has married a man with gambling problems, that she has shelved all her standards for testing reality. "So she makes one compromise after another with reality, hoping blindly that somehow things will work themselves out and that everything will be all right."[5]

Although in the short run denial seems to serve a purpose—it does keep family amity at least ostensibly intact, and permits the family to conduct their daily lives in a quasi-normal way without anxiety, depression, shame, or anger overwhelming them—in the long run it is counterproductive.[6] It obviously does nothing to solve the problem; on the contrary, it exacerbates it. The gambler takes solace in the fact that he can fool his spouse, that he can get away with his gambling. When the spouse takes his side, in effect going along with him in his gambling behavior by denying reality, she is only encouraging him. The family or marital harmony the spouse thinks she is rescuing with her rationalizations and excuses turns out to be a mere peaceful pause in a plot that is inevitably approaching a tragedy of Shakespearean proportions.

Gambling problems are what they are; they are not debt problems or financial problems or budget problems or money-management problems. They are *gambling* problems, and they will remain so until something is done to correct them. They won't fix themselves. Not seeing them for what they really are does nothing to change any of that.

MAKING GAMBLING EASIER

Another negative and unproductive response to gambling problems is called enabling. This too has become a buzzword in contemporary America, but despite its overuse to the point of becoming a cliché in the vocabulary of a therapeutic culture, it too is all too real. Like its partner in deception, denial, it too takes many forms, and it too ends up encouraging the very behavior it is intended to curtail.

"Enabling" can succinctly be defined as "any action that

makes it easier for the gambler to gamble."[7] We will outline
this often unwitting and well-meaning but nonetheless
destructive response to gambling problems in four categories:
covering up and covering for the gambler, attempting to control his behavior, bailing him out, and cooperating with him.

♣ *Covering up and covering for the gambler.* It is only a
   matter of time before bad things begin to happen
   because of the gambler's escalating condition. A
   spouse may want to conceal the problems from her
   family and friends, but in hiding the behavior she is
   only protecting him from the consequences.[8] It is also
   inevitable that a person with gambling problems will
   eventually fray his relationships at work, with friends,
   or in the extended family. He may miss time on the
   job for gambling, he may alienate friends or relatives
   by reneging on family responsibilities, and his spouse
   may take it on herself to play a firsthand role in
   patching up these strained relationships. She may call
   his boss to excuse his tardiness or absence, she may
   take his side when a family member criticizes his
   behavior. When she covers up his behavior in these
   and other ways, she is deferring the consequences of
   his gambling and indirectly green-lighting his further
   destructive behavior.
♣ *Attempting to control the gambler's behavior.* It is
   axiomatic in addiction treatment that the addict himself must hit bottom before he can begin the grueling
   journey upward. Once the gambling reaches addiction
   stage, the gambling controls the gambler, not vice
   versa. People not wanting to be helped will not and
   cannot be helped. Trying to control the gambling,
   thus, becomes largely ineffective and even counterproductive. "Most illnesses progress uninterrupted along a

predictable path unless effective intervention is applied," writes Mary Heineman. "Because many wives do not know they are dealing with an addiction when their husbands are gambling compulsively, they believe they can control or even cure the problem."[9] Spouses wanting to control the gambling will employ every trick they think might be effective, from hiding car keys, to trying to dissuade gambling friends from associating with their husbands, to obligating their husbands to frequent, time-consuming family affairs, to even withholding conjugal favors. The important thing to remember about attempts to control the gambling is this: they don't work. In addition to giving him the opportunity to blame you for the gambling, you offer him the chance to rise up in indignation at some perceived slight and go gamble away his pain.

Even the threat to leave him, although usually coming after other tactics have failed, is an attempt to control the gambling. A gambler in the throes of his addiction would likely see your leaving as a godsend—after all, the gambling has taken up residence as the monarch of his life, and its requests are his commands. If he had his druthers, he'd like to be married to you, but if it's between you and the gambling, you might want to take the gambling and lay the points. "If you say that it's either gambling or me and the kids," Coates says, "be prepared to hear, 'Then I'll take the gambling.'" Adds John M. Eades, a recovering addict trained in addiction counseling, "If my wife had left me, that would have been perfect, because then I could have felt sorry for myself and gambled. In other words, everything is fodder for the gambling addict."[10]

✣ *Bailing out the gambler.* Bailouts come in too many forms to number, but all share the same effect: They relieve the gambler from facing the consequences of his gambling excesses, and thus they arrest his plunge toward his bottom. In order to finally face his condition and do something about it, he must be forced to face the consequences of his actions, painful though they be. When you reap the whirlwind for him, you're only hurting him, not to mention yourself. Bailouts, too, run the gamut of enabling and rescuing behavior. They can take the form of your assuming the gambler's family duties—you take the son to football practice instead of him; you take the car in for an oil change instead of him—thus freeing his time for gambling pursuits. They may also show themselves in a more recognizable form: bailing out the gambler monetarily, fixing the financial quandaries he puts himself in. To pony up money to pay back a gambling loan, to arrange for a sizable bailout from your parents or to cosign a loan at a bank, to mollify hounding creditors with your personal monies may alleviate crises short-term, but they perpetuate the problem and reduce the gambler's motivation to change. Says Chaplain Killian: "You're not helping them if you bail them out. You're just ... allowing them the opportunity to go back in there and gamble more. And they will do it."

✣ *Cooperating with the gambler.* One other way spouses enable the gambling is by directly or indirectly participating in it with him. Not uncommonly, spouses enjoy gambling too, and the gambler will tap this enthusiasm to both compromise the spouse and justify his own activity. If she goes to the casino with him, how hard can she come down on him for his gambling?

If the gambler says, "What do you mean, we lost forty-five thousand? Then we both have to go gamble and try to win it back," you should resist the entreaty. On the indirect side, taking gambling-related phone messages or in other ways facilitating, or making easier, his gambling also applies here.[11]

HELP IS ON THE WAY

But enough bad news. Compulsive gambling, although generally regarded as one of the more devastating addictions, can be turned around. And although the onus of that reversal is placed squarely on the shoulders of the addict himself—he has to hit bottom, he has to want change—spouses and family members can facilitate the process.

They can "raise the bottom" by refusing to deny the problem and to bail him out. This may on the surface seem like more bad news, for the pain involved for the spouse and family is immediate and acute—you definitely *are* making things worse for the gambler, and probably for you as well, in the short run. But truth be told, things often have to get worse before they can get better. He has to reach the bottom of his vexatious slide before he can even glance at the hill of recovery ahead of him. Anything you can do to speed his downward progress is, as paradoxical as it may seem, extremely helpful to all parties involved.

NO MORE BAILOUTS

As we mentioned above, anytime you bear the consequences of the gambler's actions for him, you are erecting a speed bump in his slide toward desperation and ironically hampering his chances at recovery. Thus the shibboleth of the gambler's spouse: "No more bailouts!"

This requires tough love, and it is easier said than done. A gambling addict, a man or woman you love, coming hat in hand to beg funds or services from you, an ostensibly repentant person bent on reform and putting things right if only you would supply this little monetary relief, is a heartbreaking specter to turn your back on. "You don't want to see him suffer," says Randall E. Smith, a Denver-area therapist, of the gambler's spouse. "Or you have the illusion that, if I help him for a little bit, I think he understands now what the problem is, and if I just help him this, this one time, then everything will be okay."[12]

It won't be, for, as Rev. John Landrum of the Mississippi Coast says, "We have seen it happen time after time after time, where you bail somebody out, . . . that takes the pressure off. Then they go right back to it. And then the next time, it's usually a bigger hole they've dug."[13]

Emotional support, though, may help the no-bailout philosophy go down more easily. Smith counsels spouses to "still [be] there with the individual and for them, being able to talk with them about the issue, the problem, emotionally supporting them, but absolutely not one dime toward bailing them out."

Absolutely no bailouts coupled with emotional support is simple and extremely sound counsel. Sometimes, though, following through on the no-bailouts commitment is more difficult than it seems. Whether to bail or not to bail grows very complicated when the welfare of others is at stake, and bailing may thus on occasion become a necessary evil. Sometimes instead of "just saying no," you may find yourself "just saying yes this one time"—and with some justification.

What if, for example, your gambling addict husband has decided the family doesn't have sufficient funds to send your daughter to volleyball camp or your son to baseball camp, even though he'd promised it to them. Because he gambled the camp money away, do you ride to the rescue with your own monies? What if your elderly mother is threatened with eviction from her apartment because she's pumped all her social security checks into casino slot machines? You going to put your momma on the street? What if you yourself are threatened with foreclosure on your own home because your husband has gambled his way into five-figure debt. Do you get a personal loan to bail the family out?[14]

Write Berman and Siegel: "Accept the fact that a bailout may sometimes be needed for the sake of others. . . . Find the courage to refuse when you should and try to find the wisdom to know the difference."[15] In the end, however, bailing out your loved one, whether emotionally or financially, whether you deem it necessary or not, only perpetuates the gambling problems.

Don't expect the lightbulb of recognition to suddenly illumine his mind to the problem, either. It might, certainly. Your refusal to bail him out does communicate that you're onto his gambling and that you're not going to take it anymore; it may also tell him deep down that you love him enough to try to help him. If the gambler is not too far into his addiction, refusal to bail him out may in itself begin to turn things around. But if he's well into his addiction, don't expect him to like what you're doing. In fact, steel yourself for anything and everything in response to your refusal of monetary or emotional relief—including anger, rage, abusive comments, and anything else. Stay strong in the face of the onslaught, though, for your refusal to assist in the short run only accelerates any possible help he may receive in the long run.

FINANCIAL SEPARATION

By refusing to bail the gambler out, you are in effect drying up one of his potential money sources. But you are still vulnerable financially, for you likely hold a number of assets jointly with the gambler. Once you snap your purse closed and deny him personal financial help, he may seek to tap these joint resources, and if he continues his slide into financial doom, you may be unwittingly dragged along with him.

Thus, once the problem is identified, it is incumbent on the spouse to determine what exactly her financial vulnerability is, and to detach herself financially from the gambler. Savings and checking accounts are an easy place to start. One gambler's spouse says, "He wrote about seven or eight checks to the casinos—there was no money in our account. That was when I had gone to the bank and taken my name off of everything I could take my name off of. I wasn't going to be liable for that."

But no money is really safe from the gambler's rapacious grasp, so things like loans, leases, investments, insurance policies, retirement funds, and any possible source of credit could also be in your name as well. You may think many of them are held in the gambler's name only, but gamblers, in their desperate quest for money, may surprise you.[16] And you are responsible for a jointly held credit card, for example, even if you've never used it or didn't even know about it.

Such information is available, however, in a credit report. "Since most spouses have some joint obligations," Tom Coates says, "to pull a copy of both credit reports is not very difficult, and if you have some suspicions, the credit report will generally show you [that] some credit cards have been taken out, some lines have been drawn. Sometimes I've seen spouses . . . go ahead and forge the signature of their spouse and borrow against their home or things like that. The credit report is a good indication of what may have gone on if the suspicion exists."

Once you've determined your financial susceptibility, then you must protect yourself by detaching monetarily from the gambler. This may be problematic—even traumatic—in a family where finances have always been a cooperative endeavor, and indeed it must be handled tactfully, but in the end it is necessary to go your own way on the money.[17]

This will also entail establishing financial independence if you do not already enjoy such—instituting your own checking and/or savings account and credit rating. Dr. Linda Chamberlain of Denver counsels clients whose spouses are not stopping their gambling or are not willing to stop "to take steps . . . to protect themselves financially. Open up a second account. Put some money in it. Don't let the gambler have access to that. Do what you can to try and get things, household finances, squared away so that you have money to cover basic needs and so forth." She also tells them to get a job. "You're going to need it. Might as well get started now."[18]

Obviously, resources are available to help you disentangle yourself from the gambler and fashion a financial identity of your own. Among others, you may want to consult a lawyer, an accountant or financial planner, a banker or financial consultant in a brokerage firm, and an insurance agent.[19]

YOU'RE NOT IN THIS ALONE

Bewildered, befuddled, discombobulated, perplexed, frustrated, embittered, indignant, irate, infuriated—write these words down, put an "I am" at the front, and you have probably penned a pretty accurate summary of your feelings about the living nightmare that is being a spouse to someone with gambling problems. Help is available, however, in the form of professional therapy. Many spouses seek out counselors, for they have been put through an emotional wringer and (a) don't know what to do about it, (b) don't know how to handle their feelings about the compulsive gambler they married, and/or (c) may have developed emotional problems of their own as a result of (*a*) and (*b*). Psychologists, psychotherapists, family counselors, pastors, and other professionals are all productive resources from which to pursue help. Unfortunately, specialists in compulsive gambling are few and far between—but their numbers are growing as the addiction itself victimizes more and more of the population.

If you're anything like most spouses of persons with gambling problems, you probably think you're alone in the world as well—nobody else could possibly be going through what you are. Well, you thought wrong. Millions of spouses experience the same things you do in their relationships with compulsive gamblers, and these people are more than willing to offer you a support group to find your way through the maze of emotional and financial difficulties that confronts you.

It's a group called Gam-Anon, and it is modeled after its predecessor for spouses and families of alcoholics, Al-Anon. Begun in 1960 as an informal fellowship of those affected by gambling problems in their homes, the organization now boasts hundreds of chapters around the country, meeting in churches, community centers, and synagogues. It is a group that prides itself on protecting members' anonymity and on offering a helping hand to newcomers who may be bewildered about what they are experiencing. Whether the gambler in your life is still feeding his addiction and you want to know how you can encourage his need for recovery, or whether he's hit his bottom and is now clawing his way back to normalcy, this organization will offer a forum of friendly faces who have all been through what you're now suffering.

Gam-Anon can prove vital for the spouse's emotional well-being. Whether taking a passive or active role in the discussion—there is no pressure to talk—the spouse can put in context what is behind her and steel herself for what is ahead. Says Chamberlain: "To give these people a framework for what's going on, it's an important place to be. And particularly to have somebody else who understands the signs of what's going on, is a resource that's invaluable in these kinds of situations."

It also serves as a living, breathing manual for handling the practical issues dealing with money, time, spousal manipulation, and verbal subterfuge that have become a part of the spouse's day-to-day living. The other spouses and family members of gamblers sitting around the table have seen and heard it all, and can offer good, solid, nuts-and-bolts tips for survival, and even beyond survival, recovery.

Not inconsequentially, Gam-Anon also provides a duct through which they can vent their anger—which is considerable in many cases, "anger beyond anger," in Chamberlain's words. "When a lot of this starts to fall apart and it surfaces what's been going on, the partners and spouses are oftentimes horribly, and understandably, angry about what's happened."

This anger is a substantial hurdle to many spouses embarked upon their own recovery. The spouse thought she knew her mate. She trusted him, confided in him, shared a history of intimate and candid moments with him, had been his helpmeet, one flesh with him, carried and bore his children, and now he's gone and recklessly squandered the family's finances, jeopardized the family's future, and put his marriage in doubt. He's lied and deceived, equivocated and prevaricated, shredding every last bit of trust existing between the two of them. Who wouldn't be angry? Anger of this magnitude has the potential to be a real "issue," as they say, in any attempt at recovery. Gam-Anon provides an outlet where some of that pressure can be released.

As is true with Alcoholics Anonymous and Gamblers Anonymous and other twelve-step programs, each individual group is an entity in its own right with a personality all its own. Thus some groups may better fit your needs than others. "Some groups are really not very therapeutic and not very supportive," says Smith. "They're more staying stuck in the spot of the problem and are not offering a lot of support in helping along the way. Different groups just can be better than others." Smith recommends that spouses and family members not judge the program on the basis of an unhelpful experience at one meeting or with one group. Turning your back on all of Gam-Anon because you didn't like one meeting or group deprives you of a sounding board for your thoughts and emotions and an itinerary for what happens next. "Seek other groups," Smith urges. "Continue until you find one that's a fit for you."

One event in your history with the gambler will mark the apex, the climax, of your efforts to help him see his problem for what it is and attempt to rectify it, which is essentially what this entire section is about. It is a dramatic event that requires careful preparation and thoughtful planning. It is called an intervention.

INTERVENTIONS

Confrontations often constitute part of the spouse's early history with the addict and his addiction. At some point the spouse brought up the gambling, and if her suggestions and entreaties were positively and sincerely received and acted upon, perhaps peace was reinstalled in the household. Maybe the gambler honestly didn't know his behavior had advanced to a point beyond his control, or maybe he knew about his problem but guilt, shame, embarrassment had prevented him from talking about it or admitting it. The spouse's candid words brought the issue out into the open, he recognized it for what it was and amended his behavior, and the gambling issue became a nonissue.[20]

More likely, though, the initial encounter produced denial from the gambler, and subsequent face-to-faces elicited more denial, minimization, blame shifting, and perhaps even rage. Many of these talks probably deteriorated into tirades and/or crying jags, as the spouse, frustrated and confused and desperate to change the gambler's behavior, fell back on her emotions and her pain as ammunition, and thus bore no results whatsoever. Eventually the spouse began to choose her spots more carefully, and when those engagements failed to yield satisfaction, probably even ruled out further confrontations entirely for the sake of her own mental well-being and supposed stability on the home front. She declared "a separate peace" and concentrated on making family life run as smoothly as possible from day to day.

But it is a restive peace at best—more a cease-fire, actually—because the gambler, and the problem, have staying power. They haven't gone anywhere—in fact, the problem is no doubt escalating as you struggle to eke out an emotional and financial existence while the elephant everybody knows about but nobody will talk about continues to sit in the living room right next to you.

At a certain point it becomes necessary to up the ante.

Some experts advocate a direct confrontation between spouse and gambler, a well-thought-out, planned event that attempts to bring home to him the severity of the problem. This is a very effective way of "raising the bottom," of getting the gambler to want to get help, but it is difficult for the spouse to pull off alone. It requires precise timing, a gathering of "evidence" about the gambling, a distinct style of asking questions, and a dispassionate and impregnable resolve from the spouse powerful enough to withstand reactions from the gambler that may run the gamut of emotional responses, from uncontrollable rage to disconsolate and foreboding silence.[21]

A better option may be to stage an intervention. This type of confrontation involves the leadership of a trained professional (a psychologist, psychiatrist, addiction specialist, etc.) and incorporates the help of a "team" of people close to the gambler. Its goal, though, is identical to that of a confrontation—getting the gambler to recognize his gambling for what it is and seek help.

The strength of the intervention process comes in the numbers it musters. Every person in the gambler's life who means anything to him—spouse, mother, father, brothers, sisters, daughters, sons, bosses, coworkers, etc.—is gathered in one place with the gambler and asked to tell how the gambler's behavior has affected him or her negatively. The atmosphere of the meeting is not one of grievance but of support—these close friends and relatives are not there to complain about what his behavior is doing to them, but to communicate to him that his behavior is affecting others. This is important, for many addicts, mired as they are in their own universe, see their gambling as a personal thing only. When an addict says "I don't have a problem," says Chaplain Trennis Killian, "what they're really saying is: 'I'm not bothering you. . . . I don't have a problem that bothers you. So stay off my back. It's not bothering you.'"[22] When a group of the gambler's relatives and friends gathers to impress upon him that his behavior is indeed affecting other people—that is, them—it may break through his elaborate and fortified system of defenses. Says Eades: "It's something powerful when friends and children and moms and dads and so forth, when they tell you something, enough of them, and they're not judgmental; they just tell you the facts and that this is what's happening. We love you, we want to get you some help. It's a powerful process."

But an intervention is no slapdash affair. It involves, as mentioned above, the coordination and planning by a professional, and will probably include rehearsals. Every possible contingency is anticipated prior to the event and planned for. "If the person leaves, who's going to go get them and bring them back?" says Eades, of some of the considerations covered in preparation for the event. "Who's going to speak first? Who's going to be the person who speaks last? What are we going to do? What is the treatment plan? Are they going to treatment?"

Alas, even so dramatic a measure as an intervention doesn't

always work. Indeed, Killian puts the success rate at from 30 to 50 percent, "but that's 30 to 50 percent that we wouldn't get otherwise."

More bad news: It is basically a one-shot deal, a onetime operation. Because of its drama and gravity, "you pretty well are limited to that one shot," Killian says. "Unless years later you try it again. But, you know, you're not going to be able to try it one week and the next week try it again, or next month, or even a year later. It's generally not going to work."

What do you do then?

In a word, pray. Says Killian: "Once that . . . doesn't work, there's not much we can do but pray. And pray that there will be a time when that person will be receptive. And it does sometimes happen. We've had people go two or three years with 'No, no, no. I don't want anything to do with it,' and all of a sudden, something happens."

That something is the gambler hitting bottom.

Whether you are able to lift it or not, the bottom is a painful place to be for everyone involved, both the gambler and his spouse and family. Realizing that you have a severe problem that will not go away or fix itself, that indeed you must enlist assistance to right your life, is a blow to the integrity of any man or woman. But it is a necessary place to be as well. No one with any addiction, be it to alcohol, drugs, or gambling, ever starts clawing his way back upward without first tasting the dregs of the bottom.

It is to the process of restoring normalcy, and physical, psychological, emotional, and spiritual wholeness to one's life, that we now turn. The next chapter will deal with the treatment of someone with gambling problems.

SEVEN

From Down and Out to Out and Up

I don't know why it's different," says Mary Lou Strachan, who has been addicted to both alcohol and gambling in her life, "but I feel somehow that the urge to gamble is stronger than the urge to drink."[1] "I think gambling addiction is probably even more powerful than many instances of alcoholism," says Dr. John M. Eades, who himself suffered from compulsive gambling and now counsels addicts of all stripes. "I saw it with my own life. It is just like being totally possessed."[2] Another recovering gambler says of compulsive gamblers who have also been hooked on alcohol that he meets in recovery groups: "Every one of them says that gambling's worse than drinking or drugs to recover from."[3]

Comments like these are heard frequently from gamblers and in compulsive gambling literature. And they are sentiments with grave implications for treatment programs and recovery for addicted gamblers. For if the toll compulsive gambling takes is greater on the individual and by extension his spouse and family than other addictions, then successful treatment becomes all the more important—and problematic.

In this chapter we will explore those treatment options. But first, let's differentiate between compulsive gambling and other addictions, trying to understand what it is about gambling that makes it more difficult to kick for many.

GAMBLING VERSUS OTHER ADDICTIONS

Similarities between gambling addiction and alcoholism certainly exist. Both involve escape, euphoria, an altered self-image that comes over the addict once under the "influence," so to speak, and a similar progressive nature demanding more activity and higher doses as the condition accelerates, to note but a few.[4]

But compulsive gambling seems to be more fearsome for many. There is no tolerance threshold, no physical limits, for one thing. While an alcoholic is limited by his own biological composition, no such physiological boundaries constrict the gambling addict. Says Randall E. Smith, a counselor in Englewood, Colorado: "If you drink enough, you get a blackout and you stop. But compulsive gambling—the more you do it, the more you want to do it, the more, the more, the more you want. There is really no stop."[5] This accounts for serious gamblers' herculean feats of endurance. It is not unusual to hear of gamblers sitting at a blackjack table or slot machine for as many as twenty-four hours straight.

Some gamblers, however, experience what are called "brownouts," periods of time that recede into the haze of the gambler's past. "I was with a group of gamblers," says Christopher W. Anderson, past executive director of the Illinois Council on Problem and Compulsive Gambling who now operates his own counseling practice in Chicago, "and a guy said, 'I left my house on Thursday afternoon and woke up driving down the expressway on Monday afternoon.' I mean, he had no recollection of where he had been and what he had done. . . . Now, if we'd have taken time and [begun] to retrace his steps, he could pull that up, whereas the alcoholic probably could not."[6]

Generally speaking, though, the body of the gambler is not the thing that gives out, requiring him to cease gambling. It's his money. "You can gamble as long as your credit cards go," says Eades.[7]

Second, this addiction can set in a lot quicker than others. And it can grow to maturity a lot faster. Eileen Fox, a certified compulsive gambling counselor in Colorado Springs, has been seeing alcohol and drug abusers since 1987. She says, "The gamblers can get into trouble a lot faster" because "the stakes are higher. Once they get hooked, as far as monetary things, things can happen . . . quickly."[8] Their fall rate is much faster than that of alcoholics, who typically drink problematically for years and decades before bottoming out, or any other addicts, with the possible exception of those hooked on crack cocaine. Says Smith: "We've actually seen a person who has not gambled before go from one night the big win, the next night another big win, to a month later having the entire house mortgaged and the insurance policies cashed out, and only then was he ready to seek help."

Third, for many the high of gambling supersedes anything the other addictions offer. "I'm here to tell you," says Anderson, "that there is no drug high that can come close to the gambling high. None. None. And the cocaine addicts will tell you that, you know, they're always chasing that first high. With the gambling, it's not euphoric recall, like we talk about in substances; it's euphoric projection. I get juiced thinking about the win that is going to take place just around the corner that's going to solve all my problems."[9]

Fourth, the ultimate and terminating low can be a lot lower as well. As we mentioned in chapter 3, no addiction rivals that of gambling in attempted suicides—no fewer than one in five compulsives attempts to end it all. Not alcoholics; not soft, so-called recreational drug users; not even hard drug users like heroin addicts can match this notorious statistic. When the downhill runaway train that is compulsive gambling finally spits its passengers out, they are at the bottom of a hill so steep many don't even attempt an ascent. So great is their depression and despair that Fox feels she must enter into a no-suicide contract with her compulsive gambling patients.

And fifth, recovery is slow and painful. An alcoholic who quits drinking is "rewarded" within days thereafter with physical benefits—he feels better, his thoughts are clearer, the haze that had occluded his outlook on life starts to dissipate. A gambler, though, will feel no physical relief once he stops betting—indeed, he may even feel worse because the excitement that he thrived on is now absent from his life. Moreover, his relational and financial problems have, in most cases, only just begun. Staggering debt, joblessness, marital crisis, relational catastrophe, legal repercussions—all of it is staring him squarely in the face, often for the first time, as soon as he stops betting. "When gamblers stop," says Dr. Linda Chamberlain, "they're going to feel a lot worse for a long time. We're talking about probably anywhere from a year or more before they can even start to feel hopeful that things are going to get better."[10]

These five reasons unite to make gambling an onerous addiction to kick, more malevolent perhaps than any other. But overlaying these five differences is another, more qualitative contrast that distinguishes compulsive gambling from other addictions and presents serious implications for treatment, and that is the profound spiritual element that exists in addictive gambling.

Playing God
Anderson believes this spiritual component is key to understanding the severity of gambling addiction. Compulsive gamblers, he

says, are literally attempting to play God when in the throes of their addiction. Noting that one of the images the book of Genesis employs to present God is as the creator God (Elohim), whose primary act is creating the world *ex nihilo*, "out of nothingness," Anderson writes, "One of the primary characteristics of the compulsive gambler, as described by GA, is 'a desire to have all the good things in life without any effort,' or, the pursuit of something for nothing. It seems, therefore, that the gambler, in the process of the addiction, is literally attempting to recreate the primary characteristic of Elohim—that is, to create 'something out of nothing' through the act of gambling. . . . Pathological gambling can be described as the attempt to literally play god."[11]

Placing a bet and winning that bet is akin to creating something from nothing, in Anderson's view. "When you buy a one-dollar lottery ticket and have a shot at winning $300 million, ... I dare say that is something for nothing." Winning a wager—especially a large win—goes to the gambler's head. He feels lucky, blessed, set apart, special, and he feels he has controlled the uncontrollable, in this case Fate or Lady Luck, which takes the place of the God of providence in the gambler's thinking. "And so, part of what happens spiritually is that sense that I have control of the uncontrollable," Anderson says. "I have created something out of nothing. . . . Psychologically we refer to that as omnipotence. Spiritually, what it means is that I am living with the experience of being the creator God." In his mind the gambler did not just get lucky, but thinks, "I have done something really special here."[12]

And if he has won once, he thinks, he can win again—and again and again—and accrue many fine possessions and distribute his newfound wealth lavishly—establishing a philanthropic society, setting all his relatives up for life, and so forth. Anderson himself, when deep in his own gambling addiction, had visions of building a new wing on his church with his never-forthcoming "big win." In short, the gambler develops a grandiose opinion of himself—many compulsive gamblers are narcissists to begin with—as the supreme gambler who, through his own skill or the magic touch that has been bestowed on him, can accomplish many great things.

In other words, the gambler fashions for himself a fantasy world. It is this fantasy world that perpetuates the addictive element of gambling, for it is into this fantasy world that the gambler retreats whenever cruel reality starts to intrude. And this reality, alas, becomes ever more intrusive as his losses begin to outnumber his wins. For after he loses money, the gambler must somehow make that loss tolerable—losing, after all, is not what one who controls the uncontrollable does. To make that loss tolerable he jumps into his head and imagines the next win that is going to take place that will solve all his problems. Once he imagines that happening, he attaches all his feelings to that fantasy, and begins to live, think, and feel as if the fantasy is already true—that he's already won, in other words. This provides him temporary escape from unpleasant or intolerable feelings, and offers him a sense of well-being.

But that big win that will extricate him from his now-increasing problems is not immediately forthcoming. So each time he loses, he must go back to the drawing board, so to speak, to throw off the depression he feels from losing and to construct a brand-new fantasy. This takes its toll in time, and eventually the losses—very big by this time—create in him desperation and despair. He continues constructing new fantasies until they can no longer be sustained, at which point he hits bottom and can be treated.

This is why treatment for gamblers is often more difficult than for other addicts. When gamblers quit, what they have to do is give up their fantasy, the one thing that has sustained their mental and emotional life for however long they've been gambling. They have to give up their dreams, their dreams of financial restitution and emotional wholeness—dreams that will come true when they get the next win. "The sheriff can be coming and knocking at the door to foreclose on my house, and I'm betting that the Broncos are going to bail me out tonight and turn everything around, and when I believe that, then everything's okay," says Anderson. Alcoholics don't harbor such dreams. The alcoholic toward the end is merely drinking to numb reality—he knows his drinking isn't going to solve his outstanding crises. "That next bottle of beer is not going to pay my mortgage and keep them from foreclosing on the house and taking the car and turning off the lights and that sort of thing."[13] But the next pull of a slot machine handle, the next lottery ticket he purchases, might.

Fundamentally confusing oneself, a created being, with the Creator is as old as time—the quest for power and control vis-à-vis the Creator, to "be like God," is the original sin and harkens back, after all, to the Garden of Eden—and is a spiritual problem of enormous scope. It therefore requires a spiritual remedy of equal size, for what the gambler is asked to do when he finally hits bottom and seeks to reverse his field is, in essence, to abandon his god and find a new one. He doesn't have room in his heart for two of them—the god he has made of himself has to go.

To put it short and simple: what any therapy the gambler receives must deal with is a rather elevated case of idolatry. The fantasy—or, in effect, the gambler himself—must be dethroned as god and replaced. We will deal more with this aspect later.

THE CLIMB OUT OF DESPAIR

Once his fantasy evaporates, once he finally reaches a realization that the one big, elusive win is not "right around the corner" and that, even if it were, he would simply blow that as well on the machines and/or the tables, only then is the gambler ready to be helped. The question then becomes: What next?

For a rare few nothing comes next. They, like their fellow "rare few" alcoholics or drug addicts, quit "cold turkey" and simply move on.[14] Certainly they are beset with the problems, financial, emotional, and relational, that they have incurred and have subjected loved ones to during their addiction, and these they must resolve, but the gambling itself they leave behind and don't look back.

Many, many more, though, need organized, professional help to point them in the right direction and lead them down the path toward recovery. They need therapy of some sort, either with a skilled professional or with a group, or in both settings during the same course of therapy.

Optimally, this therapy will serve a great many functions:[15]

✣ It will successfully identify and treat co-occurring disorders like substance abuse and other problems.

✣ It will help the gambler devise strategies to replicate the benefits of gambling—escaping one's problems or limiting one's anxiety, for example, or getting the "high" the action provides—in other, more constructive ways than gambling.

✣ It will help the gambler take more responsibility for his actions, including the damage he has done in his relationship with his spouse and family—the betrayed trust and highly curtailed lines of communication—and especially the financial havoc he has wreaked, and seek to remedy these wrongs.

✣ It will debunk all the erroneous beliefs the gambler harbors about gambling, such as his view on how luck operates and how, through his "system," he can exert his skills onto the odds.

✣ It will augment the gambler's emotional skills, his problem-solving skills, his interpersonal skills, and his relapse prevention skills.

❖ It will address underlying issues such as depression, the gambler's psychological relationship with his parents, his views of success and failure, and others, if such exist.

But its principal goal is simple and cannot be overstated: to change one's gambling habit and everything that destructive habit has wrought in the gambler's and his family's lives.

Any therapeutic program is a partnership between the therapist and his patient. The therapist's cooperation is a given—you aren't paying him big bucks to be *un*interested in your recovery—but many gamblers are dragged to the couch kicking and screaming, as it were, and for these reluctant counselees, therapy may not reap the expected results. Write the authors of *Don't Leave It to Chance:* "Imagine your journey toward recovery as traveling by rowboat toward a destination you have seen, but you don't know the way. Now imagine that you find a guide who knows the way and will help get you there by working one of the oars. If you pull together you can move the boat faster and easier than you could by yourself. If only one of you pulls an oar, the boat will move aimlessly in circles."[16]

One possible setting for this counseling is an inpatient facility that specializes in compulsive gambling, where the gambler lives at the facility for upwards of a month and receives intense and comprehensive treatment. These, unfortunately, are rare in the United States, and figure to continue to be so, since the trend in medicine is away from inpatient care generally, and specifically away from such treatment for substance abuse. They are typically quite expensive as well, which is an especial deterrent for gamblers, given their depleted resources. A follow-up study at an Ohio facility indicated that, six months after completing treatment, about 55 percent of its patients had remained abstinent of gambling,[17] which is a very high percentage.

But hospitalization is not needed in most compulsive gambling cases. Richard Rosenthal, a California-based expert on gambling addiction, advises inpatient treatment only in specific problematic instances, such as when suicide, major depression, cross-addictions, or other serious conditions are involved. He believes stopping the gambling—which is, after all, the primary goal of therapy and would be also for inpatient care—can be accomplished in most cases through active participation in Gamblers Anonymous (GA).[18] Unfortunately, the success of GA-only treatment may be very low.

Outpatient care, which is similar to the inpatient variety in that the client receives treatment from a facility but does not live in the facility itself, is also available from various hospitals around the country.

Individual therapy is probably the best route to take. Pastors, social workers, psychologists, psychiatrists—if they are conversant with addiction problems—are all good avenues to pursue, as are addiction specialists. And if a given professional is not well versed in gambling addiction, he will likely refer the gambler to a colleague who is. Many gamblers, when initially seeking help, in fact prefer the one-on-one relationship a personal counselor provides rather than a group therapy session; it is less intimidating for them to talk with a professional counselor about matters they have invested so much energy to keeping secret rather than with a group of nameless unknowns.[19]

But a therapy group is also considered indispensable for successful recovery, and the counselor will hopefully insist that the gambler participate in one. This group, in many cases, will be Gamblers Anonymous.

People with Problems Helping People with Problems

Gamblers Anonymous (GA), the nation's only voluntary organization for compulsive gamblers, came about in January

1957 as the result of a "chance meeting" between two men who shared a perplexing history of trouble and misery associated with their obsession to gamble. The two men began meeting regularly to discuss this, and as time passed neither went back to gambling.[20]

They deduced from their discussions that certain internal character defects—Custer describes them as the "inability and unwillingness to accept reality, emotional insecurity, immaturity, deceit, self-indulgence, egotism and selfishness, insensitivity to the needs and feelings of others"[21]—had to be changed to prevent them from relapsing and returning to gambling. Adapting the program of Alcoholics Anonymous (AA), the granddaddy of the twelve-step regimens, they conducted their first meeting in September 1957, and have since grown to about twelve hundred chapters nationwide. GA, like other twelve-step programs, operates under the philosophy that "people with similar problems can help one another."[22]

GA has no membership requirements. Because many who attend meetings may face legal or work trouble, or may wish to escape the embarrassment and shame accruing to them in the outside world because of their gambling problems, the organization prides itself in the anonymity it provides its members, who are referred to only by their first name and last initial. Attendance at meetings is equally unregulated, and it is not unusual for a member to attend three or four meetings and then drop out of the program; conversely, many attend regularly, sometimes more than once a week if more than one "room," as the meetings are termed, is available in a city or geographical area, and often for as long as ten or twenty years. Recovery, according the program, is a lifelong journey.

Central to the program are the twelve steps, modeled on the AA twelve steps, the first of which is admitting that one has no control over one's gambling. The "Power" of AA, also called the "Higher Power," is also invoked in GA's twelve steps as the source that can restore gamblers to a "normal way of thinking and living."[23] But, contrary to a popular misconception, GA is not a religious organization, and it is certainly not affiliated with any church, synagogue, denomination, or sect. "The few references to God and to 'a Power,'" writes Custer, "are ... couched in terms that make it possible for the individual to interpret them in any way he wishes."[24]

The other steps resemble AA's and exhort the gambler to, among other things, take a fearless moral and financial inventory, confess his wrongs and be ready to have these character defects removed, ask "God (of our understanding)" to remove the shortcomings, make amends to all people he has harmed, and carry this message to other compulsive gamblers.[25] Members are urged to invest their hearts, emotions, and minds fully in these steps, to "work the program," as it is called. Full mental and emotional investment in the program, coupled with regular meeting attendance, gives the compulsive gambler the best shot at licking his addiction.

Gamblers attending their first GA meeting are often amazed—and elated—at what they find. It is typical that a compulsive gambler—living in a universe he erroneously believes revolves around himself—thinks he alone in the world is thrashing for his life under the financial and relational rubble that has descended on him. Walking into that first "room," however, changes that. "It's hard to describe my first meeting," says one recovering gambler. "It was great. I honestly thought I was the only person who had this problem, and the only person doing all these things, and lying to his wife and getting the mail and this stuff that I was doing. I honestly thought I was the only one who ever did that. And [I] came in and met a roomful of people who all had done exactly what I had done, and even more than what I had done. And so, for me it was wonderful. I was able to relate to these people."

But the room offers more than mere collegiality. It also

serves as a ruthless tribunal demanding unequivocal honesty; members have noses sensitive enough to sniff out even the slightest dissimulation, or deception the gambler might throw their way. The room is a tough, critical audience of people who have been there, done that. Nothing—none of the usual denials, rationalizations, minimizations, excuses—gets by these folks. This helps the gambler immeasurably—he is forced to be completely frank about his behavior.

Soon after the newcomer joins a room, he is submitted to a "pressure group," a group of veteran GA members (called "trusted servants") who meet with him and his spouse, if applicable, and encourage the gambler to tell all, to "come clean," in the GA parlance. The pressure group also helps the gambler reconfigure his and his family's finances, a reordering that almost always entails radical changes in how the family money is held and distributed. All possible financial resources are stripped from him—his name is removed from joint property (the house, the car, etc.) and from checking and savings accounts, his credit cards are cut in half—and he is put on an allowance. Paychecks are also turned over, with the stub still attached, to the party responsible for managing the family money.[26]

Many gamblers resist this unilateral divestment for all the usual reasons—he has always handled the family's finances and doesn't want to stop now; it is the husband's duty to oversee the family's money; it is a real comedown for the supposed head of the household to be so treated; etc.—but they do so at their peril. Says one recovering addict who relapsed after three-months' "clean" time: "What should have happened when I first went into GA was that my wife should have taken control of the finances. I should have given her control. I should have gotten rid of my credit cards, gotten rid of my checkbook—everything—for a while. And I didn't do that."

Also integral to the pressure group's function—and to

recovery—is the concept of restitution. Two of GA's twelve steps are devoted to making personal amends to individuals the gambler has wronged with his behavior. It is important that he admits his wrongs and attempts to close the rift he has opened between himself and his spouse, family, coworkers, boss, and friends and relatives. In addition to allowing him something of a return to his normal life, this act also keeps him connected to reality, to the real consequences of his gambling problems.

Equally important is financial restitution. Creditors may be knocking down the gambler's door, and the financial arrears he has thrust upon himself might seem daunting, to say the least. Thus the gambler may want to escape into bankruptcy court and/or get the financial burdens off his back as quickly as possible. This would be a natural desire for any of us, but it bodes ill for the gambler intent on successful recovery. The pressure group will advise the gambler to accept full financial responsibility for his debts, and it will encourage him to string out his repayment schedule over as long a period of time as possible. Both measures give him the best shot at recovery.[27]

Tom Coates, of Consumer Credit of Des Moines, many of whose clients come in with gambling problems, says because gambling addicts have lived years of their lives in a fantasy world, pulling them back to a world of reality "is not facilitated by taking these debts, tens of thousands of dollars in debts, or a hundred thousand dollars in debt, that they've run up and discharg[ing them] in bankruptcy court. It didn't seem real while they're running it up, and it sure doesn't seem real while discharging it." Coates advises clients to pay back at least some of the debt. "If they run the debts up and discharge in bankruptcy and walk away from it, my fear is that they [have a] much higher-percentage chance to slide back into that abyss of gambling than they would have otherwise."[28] Many creditors, experts say, will accept a deferred repayment plan if they are apprised of the debtor's gambling problems. Members of the pressure group, as well as some counselors, may be willing to intervene with creditors if necessary.

As for protracting the payment plan, this principle derives from common sense. The longer the pain lasts, the more reluctant the gambler is to return to the activity that begot the pain. Every payment the gambler must make is a forceful reminder of the bad old days when gambling ran his life. Chaplain Trennis Killian, of Riverboat Casinos Ministry, sets up a restitution plan with his clients as quickly as possible, and "we want it to be as long as we can. If it takes them twenty years to pay off all that stuff, that's great. Because that's holding over their head all those twenty years." With the debts hanging over their heads, recovering gamblers will "think twice about going into the casino. But as soon as that debt is released—ah, I'm free. And away they go."[29] The financial obligations that had prevented his return to gambling are removed.

And herein lies another difference between the compulsive gambler and the alcoholic. Follow-up treatment with a gambler is, in some ways, much more important than follow-up with an alcoholic or drug addict. Whereas the alcoholic or drug addict can be dissuaded from relapses by simply calling to mind the physical devastation and ill effects of his drinking, the compulsive gambler's mental makeup is different. "All they can remember, for the most part, once they get that [their debt] paid off, is the good things that happened," says Killian. "Some of them may buy a car with their winnings.... And that's what they remember once the bad part is eliminated, and that bad part is that debt."

GA members also provide other vital functions to help the newly repentant gambler in his recovery. They exchange phone numbers, thus offering the gambler a backup network to "talk the gambler down," that is, to relieve his tension and keep him from betting, when he cannot get to or reach his therapist.[30] As many members are businessmen, industrialists, and influential professionals, they have the wherewithal to look out for one another as per employment, and often find jobs, menial or otherwise, for gamblers first entering the program. Gamblers in recovery frequently want and need to be busy, and will accept with relish even the most servile occupations.[31]

GA, thus, with the support, encouragement, advice, and accountability it offers, is considered an indispensable part of any gambler's recovery. Writes Custer: "We say without hesitation that the most important step a compulsive gambler can take toward recovery is to get into Gamblers Anonymous and become a steady and active participant."[32]

But all that said, GA is no panacea. Just showing up at meetings doesn't get the job done. Its success depends, like that of any other twelve-step program, on the member's motivation. Many gamblers arrive at their initial GA meetings with a "footprint on their fanny," as Mary Heineman puts it, that footprint applied by a spouse, a parent, an adult child, a boss, or even the courts of the land.[33]

These unrepentant gamblers, unless they buy into the program, are destined to lead even more miserable lives than when they were gambling—primarily because they still want to be gambling but now they're *not* gambling, the one and only joy in life they may have had. GA is not going to do much for them. Says Richard Rosenthal: "It's not enough to sit in the back of the room and say nothing. Speaking at meetings, getting a sponsor, working the Steps—being involved is what's important."[34] If the gambler does not buy into the program, including its crucial first step—admitting he has no control over his gambling—the chances the GA experience will benefit him are slim to none.

Hard data on GA success rates are virtually nonexistent— systematic follow-up studies on GA members have never been conducted—and the data that do exist are far from encouraging. The one known study revealed that a mere 8 percent of GA members were abstinent after a year in the group.[35]

But the picture is not all bleak. GA is most effective as a corollary to professional therapy, experts say. "I think of self-help as a complement to treatment," Mike Brubaker says. "I don't think the retention rate in Gamblers Anonymous is ever going to improve dramatically unless we have a better treatment system."[36] According to Anderson, "When you combine [GA] with treatment, the numbers go way up."[37]

Setting the Captives Free

For all its indispensability and all its success—and it, or something very much like it, is indispensable and successful—GA does have its deficiencies in the view of some. Some Christians especially object to the ambiguity of the spiritual component—or the lack of spiritual emphasis—of the program.

Regarding the latter, Chicago-based gambling expert Christopher W. Anderson, for one, is troubled by the fact that of all the twelve-step programs adapting AA's steps—and there are many—GA stands alone in altering the spiritual component of its progenitor. GA has essentially "removed God and spirituality in favor of a rational and somewhat amorphous awakening that leaves the gambler in control," Anderson writes.[38] This removal, he asserts, reflects a symptom of compulsive gambling itself—narcissism. Another expert, B. R. Browne, argues that gamblers undertaking the twelve steps don't blame themselves for the turmoil their lives have become, as alcoholics do, but they put the finger on the gambling.[39] Says Anderson: "The alcoholic says, 'Hi, I'm Chris. I'm an alcoholic, and my problem is me.' The gambler says, 'Hi, I'm Chris. I'm a compulsive gambler, and my problem is my gambling. If I'm not gambling, I've got no problems.'"[40] In nearly half of the twelve steps of the gambling inventory, the power of God to effect change is either reduced in scope or removed altogether from the AA prototype.

These subtle but profound changes underscore Anderson's contention that compulsive gambling in itself is a deeply spiritual problem—it is essentially a confusion of the creature/Creator distinction spoken of above. Gambling addicts are playing God when in the depths of their obsession, creating something out of nothing in their minds. To turn their lives over to God when they quit gambling is not possible, "because there is room for only one [God], and I am he." Anderson explains: "If it is the experience of the gambler to create something from nothing and to experience oneself as the creator God, then how can I work a program that invites me to turn my will and my life over to the care of a higher power that is not me."[41] Thus the god of a compulsive gambler's gambling is identical to the god of his recovery from the addiction.

That god, simply put, is a false god, an idol. "Without a shift away from a god of luck to a God of Providence, true recovery is impossible," Anderson writes. "Such a shift demands that the gambler abandon control to the healing power of divine relationship."[42]

Anderson urges gambling counselors to give spirituality greater shrift in their therapy, not necessarily by talking about God per se, but by reframing issues usually addressed on a psychological level into a spiritual context. He also encourages prayer. "If it is as simple as saying 'Help' in the morning, and 'Thank you' at night, that is enough."[43]

Moving Higher than Higher

If compulsive gambling is at its root a spiritual problem, it thus demands a spiritual solution. Says Dr. John M. Eades: "I don't think people recover without a spiritual transformation. I don't care how great the psychiatrist or psychologist is."[44] But for spiritual solutions to take hold, a spiritual power of some sort, a power other than oneself, must sit at the heart of the solution. For GA and other twelve-step programs, that power is left undefined.

The anonymous Higher Power of the twelve-step protocol, the "Power greater than ourselves" and the "Power of our own understanding" of GA's particular regimen, comports nicely with a religious zeitgeist where all roads lead to the God of many names. And this indeterminate and nebulous deity, however vague and unshapen it is, seems to serve compulsive gamblers well in their recovery. In a therapeutic context, any old Power will probably do. Any Power whatsoever, be it the big tree in your backyard or the magic mountain off yonder, if taken seriously, will serve the purpose of getting the gambler out of himself and pushed onto the path of recovery.

Some counselors, though, are uncomfortable with the vagueness of it all, and they make so bold as to actually name names. They delineate this Power as the triune God, who, through the death and resurrection of His Son Jesus, offers those with gambling problems not only the cessation of the gambling itself but also full recovery.

Rev. John Landrum, who, with his wife Linda, ministers to the thousands employed at the twelve dockside casinos on the Mississippi Gulf Coast, and who specializes in gambling-problem counseling as well, has seen spectacular recovery results in his ministry. He estimates his success rate at from 75 to 80 percent.[45] Chaplain Trennis Killian, of Riverboat Casinos Ministry, who also runs a ministry for casino employees, knows of none of his clients who have completed his one-on-one counseling program to return to gambling afterward.

These two men, along with others, employ an addiction treatment program developed by Neil T. Anderson, president of Freedom in Christ Ministries.[46] Gamblers who enter their counsel are led through a seven-step process through which they appropriate the total freedom Jesus provided them through His death on the cross. If they are already Christians, and many gambling addicts are, they are probably confused about their spiritual status. When they became Christians, Jesus entered their hearts; they may even have been and are active in their churches. How is it, then, that this gambling has gained control of their lives? Are they no longer Christians? Were they never Christians to begin with? Churches may tell them to lay their problem at the foot of the cross, to turn it over to the Lord—which is good advice, of course, but kind of general in the practical application department. "The seven steps to freedom in Christ," Landrum says, "is simply a practical process in being able to appropriate what God has already done for you. But it really works."

If the gambler is not a Christian, the first task then becomes leading him to Christ. Landrum says the benefits of this program are not available to the non-Christian. "Like in baseball," he says, "[if] you run around the bases and you skipped first base, when you hit home plate, you're out. You have to hit first base, and salvation is first base."

The phrase may be very familiar, but it remains nonetheless true: in this view, "Christ is the answer" to gambling addiction (as He is to all of our problems). But for Him to be the answer, He must replace the gambling at the center of the gambler's life. "The bottom line, I feel, in any addiction, is that the person is turning control of their life over to something or someone else, be it drugs, alcohol, or gambling," Killian says. "And the only way they're going to get recovery or healing is to turn that control over to Christ." His approach entails getting clients to admit that they have no control over their gambling, and subsequently to turn control over to Christ, not to themselves. "And that's the first thing we say to them. We can't help you. You can't do it. Only Christ can."

Fortunately, many of the casino workers who enter Landrum's

office are open to a spiritual counseling program. "The casino people generally have tried everything," he says. "They're generally desperate people, and that's generally when they will come to us, knowing that . . . there's going to be a spiritual aspect to our counseling. But by that time, they don't care. They just want help."

And many of them get it. "We have seen people come in suicidal, seen people with addictions that they could not even begin to break, and literally in twenty-four hours they've walked out free in Christ."

Which brings up another difference between this specifically Christian counseling approach and that of the secular world. The conventional wisdom on addictions is that the addict never leaves the addiction behind. "Once an alcoholic, always an alcoholic," one popular saying has it. So too with compulsive gambling. Recovery is never actually achieved; it's a lifelong process that is never put to rest. Gamblers can be thirty years removed from their gambling problems, on their deathbeds with a casino not within five hundred miles, and they're still "in recovery." Only in death will they no longer have to cope with the problems of their gambling.

In the view of Landrum, Killian, and other Christians, however, Christ can heal a gambler of his addiction. "What we teach—and it's biblical," says Landrum, "is, if the Son sets you free, you're free indeed. That's not coping. That's freedom from the problem." The gambler, according to this view, is not first and foremost an addict; he is a child of God, and by definition an individual with Christ at the center of his life. As such, his identity changes, and along with it, his approach to the problem of gambling. Citing Neil Anderson, Landrum says, "Who a person believes in and what a person believes is going to determine what they do." He adds: "We generally have it backwards in our society. I have a gambling problem, therefore I am a gambling addict. Well, if you're a Christian, who you are is not a gambling addict. Who you are is a child of God who has a really big problem with gambling. Now, that may sound very similar, but . . . they are coming from totally different directions."

Many find the news that their status as believers in Christ offers them numerous rights and privileges quite liberating. Many of the people Landrum sees are so elated at learning of the authority that comes along with being a Christian, "that we have to warn them: This is not the end. This is the beginning. We've actually had people go out and never come back because they were so excited about finding out the authority that they have as Christians, what comes along with the package."

Many believe Christ can heal gamblers of their addiction. He can, in essence, remove the temptation to gamble. Says one recovering addict: "I just believe you can have victory in this area. I mean, I believe it takes a complete change spiritually. But I don't have the desire to gamble, and I often think God just took it away." He adds: "I don't think anyone can truly get through that, be healed, without having just a spiritual renewal in your life. I think the only way it happens is, Christ completely changing your heart, changing your desires."

Or He can merely allow them to recover. Killian juxtaposes the two concepts thusly: "Christ can heal. Not recover, heal. Now, that's just like anything else. I broke my back twenty-two years ago. I recovered, but I'm not healed. But I do fine. I walk around real well. I didn't for a long time. I do find in most things, as long as I don't do something stupid, I've recovered. But I'm not healed.…I feel that God heals us sometimes and sometimes we are recovered.…Sometimes people only recover. Sometimes they're healed. And only God knows why."

It goes without saying, of course, that even a gambler who is healed of his addiction would be foolish to believe he can return to gambling. Says Landrum: "We tell people that if you've been bit once by a rattlesnake, don't pick it up again."

The Christian approach outlined above does not diminish the efforts of Gamblers Anonymous, however. "We would, in no way, put down the twelve-step programs. They have helped millions of people," Landrum says, adding that any help one gets is 100 percent better than no help at all. But Landrum also tells people, "If you're ready for help,…we can guarantee the results, because God is already ready. Not to cope, but to be free of your problem." He would even offer a money-back guarantee, but Landrum's Mississippi Coast ministry does not charge counselees.

The Role of the Church in Recovery

It will not come as news to anyone reading this book that the Christian church is for sinners. It was established to serve God's people, sinners all, as a place where they can lay their many transgressions out before their Lord and Savior Jesus Christ and subsequently be lifted up by the message of the grace of their all-loving God and His total and complete forgiveness of their sins. It is a community of redemption, where the good news of God's love permeates every activity, every event, every worship service, every relationship; where love comes down from heaven above and then spreads horizontally among Christians, and out to the non-Christian world, below. So is it now; so has it ever been.

As such, the church can play a great and meaningful role in the recovery of people with gambling problems. It can be the source of the spiritual renewal a gambling addict needs to turn his obsession around. In fact, nowhere else can one under the sway of the gambling bug find people who love and accept sinners as they are than in a good Christian church.

Eades, who proposes a five-step recovery process from a Christian perspective, spells out the importance of establishing a church home for one bent on recovering from gambling addiction: "Stage Five: We will make church attendance a priority in our lives. We will join in the fellowship of Christians. We will strive for formal Bible study and will read the Scriptures on a daily basis. The mess of our gambling lives and what God has done for us will become the message we will take to other suffering gambling addicts."[47] Other pastors echo Eades's emphasis. Landrum, as part of his counsel, tries "to let [clients] know the worthiness of being involved in a good church with Christian people and letting people help them maintain their freedom." One of the first things Chaplain Killian does with his patients is get them involved in a church as well.

In addition to providing a community of grace and forgiveness, the church also offers help in other forms. One such is in accountability. One recovering gambling addict says he met with a pastor at his church every week, "but then, every week I would meet with one other elder, just for accountability—discipleship. They were really concerned about how I was treating my wife. Was I giving her freedom to ask questions." Another is financial assistance. The aforementioned recovering addict said his "church stepped up and made a commitment that they would make sure that my whole family was taken care of financially, and that needs were being met."

But people with gambling problems will want to choose their church home wisely. For, alas, some churches—and some pastors—seem to forget their own roots in sinfulness. Killian, who exhibits at religious conventions, has witnessed firsthand clergy resistance to dealing with gambling problems. "I've had pastors tell me point-blank, 'Those people don't deserve help.'...And I say, 'What happens if these people come to the Lord. They need a church.' And I've had them tell me point-blank, 'Those people are not welcome in my church.'" Often the attitude is one of quintessential self-righteousness: I don't deal with that sort of problem, but I'll pray for you.

Some of the blame for church resistance can be laid at the feet of the sinful nature that pervades all our actions and lives. Our own sanctimony and pharisaical pietism may make it difficult for a person with gambling problems to come forward in the midst of our congregations. Backbiting and gossip amongst members can be cruel, and some church people like to single out those with open problems to cover their own sinful lives. Says Eades, speaking of the climate in some churches, "We all want to pretend that nobody here has this. And that's why you have your alcoholics in the churches and your drug addicts and so forth and so on. Because nobody wants to admit that they don't have their Christian act all together."[48]

Some can also be attributed to a natural reaction to the preaching of sin. Although the church is a house where the gospel, the good news of Christ's forgiveness, takes center stage in sermons as well as in overall church life, the law must be communicated to give the gospel traction. After all, if there were no law, the gospel would lose its power—we wouldn't need it. But it is still the gospel that communicates God's love, that stands as the sole source of a sinner's hope—the law can't do any of that.

Thus a pastor preaching against gambling from the pulpit may want to keep in mind the totality of his audience, the fact that some sitting at his feet may indeed gamble and even be led into gambling problems. Are these sinners offered hope, solace, *forgiveness?* "If we say gambling's a sin and don't do it," asks Eades, "what do you do if you do it and you start having a problem? You going to go talk to your minister?…I think we should keep them away from [the casinos], but if they have a problem, let's leave the door open."[49] Adds Christopher Anderson: "How [are] you going to help me sitting in the pew of the church, which I did, wanting nothing more than to kill myself because I'd gambled away my home and my family?"[50] People suffering from the dire consequences of their own gambling don't derive much spiritual benefit from hearing that they're miserable sinners—*that* is one thing they already know. They need to be lifted up by the sweet forgiveness offered in the gospel.

Third, the widespread ignorance regarding compulsive gambling that suffuses society infiltrates the church as well. And here, education is the remedy. If more church people were apprised of what compulsive gambling is, that it is an addiction, they might change their attitudes about, and behaviors toward, those with gambling problems. Alcoholics no longer labor under the stereotypes that pervaded thirty or forty years ago—no longer are alcoholics routinely castigated as vermin with weak willpower. Experts in gambling addiction hope understanding can "elevate" their cause to similar levels. Anderson has no problem with pastors criticizing gambling from the pulpit, "but [they] better include a message on how you can recognize [how] you, as a fallible human being, can get caught up in this and what the signs are and the symptoms are."[51]

On the whole, however, the church, the community of God's people, is perfectly suited to serve as a refuge and healing place for those with gambling problems. It is a spiritual reservoir for those needing to drink the renewing waters of spiritual transformation. Many churches have, in the past few decades, opened their doors as meeting places for various support groups, be they AA, Al-Anon, Adult Children of Alcoholics, and so forth. Eades encourages churches to take their support beyond merely providing accommodation, however. He advocates establishing groups within individual congregations to implement his five-step, specifically Christian recovery process. "When you have a Christ-centered program and you're talking about prayer and reading the Scriptures and so forth, what we're trying to do is to get that person back into the church if they once were a member. The other thing is to show people love and compassion. Because that has a way of helping people."[52]

Eades sees such congregational groups being led by pastors and biblically literate laity who have received education on compulsive gambling—one of his requirements is that they attend at least twelve open GA meetings.[53] Covered by an ethic of confidentiality, the meetings themselves will deal with gambling behavior and problems and a conscious working through of Eades's five-step plan to recovery. Other components of Eades's plan resemble a typical GA format, but the groups are consciously Christian in outlook and feature a Christ-centered recovery plan. His program has been made available, in a six-week format, to at least one state Baptist convention, Mississippi, where it has been mailed to all churches of that convention.[54]

"The church is going to have to get involved," Eades says. "The church is being impacted too much to not be involved."[55]

Putting a halt to one's problematic gambling is no easy task, as the preceding chapters have made clear. But with the help of a loving God—and usually with that of family and friends and professional counselors and fellow Christians as well—it can be accomplished. This very fact is enormous comfort for the hurting addict.

But with the comfort comes a challenge—a challenge to remain "clean" from the gambling bug. And as difficult as was stopping the gambling initially, staying stopped requires an equal measure of attention and resolve.

It is to the matter of preventing relapses that we now turn.

EIGHT

Staying Stopped

The fact that so many gamblers continue gambling problematically until they bring upon themselves a mudslide of heinous consequences indicates how difficult stopping gambling truly is. Unfortunately, as low as the low of hitting bottom is, their troubles have only begun.

For one thing, they must stay stopped. This is as difficult, if not more so, than quitting the gambling itself, for a number of reasons. Life itself, without gambling, becomes a tedious, humdrum existence in which the gambler finds himself with enormous blocks of time on his hands—time he used to invest wholly in gambling action and gambling thought. The joy of his life—nay, the *love* of his life—has now been taken from him.

In addition to which, any underlying problem in his life—a strained marital relationship, a boss who's in his face constantly, children who are uncontrollable—is still there even though he has taken the huge, constructive step toward putting his life in order. The problems he had escaped by gambling didn't resolve themselves in his physical, mental, and emotional absence, and now the place to which he had fled is closed off to him as well. The pressure continues to build, but his release valve has been screwed shut.

And then there are the cravings. Anyone trying to beat an addiction knows them well. They can be short-lived and fleeting at times, but they can also be robust and unabating, arriving upon rising in the morning and departing only upon retiring at night—with sleep and sleep alone offering respite from their diabolical pull. Eades, after he had stopped gambling for several months, said cravings came upon him that "stayed with me from morning to night, powerful and relentless."[1]

All of which can lead to a setback in the gambler's recovery, what addiction specialists call a relapse. He returns to his gambling. Not all recovering gamblers experience this, but many do, and of those that do, many more than once. Sometimes the return is brief, comprising only one or two episodes before the gambler snaps to and returns to the straight and narrow. Sometimes the gambler wants the return to be brief, thinking he can control it, but finds that the gambling has a mind of its own—it quickly brings him once again into its snare. And sometimes the return is unabashedly enthusiastic, replete with throwing-off-the-shackles energy.

Like the relapse of alcoholics, gamblers pick up the action, the dollars bet and the time spent betting, right where they left off. They do not start all over again at the nickel slots or the dollar-limit blackjack tables; they begin again at whatever level they were betting when they first stopped.

The reasons for these relapses are legion, and can pretty much be anything and everything, depending on how much the gambler wants to get back into action. A crisis in the family is a frequent rationalization, as is any time of stress. One recovering gambler's excuse for hitting the tables again after ninety days' absence was that "I had had a big fight with my wife. As I look back on it now, it shouldn't be surprising that, even though I stopped gambling, I still [had] issues I had to deal with, especially with the spouse, because of all the lying and the deceit and everything else that goes on."[2] The demands of work or family life also serve this fiendish purpose, as does a major threat to the gambler's self-esteem.[3]

Even an event that would elicit great joy for most of us can offer up reason enough for a problem gambler to return to the spinning wheels. One recovering addict, having enjoyed a six-month stoppage, received a large inheritance, and "for me, that was all I needed. I could do whatever I wanted. And I did. I gave money away. I spent money like crazy....And went back full time to gambling." Gamblers in recovery can also get "sloppy," complacent about their vulnerability, and thus be lured to dangerous places or activities.

As a prelude to this relapse many gamblers engage in what Eades calls "bugging," that is, "building up to gamble." This term is derived from the alcoholism field, where the coinage is "budding," as in "building up to drink," but the process is identical. Under continued pressure of some sort, gamblers hatch a devious plan to break away and scratch their sinister itch. They keep this plan to themselves, of course, lying about it when necessary, and forge a mental and emotional strategy that will allow their return to gambling.

Eades, when under pressure at home, squirreled away over several months any extra money he came upon under the carpet in the trunk of his car, accumulating nearly six hundred dollars. He was intent on fleeing the mountains of central Tennessee for the casinos of the Delta country, in Tunica, Mississippi, six hours away. He then conjured up an excuse to get out of the house for a couple days, convincing his wife he needed "to get away for a while. That was just gambling thinking. I had been building up to gamble probably for a long time."[4] Only a serendipitous but nearly tragic event kept him from making the trip, an event he calls "the miracle on

Boswell Road." When the motivation to gamble meets the opportunity to gamble, a relapse is often in the making.

How, then, can the gambler serious about recovery fend off these relapses?

> ✤ *Use your support system.* Whether it is GA, a therapist, a pastor, a group organized by a therapist, a church group, or a combination thereof, the recovering gambler must avail himself of his support structure. Attend meetings regularly, and not in body alone but also in spirit. Participate. Talk. Listen. Inwardly digest it all. Work the steps. Hard-bitten recovering gamblers in a group setting can help those who are tempted to return to gambling, primarily because they've been through it all and have a wider perspective, a longer view, on which to rely. But it is crucial to be candid about your trials and temptations. Do not harbor these in your heart, but air them among people who can empathize with your plight and direct you away from their grasp.
>
> Listening to newcomers tell their stories also serves a purpose: it opens old wounds and reminds even the veterans of their past pain. "That's why we continue to go back," says one addict now in recovery, "to remind ourselves. Because after a number of years we can become complacent, and we can think that we have everything under control, but when the new people come in, they show us exactly where we were. And I get strength from that." Just hearing the horror stories told by GA neophytes, although sad and painful, is "helpful to us, as individuals who have already stopped, to keep us from going back." Do not be afraid to voice your little triumphs, or big victories, over cravings and compulsions either, for others can

take heart and be encouraged by your successes just as
you can by theirs.

✤ *Watch who you're with.* An alcoholic in recovery is frequently admonished to dispense with his drinking
buddies and find a new set of pals. So too with the
gambler. If you're a former track man and the "guys"
hit the races every Saturday afternoon, they'll just have
to start getting along without you. If Wednesday
nights are "girls' night out" at the casino, maybe you
can find some different "girls" for whom Wednesday
nights are Bible study nights. This doesn't necessarily
mean giving up the friendship of your former gambling compatriots, but it does mean not tempting
your recovery by consorting with them in gambling
venues. If they remind you too much of your gambling career, however, it may mean finding new
friends.

✤ *Watch where you go.* It's one thing to lead a normal and
settled life in a society in which gambling opportunities
are everywhere, but it's another thing altogether to put
your recovery to unnecessary tests. The difference
between the two depends on how strong the urges
and how great the temptations. If you can drop in on
a convenience store for a sandwich without catching
"Lotto Fever," then by all means don't deprive your
palate of those microwaved delights. If you can take in
a baseball or football contest on the tube without
having to pitch a battle against your demons, then
kick your feet up and enjoy the game. Ditto for reading the sports page in your local paper—maybe you
can safely check out the point spread, maybe you
can't. If you can surf the Web without your mouse
inevitably finding its way to an online casino, then
cruise away. But if these, or any activities like them,

fill you with yearning for action, discretion is the better part of valor.

Recovering compulsive gambler Mike Brubaker, now counseling the same, laments that he can no longer enjoy raffles and fund-raising Monte Carlo nights because of the temptations they arouse. Even winning at something so innocuous as a fast-food rub-off ticket, he fears, might put him back on the downward slope. "I always try to think through what would happen if I won anything," he says. "My mind would start racing, and before I knew it, I would be off and running. I have to keep reminding myself that even when I won, I lost because winning always led to more gambling."[5] These are all judgment calls, though, and how recovering addicts handle them will vary.

Infinitely more dangerous, however, would be to jeopardize your recovery outright, to tempt fate, so to speak. For example, to plan the family's yearly vacation in Las Vegas would probably be pretty stupid, and to accompany "the boys" to the nearby Indian casino, "just to watch," would be beyond stupid. Addiction experts learned long ago that the mere sight of a piece of rock cocaine could induce cravings in cocaine addicts, despite how long they've abstained, "urges that are beyond their control," Eades says. Thus Eades urges people never to visit a casino again: "I tell people, unless you have to, don't go. I've had people say, 'Well, I'm not going to go gamble. I'm going to go cash in all my comps that I have and we're going to eat there. We're going to spend the night there.' And I say, 'You're a fool.'"[6]

Not only that, Eades advises never even driving past a casino. "If it is possible, and it usually is, avoid driving by a casino. Out of sight is not out of mind, but it surely helps to not have to look at reminders and be tempted. What are a few extra blocks out of your way?"[7]

The casinos themselves do not make recovery any easier. One recovering addict was still receiving mailings from casinos two years after he quit gambling—he had to contact them to make them stop. Tom Coates tells the story of an elderly woman who gambled to escape the depression she felt over her terminally ill husband. When she had run through their entire savings, she realized she needed to stop. And she did. But because she had been a member of the casino's slot club, casino personnel knew quite a bit about her, including her gambling habits. "After a period of time of not seeing her," Coates says, "the casino assigned some employee to call her, say, 'Oh, Mrs. So-and-So, we haven't seen you for so long. We miss you. You want to come back out. We'll give you a complimentary meal or some such thing.'" The woman returned to gambling—and to losing. She even borrowed $12,000 she didn't have to do so.[8]

Some recovering addicts find themselves taking heroic measures to withstand the temptations. One such, with eight months' clean time under her belt, found herself alone and lonely over Thanksgiving. Her children were with their father; her family lived elsewhere. She sat at her computer, looking at a Web site that sold plane tickets online. "So here I'm sitting, twiddling my thumbs," she says. "Well, Vegas is only a hop away, you know? All I had to hit was 'Buy' the ticket. But then I also saw, Okay, last plane out is at eight. Okay, so if I wait till after six, I won't have enough time to get out to the airport and get the ticket." She physically wrapped herself up in her bedclothes until the deadline had passed.

It is certainly in their best interest for gamblers in recovery to summon the wherewithal to do whatever it takes to stave off such attacks, to fight off the cravings, the desires. Their support group contacts are of vital assistance for this task—they can "talk you down." But more even than they, a gracious and loving God awaits such requests for help in fighting the urges. Prayer is vital throughout the recovery process, but at no time is it more crucial than when the one in recovery is hit full-force with all of Satan's might.

Unfortunately, not all gamblers take the shortest distance from A to B, from stopping to recovery. Many take serious detours along the way. These relapses often leave the gambler as desperate as he was when he first stopped. For one recovering addict, his relapse left him "probably as suicidal as I ever got. Because at that point I was sure I was beyond redemption."

Fortunately for this gambler, and for all of us, gamblers or not, he wasn't beyond redemption. None of us ever are. For the God we worship is one of redemption, one who is identified and characterized by His love for His creatures and His willingness, His eagerness, to forgive them their sins. God has promised to forgive us our sins if we repent of them. And our God is a God who unfailingly keeps His promises.

The notion that "God loves you as you are" became key to this gambler's recovery. "Regardless of what I've done in the past, there is redemption for me. So, yes, this notion . . . [of] forgiveness of sins and redemption is a very strong part of my recovery. That you get another chance. And that I will even get another chance even if I blow this."

Relapses happen. That's testimony to the power of any addiction. But forgiveness also happens. And that's testimony to the greater power of God's love for each of us, His children.

WHAT ABOUT THE SPOUSE?

No single person in a male compulsive gambler's life better aids his chances for recovery than a loving spouse. Despite the pain, the anger, the disappointment that pummels them when the tidal wave of consequences comes rolling over themselves and their families, many wives decide that, in the end, the best course of action is to stand by their man. One recovering addict, when he finally came clean to his wife about his gambling, and when he told her he had also ripped off his employer of a substantial sum to subsidize his addiction, thankfully remembers his wife's reaction: "The first thing she said to me was, 'Well, I'm not going anywhere. How much was it?'" Gamblers blessed with such helpmeets should sing *Te Deums* all the day long that God saw fit to send such fine women down the aisle with them.

But these women are undergoing their own ordeal. Their lives have been shattered along with their husbands'; they must embark upon a journey of recovery as well. Trust must be restored with their mates; the lines of communication, frayed possibly to a few strands, must be rewound; all sorts of unaccustomed responsibilities, chiefly financial, have probably been thrust upon them, which they must learn to handle; even intimacy, in many cases, is in need of resuscitation. And that's not to mention any of the lingering family problems that had arisen before the onset of the gambling problems and that remain for resolution after the gambling has stopped.

The anger that often overwhelms the spouse must be dealt with as well. "How could you do this to me?" is an oft-heard refrain among the spouses of compulsive gamblers. It is a question to which there are no really good answers. Says Chaplain Killian: "Essentially, we have to convince them that if they don't help, they're basically abandoning that person. And there's got to be enough love left there somewhere to where that appeal will work. It's not easy. We've had many of them walk away."[9]

Perhaps the most helpful response is that, once the addictive stage sets in, the gambler has succumbed to something greater than himself. He is no longer who he was: The gambling has become him. A spouse, to assist both her husband and herself, will be well advised to educate herself on compulsive gambling. Through education comes understanding. And through understanding often comes forgiveness. Says Eades: "People take it very personal. And it's really not personal. It affects that person, but it's a disease in the way I see it. And that person, first, did not mean to become a gambling addict. They don't mean to make your life miserable. And anger, or anger at that person, probably is not going to help them get any better."[10]

Many spouses undergo therapy themselves to assist their recovery, either with their partner and family or alone. Many join Gam-Anon, which serves as a sounding board and tour guide for their continuing crisis. And many seek solace in the church.

The wife of one recovering addict got close to seven or eight women at her church, women who provided good counsel and built her up. They told her, in the words of her husband: "Satan is going to try to make you bitter over this. Don't let him," and "It's okay to be angry, but be forgiving." All of which fortified her tremendously in her own recovery. But the spouse of another addict found only condemnation from church folk; she was criticized for the anger she harbored for her spouse. "I needed to unload all of my anger," she says.

Stand by Your Woman
Wives of compulsive gamblers may stand by their man, but alas, when the gender roles are reversed, it's the husbands who are often first out the door. Male spouses of women compulsive gamblers oftentimes do not stand by their woman.

The reasons for this phenomenon are probably complex, but this much is obvious: Men should stand by their women with the same loyalty and love their women would proffer them.

Not to get too elementary, but a marriage is a lifelong yoking of two people, a relationship to be carried on in perpetuity, in health or in sickness, in richer or poorer, in good times and bad. Male spouses who flee their wives for this reason are not living up to their half of the deal.

And here again, education is key. Eades, who has counseled couples with this role reversal, tries to bring understanding to the situation. "I tell them that she's sick, first of all. I really explain what has occurred, and how it happened, and why she's a lot more sick than bad at this point in her life. This is why she lies, and this is why she can't spend more time with you, and this is why your marriage is going bad. There's something freeing about understanding what has happened."[11]

Unfortunately, with more and more women falling under the spell of gambling problems, this condition is likely to increase in time rather than decrease. We can only hope and pray that men will manifest the love they themselves receive from their Father in heaven to their wives, and that they will react with the same love for their spouses as their spouses would show them were the roles reversed.

NINE

Getting Them Young

One of the most troubling trends in gambling in America today encompasses those at both ends of life's continuum—the young and the old. Both adolescents and the elderly, in increasing numbers, are developing gambling problems. Now, the elder set in America has always comprised folks with gambling problems, but rarely have they *become* problem and pathological gamblers in their elderly years. In the past, the problems developed much earlier in life and went undiagnosed and untreated until they were older. Similarly with young people: Adolescents with gambling problems are a new phenomenon. Says Valerie Lorenz, a nationally recognized gambling therapist in Maryland with over twenty-five years in the field: "We never saw a teenage gambler ten years ago. Now we see them regularly."[1]

In addition to being particularly vulnerable to gambling problems, the youth and the elderly, each in its own way, present difficulties in detection and treatment that are peculiar to their age groups. In this chapter we will explore the dangers faced by the first of these two age groups, offering a summary of the scope of the problem, followed by some guidance in how to deal with an adolescent who develops problems with gambling. (Gambling by the elderly is discussed in the next chapter.)

ADOLESCENCE JUST GOT HARDER

It is arguable, of course, but the children of today have it a lot tougher than their parents' generation in many respects. Certainly when it comes to creature comforts and the convenience of life in general, they don't—the technological strides made in our society over the past twenty years make the domestic lives of their parents' youth look like tableaux out of a frontier novel. But in other matters, in critical issues of spiritual and moral and ethical import, what was black and white a mere generation or two ago is now seen through gray-tinted lenses. The taboos on premarital sex, illegitimate birth, homosexuality, and even receiving handouts from the government have been largely dropped; the sanctity of marriage has withered under an all-out secular assault; and some heretofore universally abhorred practices, like abortion, have been made acceptable, if not actually commendable, behavior in some sectors of society.

So too with gambling. The generation now reaching puberty never knew an America where playing games of chance was morally condemned and secularly discouraged. Not only has a wave of legalized gambling swept the land, but if you pay attention to the advertising, you soon learn it has become the civic duty of the citizenry to engage in some forms of gambling, to wit: the lottery. Couple this reversal of public sentiment with the natural tendency of the young to take risks and "taste" life in its many flavors, and it comes as no surprise that teenagers have become one of the most endangered age groups when it comes to developing gambling problems.

The findings are sobering:

* ✤ The National Research Council (NRC) of the National Academy of Sciences, in a 1999 report, indicates that "preliminary evidence suggests that the earlier people begin gambling, the more likely they are to experience problems from gambling."[2]
* ✤ This same report indicates that seventeen out of twenty, a full 85 percent of adolescents, have gambled during their lifetimes, and 73 percent have gambled in the past year.[3]
* ✤ It also estimates that approximately 6.1 percent of adolescents are pathological, or compulsive, gamblers, three times the number of adults. When compulsives are combined with problem gamblers (those manifesting lesser difficulties from their gambling), the rate soars to about 20 percent.[4]
* ✤ Another survey showed that between 9.9 and 14.2 percent of youths had developed problem gambling, while an additional 4.4 to 7.4 percent could already be classified as compulsives.[5]
* ✤ Teens are two and a half times more likely to develop gambling problems than grown-ups, according to Dr. Durand Jacobs, who conducted a four-year study of adolescent gambling.[6]
* ✤ A Louisiana survey of 12,000 sixth- through twelfth-graders found that nearly 6 percent were compulsive gamblers while 16 percent could be termed problem gamblers.[7]
* ✤ One in ten teens has broken the law—drug peddling, prostitution, or stealing—to finance debts related to gambling.[8]

Other studies and anecdotal evidence suggest that teens are pushing the envelope with the gusto endemic to youth, trying to gamble even though they're too young to legally do so. High school students in Atlantic City, New Jersey, for example, flock to that city's many casinos, with 64 percent, according to one survey, having gambled at least once therein and 21 percent visiting more than ten times.[9] On the national level, the NRC, analyzing thirteen studies, found that a median of 27 percent of adolescents said they had gambled in a casino.[10]

Individual cases are particularly troubling. In 1989 one fourteen-year-old kid spent almost a full day playing roulette in an Atlantic City casino, downing complimentary alcoholic drinks as he played. Another youth had achieved grizzled-veteran status in one Atlantic City casino by the time she was sixteen, wagering thirty dollars a hand at blackjack and receiving the commensurate comps—rooms, lobster and champagne dinners, show tickets—from casino management. Another youth played so much that he was extended a $2,500 line of credit by one casino.

Another underage gambler from Washington, D.C., made a mistake one day: He hit a $50,000 jackpot. *Him* they noticed. As any substantial winnings must be reported to the federal government, the casino needed to see some ID from the lad. They then "discovered" he was nineteen. David Johnston writes that in New Jersey, Nevada, and other states where casinos are legal, "so long as kids are losing money the casinos have no incentive to throw them out. And if they win, the casinos suddenly take a keen interest in their age because if the player cannot prove he or she is twenty-one, then the casino gets to keep the money."[11]

But the casinos are getting wise to this problem—they're starting to talk the talk at any rate. Some, in fact, have aimed high-profile campaigns at potential underage transgressors, crusades that conspicuously avoid mentioning the obvious "possibility" of losing money at the slots and tables in favor of imploring youth to defer their gratification of these forbidden fruits until they're of legal age. "These are, at best, hollow public relations ploys," writes Robert Goodman. "At worst, they add to the mystique of gambling and actually encourage more gambling."[12]

Casinos are perhaps most influential, however, in training up a new generation of gamblers. Las Vegas's transmogrification from "Sin City" to "Disney World with Gambling" is clearly geared for the family crowd, and families by definition include children. The kids may be kept from the machines and tables themselves, but they must walk right past them to get to the amusement rides, theme parks, and movie theaters. When occupying themselves in the kiddies' arcades, they play virtual copies of the games on the floor. Also, trends in slot machine manufacturing itself seem geared toward the younger set, now featuring child-enticing themes like Candyland, a board game popular with very young children, and for older kids, slots based on Monopoly, *The Three Stooges*, the Pink Panther, *South Park*, *I Dream of Jeannie*, *The Addams Family*, and Popeye.

This so troubled a broad coalition of conservatives, progressives, religious leaders, and academics that they requested the Senate and House Commerce Committees to "investigate whether the gambling industry is luring impressionable children to gambling or casinos by employing slot machines bearing cartoon characters and other themes popular with children."[13]

Toy-like video games of blackjack, poker, and roulette are also making their way into the market, complete with disclaimers that they are for entertainment and not gambling purposes—a trend one author calls "gambling preschool."[14] Louisiana casino self-aggrandizement is equally subtle and deceptive. Casinos there have attached cards, dice, and T-shirts sporting casino logos to donations of computer equipment and library books to that state's schools.[15]

Casino gambling is being stripped of its stigma. No longer is it seedy, sleazy, underworldish—it's safe for the whole family now. And no longer can it be done only in Nevada, a place kids would rarely visit as part of a family vacation. Now it's everywhere, perpetuated by an aggressive industry doing what all industries try to do: Get more customers. The message this industry sends toward adolescents focuses not on the dangers of its "product" but only on age: gambling is a fun, enjoyable activity, but you'll have to wait a few years before you can participate in it.

Casinos may be training up our children in the ways of the slot machines and roulette wheels for revenues to be reaped later, but on the whole, casinos play a minor role in adolescent gambling. Lotteries, cards, and sports betting are more popular because they are more accessible with the younger set. Because they are sold at often-busy convenience stores where clerks are encouraged to dispatch customers quickly, lottery and keno tickets are a big draw for teens. One sting operation conducted at ninety Massachusetts locations revealed that 66 percent of minors, some as young as fourteen, were able to illegally purchase keno tickets.[16] Other surveys revealed that teens were also buying illegal lottery tickets in significant numbers.[17]

The lottery serves as a gateway for gambling, a portal through which gamblers enter en route to other forms of wagering. Kids particularly are vulnerable to this. Dr. Durand Jacobs, a California gambling expert, says teens, once hooked on the lottery, quickly move on to other games of chance.[18]

If casinos and state-sanctioned lotteries and keno games, with their supposedly "strict" regulation, are unable to prevent underage people from gambling, what then of sports betting and Internet gambling, technically illegal forms of wagering that are nonetheless rampant in our society? Sports betting has thrived in this country ever since there have been sports, and it has been illegal just as long. But now it has expanded its grasp into the adolescent world. A Gallup Poll conducted in 2000 found that 18 percent of teens from ages thirteen to seventeen admitted to gambling on college sports, which is double the rate for adults (9 percent).[19] Says Arnie Wexler, who conducts seminars and workshops on compulsive gambling: "For most kids their first initiation to gambling is either [betting on] cards or sports gambling." Lorenz figures that nine of ten teens she works with have sports-gambling problems.[20]

Particular incidents put a face on these numbers. One San Francisco high school "bookie," arrested in 1992, had taken in $30,000 worth of action on basketball and football games from classmates at three other high schools. In 1995 in New Jersey, a high school betting ring was uncovered that pulled in $7,500 per week and was tied to organized crime.[21]

Once they get to college, the temptations for young people only increase. Bookies are ubiquitous on our nation's campuses, and students have no problem placing illegal wagers when they want to. *Sports Illustrated,* in a three-part story, described gambling on campus as "rampant and prospering." The special report revealed "how easy it is for students to bet with a bookie, become consumed with wagering, and get over their heads in debt." Indeed, NCAA executive director Cedric Dempsey calls sports gambling "as big an addiction problem on college campuses as alcohol."[22]

Internet gambling is even harder to police; the virtual casino offers anonymity and no restrictions whatever for those who want to take their action online. Teens are as close to gambling on the Web as they are to their bedroom computers, and can access it twenty-four hours a day. Although most online wagering sites require the gambler to apprise them of his age, they make little or no attempt to verify the accuracy of that information. Accounts can be set up with a credit card number, or even a debit card number—either the teen's own or his parents'. And a lot of money can be lost. One witness before the House Subcommittee on Crime testified in March 2000 that he had gambled away $5,000 of his dad's money on the Web, using his dad's credit card number to play blackjack and roulette.[23]

The 1999 final report of the National Gambling Impact Study Commission puts the situation tersely but accurately: "Parents simply cannot rely upon the government or the industry to prevent underage gambling."[24]

Recognizing the Problem

In addition to sex, alcohol, and drugs, now parents trying to raise their kids right in a hedonistic, relativistic world must grapple with the problems brought on by the accessibility and state sanctification of legalized gambling as well. Although for many teens, especially boys, gambling is but one of a number of "rites of passage" through which they test their impending manhood, eventually growing out of it as they mature, for others the gambling takes on a life of its own and they grow into problem and pathological gamblers. This is a difficulty made infinitely more irksome not only by the fact that teens can get hooked more quickly than adults,[25] but also because gambling problems in teens are more difficult to detect and treat than those in older adults.

The course of the addiction, however, remains similar to that in more mature problem gamblers. The entry point for teens is usually restricted by age to card games played for fun or the purchase of a lottery ticket; they are lured to gambling because it looks fun and interesting. If that first experience was enjoyable—either in how it made the teen feel or the bad feelings it allowed him to escape—the teen will return. If he returns often enough, eventually he will become psychically dependent on gambling, and will be unhappy or tense and out of sorts when not actively engaged in it.[26]

The stages through which an adolescent progresses are similar to those of an adult: He may enjoy a winning stage, after which he will suffer through a losing phase and a desperation phase. And toward the end, he may revert to crime to get his gambling money, justifying it in his mind, just as an adult does, as a loan that he fully intends to pay back. Teens also consider suicide a way out of their ever-growing problems.

As with adults, a teen who suspects he has a gambling problem could resolve his confusion by honestly answering a questionnaire developed by Gamblers Anonymous (GA) especially for young people. These queries were adapted from GA's "Twenty Questions," designed for adults, and go like this:

1.   Have you ever stayed away from school or work to gamble?
2.   Is gambling making your home life unhappy?
3.   Is gambling affecting your reputation?
4.   Do you ever gamble until your last dollar is gone, even your bus fare home or the cost of a burger or a Coke?
5.   Have you ever lied, stolen, or borrowed just to get money to gamble?
6.   Are you reluctant to spend "gambling money" on normal things?
7.   After losing, do you feel you must return as soon as possible to win back your losses?
8.   Is gambling more important than school or work?
9.   Does gambling cause you to have difficulty sleeping?
10. Have you ever thought of suicide as a way of solving your problems?[27]

If your child honestly "aces" this test, he may not have a gambling problem—and you can delete one item from your worry list. But truthfulness is not a character trait of adult gamblers, much less kids with problems. If your child lies in response to these questions, he is not only hurting himself in the long run, but is also making your life as his guardian far more difficult. Then it becomes incumbent on you, as his parent, to ascertain on your own whether or not he has a problem. You must look for clues.

Of all the tip-offs available to parents, perhaps the money angle is the most fruitful to pursue. If they have their own money, kids will use their wages and dip into their checking and savings accounts to finance their gambling. They will also tap others—friends, parents, siblings, relatives, and even an official lending institution.[28] Like their elders, young gamblers must also "juggle" their finances to keep solvent and still allow them sufficient funds to wager. A study conducted by Dr. Henry Lesieur and Robert Klein of 892 eleventh- and twelfth-graders in four New Jersey high schools "found that almost 7 percent of the young gamblers had borrowed from four or more sources or had sought the assistance of a relative to pay off a heavy debt."[29]

If you suspect your youngster has a gambling problem, follow the money. Does the child seem frequently to want more money than usual from you, above and beyond any allowance you might give him? Does he have money you can't account for—does he flash newfound and unexplained wealth? Does he hit siblings or relatives up for loans quite a bit? Has lack of money prompted him to break the law in some way? How about *your* money—have you noticed some of it missing? Same with your credit cards—have you "lost" any lately that you can't remember losing? Have you come upon gambling "evidence" in his room or among his things—losing lottery tickets, track paraphernalia, literature on betting, even "souvenir" chips he stole from a casino?[30] A yes answer to any or all of these questions might indicate a problem.

Far more difficult to figure out is a child's activities. Children, like adults, need time to gamble, but tracking their time schedules may be even more problematic than accounting for an adult's. Some kids engaged in sports gambling will necessarily spend a lot of time on the phone, and will most likely be quite reticent about the identity of their conversation partners. Your child may also be receiving more calls from strangers than usual—that would be his bookie. Or he may place or receive calls at particular, and regular, times of the day—in time to place a bet before evening ball games start, for example. Most kids don't follow strict time schedules for their phone calls, and one who does may be offering a clue to a gambling problem. If he continues to be absorbed right to the end of a blowout football or basketball game, long after the outcome has effectively been decided, he might have bet the point spread. If he's quit extracurricular activities, ditched school, or blown off his studying, although not endemic to gambling behavior alone, this may indicate that gambling is becoming more important in the teen's life. If your child has made new friends who seem to have little in common with him, they might be gambling buddies.[31] Any or all of these behaviors might indicate your child is gambling, perhaps even has developed problems with gambling.

Also visible to parents is any change in the child's emotional life. Here parents must utilize what they know about their child, and notice whether dramatic changes have occurred in how he comports himself around the family. If he has gone into a shell, withdrawing from family and friends, or become distant and silent, it might indicate gambling has achieved more importance in his life. Also, if he has been lying or cheating, this may also indicate a gambling problem. Admittedly, changes in the child's emotions may indicate any number of other issues, but one possible explanation is gambling.

What You Can Do

Let's say you've determined your child has a gambling problem. What do you do then? The answer to this vital question is complicated by the child's lack of responsibility in the world.

You can prevent his continued gambling as best you can, removing his opportunities to wager as much as possible. This would seem a worthwhile goal, and in some cases is. But in the end it is a mere temporary solution, for the root cause of the gambling remains untreated, in remission as it were.[32] Kids who develop gambling problems, like their adult counterparts, will have to get a handle on it by themselves—they must face the consequences of their gambling and come to the realization that gambling is destructive and they can't engage in it.

Getting them to that point is where the difficulty enters. Denial is much greater in young people because they likely feel very few of the consequences of their harmful actions. Most adults who run up credit card bills face immediate consequences. But "young people who are still living at home," says Dr. John M. Eades, an addiction specialist living in Tennessee, "really can't get the full impact of what's going on. Because they don't have that many responsibilities, they're not going to be losing a good job and so forth and so on."[33] Nor will those who remain at their flickering computer screens till all hours gambling away their parents' bank books necessarily be punished for their lethargy the next day, especially during summertime. It's hard enough to fight through the denial of an adult, says Eades, "but teenagers haven't really experienced any losses. They haven't lost a wife because they don't have one. And they haven't not paid the dental bill . . . because they don't have any."

Exacerbating the problem is a parent's natural inclination to rescue a child. This is understandable, and in many ways commendable. Kids are still growing emotionally as well as physically; they don't command the same degree of self-control as grown-ups, nor should they be expected to. And they aren't as responsible as adults either—that's what being a teenager is all about, after all. But the authors of *Don't Leave It to Chance* do not recommend that parents instinctively bail their kids out of their jams just because they're still kids. "The temptation to hold a young gambler less responsible for his or her gambling is ill-advised," they write. "The truth is that youngsters, like their adult counterparts, can overcome their gambling only by finding ways to control it."[34]

As for financial debts, parents may be obligated to step in and make them right if the child is under the age of consent; they may also feel an ethical obligation to do just that. But as far as their own control of the young person's money supply, that depends on his age. Clearly, those just entering adolescence are totally dependent on their parents for their day-to-day support, which includes their access to money, and parents can quite effectively monitor this.

With kids who are away at college, it becomes more problematic. Tom Coates of Consumer Credit of Des Moines has seen kids drop out of college "because they rack up enough debt and they can't pay their ongoing school bills that the family sent them money for, and they end up dropping out of college, because of their indebtedness."[35] If parents are involved in his tuition or in any way financially contributory to his education, consequences can be allowed to fall where they will. At the very least, parents can install themselves as financial advisors to their child's life, demanding periodic reviews and even tying continued financial support to the child's willingness to cooperate.[36]

In the end, prevention is no doubt easier than dealing with the problem once it arises. Prevention primarily entails education, and necessarily begins at an early age. Whether your kids bring the topic up or not, you should talk with them in a way that is appropriate to their age about the dangers of gambling. Our society will give you plenty of opportunities to broach the topic, as advertising for gambling is as widespread

as the gambling itself. Secondly, teach them about good judgment and self-control, both critical components of successfully withstanding the allures of gambling. And thirdly,
channel them toward alternative activities with which to play
out their need for stimulation and excitement, for discovering
new things.[37]

For those kids who have already succumbed to the sirens
of the gambling industry, education may not be as productive.
Eades recommends gathering evidence and confronting the
teen, with the intention of getting him to see his behavior as
problematic. Gamblers Anonymous is of course also an
option, and parents can recommend their youth attend meetings of this self-governed organization, which puts no stipulations on the age of its members. Individual therapy is also
helpful, but it may take quite a bit of this before results are
seen. "Once it starts," Eades says, "once they get addicted, the
denial is so pronounced, it may take a long time."

If people toward the beginning of life's journey are falling prey
to the gambling bug in record numbers, so too are those further down the path, toward the end.

Addicted seniors may be a new phenomenon in our
nation, but they are no less problematic than young gamblers
for concerned loved ones. A father or mother, grandfather or
grandmother, who succumbs in his or her dotage to the allure
of gambling presents peculiar problems that scream out for
attention. The age and position in the family hierarchy of
these elders make these challenges even more difficult to deal
with in many cases than those with our youth.

We now take up the troubling specter of senior citizen
gambling addicts.

TEN

Getting Them Old

From the New Jersey suburbs of New York City to Philadelphia, from Chicago to Denver, and from Kansas City to Nashville, and all points between, they pile into buses that will whisk them off to a place where they can forget their worries and reinvigorate their souls. It is a bus ministry to turn even the most aggressive megachurch green with envy, but it has nothing to do with organized religion. For these convoys of buses are packed with senior citizens making daily pilgrimages to a different kind of shrine—to a casino.

Seniors have become a cash cow for the gambling industry, one of the—if not *the*—demographic groups most responsible for the casino industry's rising profit line. The National Gambling Impact Study Commission found that, in 1998, half the people over age sixty-five had gambled in the past year, up dramatically from the 23 percent recorded in 1975.[1] It is estimated that people over sixty account for 65 percent of the revenue raked in by the mammoth slot farm that is Atlantic City.[2] Bus riders to this New Jersey seaside resort vaulted from 743,000 in 1978 to 12.6 million in 1985,[3] and one newspaper report from the year 2000 indicated that 75 percent of the passengers on 375,000 buses to Atlantic City were seniors.[4] Although hard evidence is elusive, eyewitnesses suggest that the weekday daytime trade at Midwestern casinos also "skews old," to use advertising parlance. Says Chaplain Trennis Killian, of Riverboat Casinos Ministry: "If you go into a casino in the Midwest right now during the day during the week, the average age in there will be about sixty-five."[5] Even glamorous Las Vegas, home to high rollers and the young and the restless, says 30 percent of its visitors are sixty or over.[6]

In a certain respect, this is all understandable—albeit lamentable. The elderly in our culture are not revered as they once were. In fact, many times they are regarded as useless family appendages—or worse, nuisances—hanging around to bother society and their kids until they pass on. Casinos offer them the respect society, and perhaps even their extended family, have not bestowed on them. Casinos, in short, meet many of their felt needs. Once these elderly people stride through a casino's doors, they may engage in a unique kind of sociability—others are around, but the others won't bother them per se—in a safe environment where nearly everybody, from security guards to cocktail waitresses, if they are regulars, may know their names and their food and beverage preferences. This offers escape from any and all of the problems of their sunset years—emotional, psychological, even physical.

The independence elderly people feel in a casino is also intoxicating, "especially if they are in or have been in a relationship where the spouse is domineering or controlling or if physical ailments or disabilities have kept them from a 'normal' life," according to the Arizona Council on Compulsive Gambling. The feeling of excitement and living on the edge they may experience, especially if they hadn't gambled in their younger years, can also be liberating. Casinos hike their self-esteem, offering a false sense that it is now "their turn," their time in the sun devoid of the demands of their family members. And of course, there is that chance that they will walk out of there with more money than they walked in with.[7]

Casinos, in short, become an integral part of their lives, meeting needs that could better be met by other entities—like the church. The fact that seniors would rather sit in front of their slot machines instead of in their pews on Sundays—"because Sunday becomes a gambling day," says Eades—offers an indication "that we're not meeting some of the needs of our elderly."

Rev. John Landrum, who ministers to casino workers and addicts on the Mississippi Coast, tells of one elderly woman who thrived on the treatment she received from casinos and developed gambling problems in the process. When she walks into a casino, she says, "'they know my name, they know what I like to eat, they know what I like to drink, they give me a room, they treat me like a queen.' And she had quit going to church. She said, 'I got tired of going to my church, where they acted like they didn't care if I came or not. Most of the people didn't know my name, didn't care to learn it. But I can go to the casino down there on the river, and they treat me like a queen, and that's why I do it.'"[8]

A majority of these elderly gamblers, unlike this woman, keep a rein on their desires. But some don't, and they submit to the gambling bug and its many dangers. Hard figures on seniors, alas, are difficult to dig up, and a correspondence between the increase in senior gambling and a resulting rise in problem and pathological gambling among the elderly, as common sense would suggest, cannot be proven statistically.

However, the Council on Compulsive Gambling of New Jersey puts the number of seniors that "cannot gamble without severe consequences" at 5 percent.[9] It also indicates that the number of callers to the 1-800-GAMBLER hotline who were over the age of fifty-five, 13.9 percent, has held reasonably steady for the past ten years.[10] The numbers from Arizona, though, shed more light on the problem. Of callers to the Arizona Council on Compulsive Gambling hotline in 1998, 25 percent were from or about people fifty-five or older and 9 percent concerned those sixty-five or older; in 1999 the numbers came in at 39 percent and 8 percent, respectively. The council adds ominously: "Nearly 86% of those had not had a gambling problem until recently and met our criteria of Escape Gamblers."[11]

Whatever the numbers, they do not do justice to the destruction gambling problems wreak on a senior's person and finances, not to mention those of his children and grandchildren. The elderly lose more from gambling problems because they have less to lose. Many are on fixed incomes with little or no disposable money. Many jeopardize a comfortable retirement by blowing their savings on the slot machines. (Most late-onset gamblers, as seniors typically are, are escape gamblers who favor the slots.) Many descend even to the point of pumping their social security checks into the machines and forgoing expensive medication, in some cases. Dr. Linda Chamberlain, a Denver therapist and gambling addiction expert, says the elderly are "one of the more vulnerable groups. They have limited incomes that they have to survive under, and they have no real resources for getting income in, in terms of going to work or learning new skills or something like that." The elderly, she says, are some of the most problematic compulsive gamblers she sees in her practice, "because there's nowhere for them to go. There's no way that they're going to recoup their losses."[12]

It thus behooves the children of seniors to keep a sharp eye out for gambling problems in their elderly loved ones. Often the onset of the behavior comes on the heels of what psychologists call "predisposing factors"—a broad rubric under which can be classified everything from boredom, stress, grief, depression, loneliness, and lack of hobbies or leisure activities to health problems, chronic pain, fear of death, relationship difficulties, and a controlling or domineering spouse.[13] Particular tip-offs to look for mirror those for younger but mature gamblers, and include the following, among others:

* a preoccupation with gambling and related activities;
* talking only about wins, not losses;
* becoming secretive or lying about the gambling or their whereabouts;
* missing important family functions;
* allowing gambling to become a preferred type of entertainment in their lives, to the exclusion of other activities they had enjoyed in the past, like a bridge club or going to the senior center and so forth;
* having trouble meeting monthly living expenses;
* depleting their financial reserves;
* extending credit lines for gambling money;
* borrowing money from family members with vague explanations for the money's use;
* giving up on friends, or conversely, failing to make new ones after a geographical move.[14] (See also chapter 5.)

Recognizing a problem is only a first, and very preliminary, step in the process. Now you must deal with it. Consider the sensitive nature of *this* project: You, a child of the man or woman with a gambling problem, have for your formative years been dependent upon this man or woman's generosity. It's always been the parent's money you spent, the parent's rules you lived by, the parent's discipline that was meted out, and now the roles are reversed. It's you tightening the purse strings; it's you setting down the boundaries; it's you circumscribing the behavior. To say that many adult children may be uncomfortable in this new role is to employ understatement unheard since Calvin Coolidge left office.

Tact is a prerequisite, of course, and when coupled with love, may yield positive results. The authors of *Don't Leave It to Chance* offer a number of tips for dealing with problem gambling seniors. Adult children should try to uncover the senior's motivation to gamble and show great respect for his independence. Zeroing in on practical necessities that the senior needs in order to gamble—transportation issues, time alone, and so forth—may also uncover strategies for controlling the frequency of the gambling. It is also possible, if the gambler takes a more passive role in the activity—relying on friends to organize a casino visit or being enticed by mailings from casinos, etc.—for the family to mediate with the source. Sweepstakes firms often target the elderly "because they are vulnerable to gambling," the authors write, so direct and firm confrontation with the relevant businesses may stop those mailings and thus remove that temptation.

If a medical illness like dementia or Alzheimer's disease is involved and the gambler suffers from diminished capacity of some sort, more drastic steps, which would necessarily include the elder's physician, are needed. In these cases family members must take a more active role in providing control over the gambler's behavior. Seeking legal control over the gambler's finances may also be necessary.[15]

When broaching the topic itself, lean toward an indirect approach. "Our experience with families suggests overly aggressive approaches can alienate the gambler, reducing the opportunity for influence," write the authors of *Don't Leave It to Chance*.[16] Success may be enhanced by recruiting those influential to the senior—a pastor, for example—to consult with the gambler. If the senior asks for a loan from the family, then the children can be more direct. Chamberlain suggests saying something like the following: "We have concerns about your gambling. We appreciate that you're responsible for your finances, but if you borrow money from us, then we want to know what's going on. We want to see what's going on." The elder may of course say no—indeed, he has every right to do so. "But you have every right to say, 'I can't support you anymore then.'"

Because of their age and position in life, seniors will be hard pressed to make restitution for any debts they may have incurred through their gambling. Being in their "golden years," most likely retired and with no active means of income, "they don't have the ability to provide the time and effort ... necessary to create the restitution," Tom Coates says. "They may, but many times they don't."[17] In addition to effectively deferring the consequences of their gambling and delaying their quest for seeking help, this also devastates the senior in the short term. What money or assets he had will doubtlessly be taken out of his hands, and he may have to move in with, and indeed, become totally reliant on family. Seniors in this predicament, says Chamberlain, "essentially ... become prisoners—hopefully, under benign keepers, but that's not always the case."

When adult children see their anticipated inheritance dissolve before their eyes, and when the vision of their parents entering a fruitful and enjoyable ten or twenty years of retirement also dissipates, adult children can become very upset. "It's gone," Chamberlain says. "And they're burdened with now taking care of them, financially, physically, and in every other way, with no end in sight.... It's a horrible stress on families."

The same means of treatment that are open to younger folks are available for seniors as well—individual therapy, GA, etc.—and family members would be well advised to urge these options on their loved one. But the times in which they were raised, and the attitudes with which they were indoctrinated, often hinder the willingness of the elderly to seek help. The seniors of our age are a proud generation, a generation that grew up on and embraced wholeheartedly axioms that to following generations have become mere bromides: "Don't throw good money after bad"; "Save for a rainy day"; and so on. When they finally realize what they have done, that they have in fact violated these precepts, the shame they feel may match their depression.

Adult children, with love, tact, and devotion, and with the help of others, be it a pastor or a therapist or a self-help group, can deal with this problem, difficult as it may be.

Much of the rise in teen and elderly gambling problems can be attributed to the increasing accessibility of legalized gambling in our society. Elderly women camping out in front of slot machines for twelve hours at a time, returning day after day to feed valuable monetary resources into the insatiable slots, were not a problem prior to the invasion of casino gambling onto our rivers, coastlines, and Indian reservations. As for our youth, although trying one's luck in back alley craps games and small-stakes poker games with "the boys" has always been present in our society, youth were not getting hooked on gambling while still youths to the same degree before lotteries and Internet gambling arrived on the scene.

Unfortunately, there is little relief in sight. Elected officials at all levels of government seem to show very little willingness to curb their voracious appetites for the "painless taxation" legalized gambling proffers. Indeed, many are even now promoting more opportunities for legal wagering in our states.

Christians concerned for the welfare of their children and of their elders must prepare themselves to join this battle, to fight for a retrenchment of legalized gambling in our society. But to fight the fight one must know the battleground.

The remainder of this book will tour this battleground on all its fronts—moral, economic, and practical. It will address this question: Is gambling good for us, both individually and corporately as a nation?

We begin with the former, gambling's morality for us as individuals.

ELEVEN

Sin or Recreation?
The Morality
of Gambling

Broad, sweeping generalizations about gambling fall easily from one's lips and are, far more often than not, true: Gambling is foolish—no, even stronger, it is *stupid.* A gambler, if he plays long enough, will lose, probably quite substantially, thus putting at risk his own welfare as well as that of his family. Gambling can hardly be considered a wise investment of resources. The atmosphere that surrounds gambling gives rise to crime, both organized and otherwise, and all manner of temptations. The list of such negatives could go on and on.

But the question persists: Is it immoral for Christians to gamble? Is it, in short, a sin?

The answer to this question is complicated somewhat by the fact that neither the word "gamble" nor its cognates appear in the Bible. Nor is the topic of gambling directly addressed anywhere in Holy Writ. Scripture does mention casting lots, which, from what we know, probably took the form of a game played with primordial "dice"—they were sheep knucklebones. Those wanting to discern God's will in a given matter tossed these knucklebones to the ground and "read" them.

Thus did the Old Testament Israelites cast lots to determine which tribes got which territory in the Promised Land (Josh. 18–19, etc.), which goats were to be sacrificed on the Day of Atonement (Lev. 16), and who was to do what in the temple (1 Chron. 24:5), to name only a few biblical instances. Lots identified Achan as the party guilty of disobeying the Lord in the conquest of Jericho (Josh. 7:14) and Jonah as the cause of a storm at sea (Jon. 1:7). Lots were also used to determine Judas's replacement among the Twelve (Acts 1:15-26). This casting of lots may have utilized the tools of gambling, and indeed may have resembled a modern game of craps, but it was *not* gambling. Writes Rex. M. Rogers: "No fate, chance, or luck is involved in the casting of biblical lots. It was an ancient practice used in decision making. That decision recognized the sovereignty of God in all things, including the lay of the lot."[1] Even the Roman soldiers at the foot of the cross, who "divided up [Christ's] clothes by casting lots" (Matt. 27:35), were not technically gambling. No risk was involved in their enterprise, nor did the winner of the robe gain at the expense of the losers; the lot casting was essentially an antiquarian version of "rock, paper, scissors" or drawing straws.

Because the Bible does not address it directly, Christians down through the ages have differed as to gambling's morality. The early church seemed to view it quite harshly. Augustine, for example, attributed its invention to the Devil,[2] Tertullian denounced it as well,[3] and clergy and laity who gambled in the early church were threatened with excommunication.[4] Thomas

Aquinas seemed to fudge on gambling's immorality somewhat in the late Middle Ages, emphasizing that within divine providence could be subsumed the workings of luck,[5] but the Reformers spoke out against it. Martin Luther contended that gambling money could not be obtained without sin, and John Calvin's Geneva outlawed it, with transgressors being fined.[6]

Presently there seem to be two (maybe three, depending on how you count) views held by Christians about gambling's morality.

A QUESTION OF CHRISTIAN FREEDOM

Some Protestants contend that gambling is in many—if not most—instances sinful, but that its sinfulness depends on the gambler's motivation. The issue for these believers, as with their fellow Reformed Christians who see gambling as always sinful (discussed below), is the Bible, but with a difference. They are concerned not primarily with what the Good Book may say about gambling, but with what it does *not* say.

Because the Bible offers neither an explicit nay nor yea on the topic, gambling, according to this view, enters a kind of moral demilitarized zone where the freedom is granted individual Christians to reach their own conclusions about its morality. Theologians tag topics such as these—which they believe fall between biblical commendation and condemnation—with the Greek word *adiaphora*.

The church from its earliest years has grappled with such questions. In the New Testament the issue was whether Gentile Christians should be forced to adopt Jewish practices—food laws, circumcision, etc. Since then, according to one writer, the church has grappled with "the language in which she worshiped, the translation of the Bible she studied, the vestments her clergy wore, the form in which the bread and wine of Holy Communion were served, whether or not her women could come to church without a hat or wearing slacks, whether buying insurance or smoking tobacco or drinking alcoholic beverages was permissible for her members—these and many other issues have come under the scrutiny of the church. All had to be dealt with in the light of the doctrine of adiaphora."[7]

In fact, proponents of the "it depends" view of gambling go a step further: They maintain that where the Bible is silent, Christians are cautioned against making unambiguous decrees about the sinfulness of a matter. "Where God's Word does not clearly declare a certain behavior sinful," writes the author of the Lutheran Church–Missouri Synod's position paper on the topic, "we must refrain from binding the consciences of others. We must neither take away from nor add to Scripture." Simply because an activity can lead to sin—and indeed, often does— does not justify banning that activity under this view. Everything from dancing to smoking to drinking to movies to card playing to certain types of music have been censured by certain Christian groups because of what they could lead to, not necessarily because of what they are. This, the Missouri Synod says, is not dissimilar to the ancient Jewish practice employed during Jesus' day. "The rabbis built a so-called 'fence around the law' in order not to commit a sin by oversight, and in so doing they placed terrible burdens upon God's people."[8]

These Christians believe such "fence building" poses great dangers. Christians coming under its sway can become "fascinated with regulating the believer's life in minute detail" and are susceptible to "falling prey to a Gospel-denying legalism, which makes 'godly behavior'—that is, the avoidance of evil and the doing of good—the standard for a right relationship with God."[9]

Can gambling be sinful under this view? Absolutely. May gambling be an example of the sins of greed and covetousness? For sure. But is it *necessarily* so? This position says maybe not.

Same with the other potential sins of gambling: It certainly can displace the triune God in the gambler's thinking, but does it in all cases do so? It can be poor stewardship, but if done for recreation with a predetermined sum of money, is it always such? Does it in every case destroy a biblical work ethic? Questions such as these are asked by those who see the dangers of gambling but do not want to, by extrapolation, definitively pass judgment on its morality. Given the possibility that gamblers' motivations are not greed or covetousness or idolatry, is it right for well-meaning Christians to lay the prospect of sin upon their consciences?

It is in the interest of Christian liberty, and faithfulness to the doctrine of Scripture alone, that proponents of this school "must refrain from declaring that each and every act of gambling is in and of itself contrary to the Word of God and therefore sinful."[10]

This does not give Christians carte blanche when it comes to gambling, however. Christians operating under their God-given freedom must examine their consciences before they enter a casino or lay a dollar on the counter for a lottery ticket. If greed or covetousness or idolatry is in their hearts, their gambling becomes sin.

And even if it's not, even if their gambling is motivated by innocent desire for recreation, a conscientious Christian will also want to weigh whether what is permissible is in addition profitable, as the apostle Paul so poignantly asks in 1 Corinthians 10:23-24. Might his gambling cause another to stumble? Might it send confusing signals to his children?

Indeed, every Christian must thoroughly consider whether it is right to support with his dollars a predatory industry that is inherently reliant on exploiting the poor, the vulnerable, and the sick. No Christian, regardless of his personal views on the subject, can escape the broader social implications of his activities.

THE CATHOLIC VIEW

The Roman Catholic Church has carved its own niche in the debate over the morality of gambling. Long have raffles and bingo games been a part of Catholic culture, with more than a few sanctuaries and rectories built with church-sponsored gambling dollars.

Officially, the church sees no harm in gambling, as long as certain conditions are met. "The teaching of the Catholic Church on the morality of gambling is clear," wrote the Catholic Bishops of Florida in 1994. "People are entitled to dispose of their own property as they will, so long as in doing so they do not render themselves incapable of fulfilling duties expected by reason of justice or charity. Gambling, therefore, though a luxury, is not considered morally wrong in itself, but it may become morally wrong when it interferes with one's other duties or responsibilities. Gambling itself, then, according to Catholic tradition, is morally neutral depending on the individual circumstances."[11] Both the *New Catholic Encyclopedia* and the *Catechism of the Catholic Church* corroborate this view.[12]

Despite the official position on gambling's moral neutrality, some clerics in the church have seen a problem with the church's reliance on it. Joseph Cardinal Bernardin, for example, the late prelate of Chicago, called on parishes to get away from the practice. The research theologian of the Catholic Archdiocese of Chicago, Father Michael Place, sees parishes supporting themselves not on gambling but on contributions as the church's goal.[13] Other Catholic clergy express concern for their flock. One bishop, in a letter to his people, warned of the dangers of bingo and raffles. "I am convinced," he said, "that we will never teach our people the stewardship of money as long as any of these means are used for the purposes of church support."[14]

Legalized gambling's pernicious effect on the poor makes

the Catholic Church, with its historical emphasis on charity, a natural opponent of expanded gambling venues. In this fight they join various Protestant groups. For example, Chicago Catholics, with Protestant and Jewish colleagues, came out strongly against the multibillion-dollar casino proposed for downtown Chicago in the early 1990s. "The church and its allies," Timothy L. O'Brien writes, "said that the casinos would bring misery to gamblers and that educational funding shouldn't be linked to such unpredictable sources as gambling revenue."[15] The proposal was subsequently voted down.

The bishops in Florida cited the impact new casino and/or riverboat gambling in their state would have on low- and moderate-income families, along with the effects on neighborhoods, housing patterns, the homeless, and public morality. They also lobbied to keep the new gambling ventures out of the state.[16] In Michigan, church officials also warned against expanded gambling, citing their own experience with bingo and raffles as evidence of gambling's shortcomings. "Despite the revenues bingo brings in, the Church must still close schools, consolidate parishes and scale-back important programs. There is little reason to expect that the state's experience with gambling will differ significantly from that of the Catholic Church."[17]

One ironic—some may call it hypocritical—outcome of the Catholic embrace of gambling, however, is that it undercuts their moral authority to speak out against the issue.

GAMBLING IS SIN

The Bible may not directly prohibit gambling, but that does not mean it provides no guidance on the issue. Because a multitude of scriptural principles bear directly on how Christians should view this activity, Focus on the Family joins much of conservative Protestantism in maintaining that the act of gambling—whether permitted by the state or not—is inherently sinful.

Chief among the scriptural principles that condemn gambling are concerns that it is based on greed and covetousness; that it violates Christ's command to love our neighbor; that it replaces the God of providence with a deity of luck and fortune, thus eroding the concept of the sovereignty of God and indeed constituting a sin against the first commandment; that it is bad stewardship of time and talents; and that it destroys the work ethic. These points will be taken up in the discussion that follows.

Greed and Covetousness

We live in a materialistic society—arguably the most materialistic in history—and are continually tempted to want more and better possessions. Some people, for example, become workaholics primarily to assuage their all-consuming desire for bigger and better things; others may exploit friends for personal gain. But nowhere in a society is this desire for material possessions more distilled than in a gambling setting, where the peripheral niceties are abandoned and one and only one thing takes center stage: the winning of money.[18] Opinion surveys reveal that two-thirds of those who gamble do so first and foremost to win money.[19] Few are the people who do not, deep down, hope and wish to walk away from a gambling experience with more money than they brought to it. Indeed, it is almost impossible to conceive of sustained gambling—or even individual, casual gambling encounters—that does not have this desire at its heart.

When people gamble with a desire for riches, when their focus is acquiring wealth for its own sake, they have planted both feet fully within the orbit of greed. Writes R. Albert Mohler, Jr., president and professor of Christian theology at the Southern Baptist Theological Seminary in Louisville: "The basic impulse behind gambling is greed—a basic sin that is the father of many other evils."[20]

And greed does not warrant even a neutral, much less a positive, word in Scripture. The New Testament is replete with warnings about it, some emanating from no less an authority than Jesus Christ Himself: "Watch out!" He told someone who sought His assistance in the division of an inheritance. "Be on your guard against all kinds of greed; a man's life does not consist in the abundance of his possessions" (Luke 12:15). The root sin of the rich young ruler (Mark 10:17-23), as well as that of Ananias and Sapphira in Acts 5 and Judas's betrayal of the Savior, was also steeped in greed.

Money, of course, is not evil in and of itself, but "the *love* of money is a root of all kinds of evil" (1 Tim. 6:10, emphasis mine). "There is nothing wrong with gold," writes Reformed theologian Norman L. Geisler. "It's greed that the Bible condemns. Having loot is not an intrinsic evil, but lusting after it is wrong. Possessing wealth is not wrong in itself, but being possessed by it is."[21] The essence of gambling is wrapped up in this avaricious attitude, this love of money.

One commandment (in some faith traditions, two) warns specifically against a related sin: coveting, desiring that which does not belong to us. "Desiring what belongs to another is wrong," Geisler writes. "Gambling is an example of coveting what does not rightfully belong to us, a strike-it-rich scheme. ... The desire to win money that we did not work for is covetousness pure and simple."[22]

The fact that this money is acquired in what is tantamount to a zero-sum economic world makes it very difficult to avoid covetousness. Gambling is unlike a traditional business transaction, in which both product purchaser and product producer stand to gain from the arrangement. With gambling, money simply changes hands from the gamblers that are losing to the gamblers that are winning; the only consistent winner is the gambling impresario, who makes his money from a cut in the action. Therefore the desire to win is closely coupled with an attendant desire that another lose—indeed, you can't win *unless* another loses.

Many of those who lose consistently in this transaction suffer commensurably. Families touched by gambling addiction are at greatly increased risk of divorce, bankruptcy, child abuse, domestic violence, and suicide. Thus gambling also violates the command to love our neighbors as ourselves (Mark 12:31).

Trust God or Mammon?

God has given us a choice: We can either trust Him, or we can trust mammon, a biblical word from the Aramaic that means wealth or profit.[23] To trust in mammon is, in effect, to rely on a god other than the true one, to commit the sin of idolatry. Instead of putting our faith in the triune God to supply us with all earthly needs—as we regularly pray in the fourth petition of the Lord's Prayer—those who trust in mammon cast their lot with an idol. "While we ask for God to give us our daily bread on the one hand," writes one commentator, "we at the same time squander that 'bread' and look to goddess chance or lady luck for blessing."[24]

This god of luck or chance is by definition a capricious god, one who regularly does not deliver on his promises. But it is particularly seductive to the poor, to those for whom gambling offers the illusory—and ultimately desperate—hope of bettering their lives. The widespread availability of legalized gambling encourages these poor to place their faith in luck instead of in the true God who alone can provide. Jesus criticized people for fretting themselves about material concerns—what they would eat and drink and wear—and maintained that God was already well apprised of our needs and dedicated to meeting them. "Seek first his kingdom and his righteousness," our Savior said, "and all these things will be given to you as well" (Matt. 6:33).

But this principle also applies to the more affluent. In his *Large Catechism*, Luther wrote: "Many a person imagines that he has God and everything he needs, provided he has money and property. He relies upon these, boasts about them, and feels so immovably secure that he cares about no one. But look, he too has a god, named mammon, that is the money and property to which he has given his whole heart. Mammon is the world's favorite idol. One who has money and property has a sense of security and feels as happy and fearless as if he were sitting in the middle of paradise. On the other hand, one who has nothing is as insecure and anxiety-ridden as if he had never heard of God. Very few can be found who keep a cheerful spirit and neither fret nor complain when they are without mammon. The desire for riches sticks glued to our nature right up to the grave."[25]

If any single activity promotes discontent with our current situation, it is gambling. To trust in the illusory—and probably not forthcoming—big win is to trust in a god other than the true God. It is idolatry, pure and simple.

The Stewardship Principle

The Old Testament figure Job summed up our standing in this world quite well: "Naked I came from my mother's womb, and naked I will depart" (Job 1:21). We came in with nothing; we'll go out the same way. All that we possess in the meantime—time, money, possessions, life itself—is not ours but God's.

The question then becomes: How will we use what God has given us? There are basically two ways we can go on this. We can use our time and talents in ways that are pleasing to Him—for care of our family, our friends, our community, our nation; in short, our neighbor. Or we can use them in ways that please us to the exclusion of the needs of others. Born into sin, our natural tendencies lean toward the latter, organizing our lives and talents to serve mainly ourselves. Gambling exacerbates this tendency, for gambling has no concern for the neighbor; indeed, for a gambler to win, a neighbor must lose. Gambling is all about no one but the gambler.

Simply put, gambling is bad stewardship of both time and talents. Our time is not our own. But that doesn't mean a life of sixteen-hour workdays. God certainly ordains rest—He commanded one day a week of it, in fact—but one must ask how re-creating (the meaning of the word "recreation") gambling is. Rather than revitalizing us to recommit our daily life to better service of God and neighbor, it does the exact opposite, sapping us, debasing us, and demoralizing us.

Gambling can also lead to obsession, thus distancing us even further from the responsibilities of family and life. A gambler is particularly vulnerable to this, as you have seen in the preceding chapters. Indeed, one big win early in a gambler's career can transform what was thought of as recreation into an all-consuming addiction. Time spent gambling is difficult if not impossible to justify, given the many loftier, more fruitful pursuits we could be engaged in.

As for talents—that is, our money and possessions—they are not ours either, not even so-called discretionary income. In God's economy there is no such thing. "Our use of what God has entrusted to us is not 'discretionary' in the sense that we are free to do with His gifts as we please," writes one commentator.[26] Indeed, the whole point of Jesus' parable of the rich man in Luke 12 is that what we possess is not ours. "Yet, at the heart of the gambler's fancy," writes Geisler, "is the belief that, 'I have the right to do what I want to with my possessions.' Wrong! According to the Bible, ultimately they aren't *our* possessions, and I certainly have no right to gamble away God's goods."[27]

It is incumbent upon us, as followers of Jesus, to spend the money God has given us, with which we will care for our families and neighbors, in a responsible way. Gambling does not pass the responsibility sniff test. "Gambling's ostensible purpose is financial enrichment," writes the author of the Missouri Synod's position paper on the subject, "and yet it almost always leads to financial loss. That loss almost always impinges directly and in harmful ways on the well-being of those whom God calls us to care for and to love."[28]

Destroying the Work Ethic

Directly related to our stewardship is our work ethic. The gifts we have been given must be developed for the glory of God and the welfare of our fellow man. "He who works his land will have abundant food," King Solomon wrote long ago, "but he who chases fantasies lacks judgment" (Prov. 12:11).

And when it comes to fantasies, gambling leads the field. "Gambling encourages people not to work and to throw their money away on blind wishes," Rogers writes. "By gambling, people attempt to avoid God's principle, 'By the sweat of your brow you will eat your food' (Gen. 3:19)."[29]

A constant thread weaving throughout both the Old and New Testaments is the dignity of honest work. Sloth and indolence take heavy broadsides in the Wisdom Literature (for example, Prov. 10:26; 19:24; 21:25; 22:13; 26:14; Eccles. 10:18), as does idleness from the pen of the apostle Paul (2 Thess. 3:6-13). The labor of our hands (and minds) is the means through which we support our families and fulfill our social responsibilities.

Gambling promotes the antithesis of this industriousness, for it promises something for nothing and financial reward disengaged from labor. (In fact, much of the advertising for state lotteries, for example, goes so far as to belittle hard work and industriousness.) "The gambler is an economic hitchhiker," Geisler writes, "a financial freeloader who wants pleasure without work. However, human beings need to work. According to the Bible, working is a divinely appointed function of life, one that gambling vainly attempts to bypass."[30]

Regardless of their personal views on the intrinsic evil or moral neutrality of gambling, Christians can join one another in fighting the civic battle against the expansion of this now-legalized vice. One need not think every instance of gambling is sin to argue that the further proliferation of legalized gambling in this country is bad public policy.

And alas, whether they're proposing to park a casino on a riverbank near you, to expand your state's lottery, or even to loosen governmental rules and regulations for that nearby horse or dog track, gambling interests are mounting an ardent campaign to augment their already significant national market base.

How ardent—and how successful—their efforts have been is the subject of the next chapter.

TWELVE

The Changing Landscape of Luck

I t is hard to fathom just how large the gambling industry has become in the United States. Indeed, in an economy that has enjoyed almost continuous growth in the past two decades, an economy that is the envy of the industrialized world, gambling is a growth industry with no peer. Hard figures on gambling's rise are illuminating, and we will cite them as the chapter unfolds, but none more succinctly captures the astronomical growth of this industry than this: revenues from legal wagering increased almost *1,600 percent* between 1976 and 1997.[1] Writes Andy Hjelmeland: "Perhaps no American industry in the 1990s, with the possible exception of computer software and online technology, has grown as rapidly and permeated society as thoroughly as legalized gambling."[2]

Which brings up the question: Why has gambling increased so rapidly in our country's recent history? The answer to this question lies at least partly in our history, for to understand the present, we must understand the past.

AN HISTORICAL PERSPECTIVE

Gambling has been around since the beginning of time. The ancient societies—the Chinese, Indians, Persians, Egyptians, Japanese, Greeks, Romans—all engaged in various types of wagering, and our own nation's beginnings prove no exception. Columbus's journeys, for example, were partially funded by lotteries, and the first government-sanctioned lottery in England, in 1566, helped Queen Elizabeth I finance her Virginia colony.[3]

During our colonial days, lotteries were prevalent, and these lotteries proliferated well into the nineteenth century. Many municipalities, their power to tax curtailed by law and the bond market still in its infancy, turned toward gambling as a viable—often the only viable—way to finance public works projects.[4] Between 1790 and 1860, Hjelmeland writes, twenty-four states inaugurated lotteries, and in 1831 alone, 420 lotteries sold over $66 million in tickets, a sum that exceeded the federal budget of that year by five times.[5]

This is not to say, however, that these early forms of gambling faced no opposition. Both the Pilgrims and the Puritans believed gambling destructive of a good work ethic, producing sloth and profligacy. The Puritans enacted the first law in the New World against gambling in 1638. Cards and dice were prohibited by the Massachusetts legislature in 1670, and in 1682 the Quakers abolished gambling in their colony as well.[6]

It was corruption, however, that finally turned the tide against gambling in the newly founded republic. As these lotteries grew in size, expanding from glorified raffles conducted among friends and acquaintances into large, private operations, they could no longer be efficiently run by individuals, and middlemen rose up to administer the games and distribute the prizes. Many of these brokers were corrupt, skimming off profits for themselves or rigging the winners, and antilottery sentiment rose to the point that, at the beginning of the Civil War, only three states still allowed legal lotteries.[7]

Other forms of gambling also proliferated during our antebellum decades. The invention of the steamship in 1812, coupled with the founding of ports up and down the Mississippi River, begat the era of the riverboats. With the riverboats came "under the hill" districts in river towns from Memphis to New Orleans, rough areas notorious for the vices they offered, one of which was card games. The purveyors of vice in these tough parts of town were generally reviled among the populace. When some of the more intrepid among them sought to expand their market base beyond the wharves of Vicksburg, Mississippi, a group of vigilantes mustered, capturing and hanging five of them. The Mississippi itself, though, was the province of a better-dressed and infinitely more cultured brand of thief than their fellow cardsharps on shore.[8] But Maverick and Yancy Derringer, noble figures possessed of a yen for justice and worthy proclivities, they were not.[9] In fact, they were the antithesis of these heroes of 1950s' TV series, cheaters who hustled games with marked cards and often worked in teams, separating the gullible, wealthy river travelers from their money.

The atmosphere farther west, on the frontier and beyond, was equally wild. Gold and silver rushes attract a distinct type of clientele—natural risk-takers. Thus it makes some sense that those rushing west to make their fortunes as prospectors would be open to losing those fortunes in like manner. San Francisco's "Barbary Coast" area became, in essence, the mid-nineteenth-century progenitor of the Las Vegas Strip—with large, gaudy gambling halls offering casino-like games and relying on percentages, rather than cheating, to take their profits.[10] Antigambling sentiment, peaking in 1855, shut down these proto-casinos, however.

The cow towns of cattle drive country—from Texas to Kansas—offered similar "delights," but the Homestead Act of 1862 and the completion of the transcontinental railroad in 1869 helped denude the West of its wildness, the former offering free land to settlers, the latter a transportation network to move supplies in.[11]

All told, by the time hostilities broke out between the states in 1861, what gambling scholar I. Nelson Rose calls the "first wave" of legal gambling in America was grinding to a halt.[12] Almost all of the lotteries had by that time been outlawed, shut down because of the venality of their operators.

Rose's second wave began shortly after Appomattox, as various Southern states, decimated by the war, sought to rebuild their infrastructure with capital derived from lotteries. Within thirteen years of the cease-fire, however, only Louisiana still operated a legal lottery. The Louisiana Lottery Company was founded on corruption—the company responsible for administering it bribed state legislators to obtain its permit. It eventually fell by corruption as well, as the lottery company influenced elections and continued to buy votes in the state legislature. Congress passed laws forbidding use of the mails for lottery purposes—over 90 percent of the tickets were sold outside the state—and in 1893 Louisiana failed to renew the lottery company's charter. By 1894, no legal lotteries existed in the United States.[13]

For nearly seventy years the United States was free of legalized gambling (outside of Nevada and selected horse and dog tracks in other parts of the country). But with the inception of a lottery in New Hampshire in 1964, a third wave of legalized betting was inaugurated in this country, which has continued until this day. Once the Granite State cracked open the door to legalized gambling again, New York, two years later, and other states quickly barged their way through. In the 1970s twelve states legalized lotteries. Moreover, other forms of gambling quickly shed their stigmas and taboos as well. In 1978 New Jersey joined Nevada to double the number of American states permitting legalized casino gambling, allowing gambling halls to open in Atlantic City. A decade or so later, Native Americans began to open casinos on their reservations throughout the country, and in the 1990s various states authorized casino gambling in selected cities.

In less than thirty years, an activity that had been generally discouraged and frequently decried for almost seventy years transformed itself into something that is not only permitted, but even encouraged by none other than the governments that had outlawed it in the first place. This is a remarkable turnaround, and it brings up an important question: How did it happen?

VICE MADE NICE

Governments at all levels need money to operate. To get that money they impose taxes on their citizens. The citizens, although reaping benefits from the services their tax money finances, often do not like these taxes, or believe they are too high. Therefore, if a given government can come upon a plan that provides it with its citizens' money, without its citizens blaming it directly for taking that money from them, as it does at tax time every year, this plan will be plenty popular with politicians. Politicians, after all, want to provide their constituents with ever-expanding services, and yet convince them that they are not taking too much of their money to do so. Walking this thin line between services and taxes is often the primary trick to getting reelected.

State lotteries make this thin line a lot wider—and safer.

A lottery sanctioned by a given state allows politicians to feed their voracious appetites for revenues without paying the political price that comes with raising taxes. A lottery lives up to its moniker as "painless taxation"—painless for politicians, that is.

Thus are many politicians fully behind state lotteries. That government officials, trusted servants of the people, would endorse and even promote a gambling venture is not a morally neutral event, though. Write the authors of the National Gambling Impact Study Commission (NGISC) report, summarizing one view of the effect of lotteries on the growth of legalized gambling: "States have become active agents for the expansion of gambling, setting the stage for the introduction of commercial gambling in all its forms."[14] By permitting—nay, encouraging—their constituents to gamble, they are undercutting the moral arguments that have shunted this vice off to the sidelines of legal activity for the past seventy years. They are, in effect, making vice nice.

"More than any other form of modern gambling," writes Timothy L. O'Brien, "lotteries have brought betting out of the closet. Propelled by festive media coverage and sustained by the government's seal of approval, lotteries have helped transform gambling's seedy image."[15]

With the taboos on gambling gradually crumbling in the 1960s and 1970s, it became only a matter of time before other, more profitable forms of gambling would reassert themselves on the national scene. Casinos arrived in Atlantic City in 1978—to great national hoopla and anticipation. One of these Atlantic City gambling halls bore a name familiar to anyone who has ever traveled the interstate highway system—Holiday Inn. This firm's entrance into the market, one author says, proved a turning point in the public attitude toward gambling, for now the money reaped by this erstwhile vice was suddenly not so dirty. The line between legitimate and illegitimate ways to make one's living was growing a lot fuzzier.[16]

Since that time, of course, gambling companies have become publicly owned, entering—and thriving on—Wall Street, thus canonizing gambling's place in the legitimate economy. They are just another, albeit extremely powerful, corporate player in a booming economy. Their proprietors are not mafiosi calling the shots from smoky basements in Chicago or Detroit, but suits in corner offices with MBA shingles on their walls. Their paid lobbyists roam the corridors of power and twist the arms of politicos with the same impunity as that enjoyed by other big industries. The vice called gambling, once largely condemned, has gone legit.

Gambling itself has had a moral makeover. In fact, it's not even called gambling by its promoters anymore—now it's "gaming," a euphemism designed to convince people they aren't really doing what they're doing when they push money across the felt or feed those gluttonous slot machines. "They dropped the B&L out of gambling and called it gaming," says Rev. Thomas Grey, one of the nation's leading antigambling activists. "We call that in the Army putting foo-foo dust on something. You take it from one thing and make it another."[17] This "gaming" industry has tried to persuade the American public that it is not what it is, that it is really just another part of a booming leisure and entertainment economy, a wholesome alternative to movies, the theater, the symphony, or the local professional sports franchises.

This effort seems to be working. While in the early 1970s most people disapproved of gambling, by 1982, according to a Gallup Poll, 80 percent of Americans were in favor of some form of legalized gambling.[18] A casino-funded study in 1996 revealed that 92 percent of American adults endorsed casino gambling as entertainment either for themselves or for others (8 percent deemed it unacceptable for anyone).[19] A 2000 study, also funded by the gambling industry, showed that 80.3

percent of Americans approved of casino gambling either for themselves or for others (as opposed to the 16.8 percent that found casino gambling not acceptable for anyone).[20] Although the latter study shows a negligible decline in public acceptance of gambling, it is clear that a majority of Americans see very little problem with legalized gambling.

So great has been its public acceptance as a "harmless recreation" that when Las Vegas, worried about losing its market niche, reinvented itself in the early 1990s as "Orlando West," with theme parks and spectacular attractions for the whole family, many parents began bringing the kiddies for a frolic in the Nevada sun.

Gambling has been largely de-stigmatized; Americans today can gamble without any threat of moral censure from the government or from secular society. And Americans, for their part, have responded to gambling's moral makeover by turning it into a $60-billion-a-year industry, offering its customers myriad ways to play with their money.

Let us now take a closer look at the elements of this industry.

DREAMS ON SALE FOR A DOLLAR

Today's lotteries are a different animal than those employed during the eighteenth and early nineteenth centuries. Tickets for the early lotteries were often quite pricey, thus narrowing the customer base, and prizes were awarded only once or twice a year.[21] It is also possible that they were conceived of more as charitable contributions than as outright gambles. Lottery historians Charles Clotfelter and Philip Cook cite the observations of a nineteenth-century writer who said "the most reputable citizens were engaged in these lotteries, either as selected managers or as liberal subscribers. It was looked upon as a voluntary tax ... with a contingent profitable return for such subscribers as held the lucky numbers."[22]

The lottery New Hampshire instituted in 1964—the one that jump-started our current wave of legalized gambling—shares a number of characteristics with these early versions. Tickets went for three dollars each and could be purchased only at liquor stores and racetracks; two drawings were slated per year.[23] Additionally, in what would become a recurrent justification for establishing this particular form of gambling, the lottery was instituted as a means of avoiding direct taxation of the populace, in this case a state sales tax politicians believed was needed to aid education (this proud New England state had neither a state income nor sales tax in the early 1960s).

New York followed with its own lottery two years later, and New Jersey four years after that. By the time the 1970s had drawn to a close, fourteen states ran lotteries, and through a process that was tantamount to trial and error, many of the bugs to lottery success had been worked out.

Some rules for lottery success included the following: Drawings had to be frequent; jackpots had to be big; distribution of tickets had to be widespread; players had to have a choice of games; and winners had to be regaled with their fifteen minutes of media sunshine. In 1975, with what one author calls the "masterstroke" of lottery success, players were allowed to choose their own numbers via computerized games, and discover, the very day they bet, whether they had won (thus mirroring the old "numbers" game). In 1976 New York rediscovered the old Italian game of lotto, in which players are permitted to choose six numbers from a larger field of numbers, thus giving them a feeling of control. The Empire State's innovative decision to link the game up by computers for weekly drawings shot the jackpots into otherworldly territory, into the double-digit millions. With Massachusetts's introduction of scratch-off tickets in 1974, by the end of the decade, a portrait of the modern lottery business was almost complete.[24]

So great was the success in most of these states that in the 1980s and 1990s, twenty-three more states and the District of Columbia joined the lottery brigade, thus putting the number of states with legal lotteries at its current thirty-seven, plus the District. With the expansion has come dramatic revenue growth. In 1997 lotteries accounted for $34 billion in sales, with a per capita expenditure of $150 per annum, up from the $2 billion and $35 per capita registered in 1973 (when seven states were in the lottery business).[25]

These lotteries provide states with bushels of revenue, offering politicians what is tantamount to "found" money to disperse as they would. In Massachusetts, a heavy lottery state, 13 percent of the state's entire budget emanates from lottery sales.[26] As for the player, in return for laying his dollar on the counter, he gets to scratch his ticket or pick his numbers and hope—a far-fetched hope, to be sure—that what he finds beneath the scratches or on drawing day will markedly improve his life.

So much for the upside—if that *is* an upside. On the downside are these uncomfortable facts: First, the player is unlikely to win much money for his efforts. What he will probably win, if anything, is the opportunity to play another lottery ticket or two. Even with that, in the end the odds will beat him. *Texas Monthly* bought 500 $1 tickets in the Texas lottery as an experiment. Staffers sat around playing them all, and when all was scratched and done, they had 100 winning tickets—most for $1 and $2, some for $4 and $5, one for $20. They walked out with only $211 of the $500 they brought in. One can only hope the scratching enjoyment they derived was worth the $289 they lost.[27]

But most lottery players don't play simply to keep playing—they play to win the "big one," the jackpot. As for the chances of hauling that home, as our New York friends might say, *Fuhgeddabowdit!* The odds of winning a jackpot in a state lottery are in the more-likely-to-be-eaten-by-a-shark category (for winning one of those humongous multistate Powerball jackpots, they're in the more-likely-to-be-eaten-by-a-shark-while-in-your-bathtub category). Lottery odds are the worst in all of gambling. As for the supposed control offered by lotto-style games, in which the player can choose his own numbers—as long as you aren't picking the winning numbers down at Lottery Central, picking *your* numbers doesn't help you. Although it is true that somebody has to win, the odds are very much against that somebody being *you*.

Impossible odds are probably the least harmful aspect of this sorry business, though. The real ignominy is the state's complicity in it, and the lengths to which states will go to ensure that they receive their regular revenue "fix." To call it ironic that government, once the tight regulator of gambling enterprises, now actively pushes this vice onto its people so as to keep money coming into its coffers, is to describe this act with unforgivable Christian charity. As the NGISC report poignantly asks: "How can a state government ensure that its pursuit of revenues does not conflict with its responsibility to protect the public?"[28]

So often and so long have states now milked this cash cow that they have grown dependent on the revenues it provides— they have become compulsive gamblers in their own right. And, like all compulsive gamblers, they will go to great lengths to get the money they need to satiate their hunger. To keep the customers coming back, these states must continually improve the "quality" of the lottery experience and advertise the games to their constituents.

Better Games, Bigger Prizes

Lottery games have come a long way from the semiannual drawings of the 1964 New Hampshire lottery. In addition to expanding the types of games to "numbers," lotto, and keno, dramatic advances have been made in the scratch-off, instant-winner games, many of which now keep the player involved in the game until the last scratch.[29] Massachusetts is the trend-setter in this department, where residents spend on average $505 each on the lottery every year (compared to New York's $198, Texas's $187, Illinois's $140, and California's $73). According to O'Brien, they offer "a wide variety of instant games with various prices and features on the street in order to attract as many different types of gamblers as possible."[30]

More troubling, however, is the introduction of video lottery terminals (VLTs) onto the lottery scene. These games often mimic casino-style gambling, and closely resemble slot machines in the action they provide. Slot machines, as you learned in chapter 2, can be highly addictive, and so can VLTs. The number of Gamblers Anonymous meetings in Oregon, for example, increased ten times within five years of the introduction of these electronic machines into that state,[31] and South Dakota researchers found a direct correlation between gambling addiction and VLTs in their state as well.[32]

Big lottery drawings—like Powerball and the Big Game—also find themselves responding to what is called "jackpot fatigue." If a store owner was hawking tickets to a million-dollar prize twenty years ago, customers would have lined up around the block on the days preceding the drawing, and the media would have been swarming his shelves recording sound bites from players already planning how to spend the money they would win. Offer it now and he would have an empty store. Gamblers are no longer titillated by a mere $1 million or even $5 million payout; our tolerance threshold has risen to the point that it takes jackpots in the $40 million range—at a minimum—to get the sales necessary for the state to get its "fix."[33] Even the national media got crazy about the $295 million Powerball jackpot in the summer of 1998. It's unlikely a "mere" $295 million will get their attention next time.

One expert sees in the growth of the lottery in our country the signs of a national gambling addiction. Christopher W. Anderson, past executive director of the Illinois Council on Problem and Compulsive Gambling and a gambling therapist in Chicago, says the ever growing collective tolerance threshold of bigger and bigger jackpots, coupled with the frequency of lottery drawings—going from monthly to weekly to daily to multiple times per day to quick picks and instant scratch-off games—in large part mirrors the progression of the addiction in an individual. "All the primary characteristics of addiction, the progression of addiction, we can measure very clearly in the state lotteries," he says.[34]

Selling the Hope

But better games and bigger prizes do not a successful lottery make—at least not all by themselves. People have to know about these games and prizes, and they must be encouraged to indulge. Thus is forged the weird alliance between government and gambling, wherein our trusted civil servants must play on the human weaknesses inherent in all of us in order to keep themselves in walking-around money. The government must, in short, advertise its lottery—enthusiastically, unapologetically, and rampantly.

Which demographic groups are most likely to succumb to this advertising? The ones that have the most to gain (and lose): the poor and disadvantaged, and people with gambling problems. To summarize we will cite the NGISC report: "The top 5 percent of lottery players (who spend $3,870 or more) account for 51 percent of total lottery sales."[35]

Regarding the poor, according to Dr. Charles Clotfelter, a Duke University professor and lottery expert, people earning less than $10,000 a year outspend every other income group, popping an estimated $597 per year on tickets. Dropouts from high school pay out four times the money college graduates do on lotteries, and blacks spend five times what whites do.[36] Joshua Wolf Shenk writes: "The charge that lotteries are regressive—that is, hitting lower-income residents the hardest—makes intuitive sense, since the pitch of wealthy fantasies clearly resonates most strongly among those who are least affluent."[37] Although it is difficult to prove that lottery agencies actually target the poor with their advertising campaigns, the anecdotal evidence is quite compelling.

For example, the Massachusetts lottery seems to saturate poor neighborhoods in the state with lottery outlets, while in more affluent areas these outlets are few and far between. Chelsea, a poor neighborhood, boasts one lottery retailer for every 363 residents, but the ratio in Milton, a well-to-do suburb, is a whopping 1 to 3,657. Perhaps as a result, residents of Chelsea fork over nearly 8 percent of their incomes on lottery tickets, or in actual money terms, over $900 a year.[38] In another depressed Massachusetts neighborhood, Mattapan, residents line up down the sidewalk outside one lottery store on the day Social Security and welfare checks arrive.[39] In Florida also, lottery outlets are more concentrated in impoverished neighborhoods than in wealthy ones.[40] The economically depressed in other states also spend a disproportionate amount of their income on the lottery.[41]

A coincidence? Could be. But a look at some of the advertising campaigns used by lottery agencies would seem to point in the other direction.

♣ New York has used the slogans "A Dollar and a Dream" and "Hey, You Never Know" to promote its state lottery, adages that encourage people to play the lottery to get rich. Once they're rich, their problems are solved.[42]

♣ A District of Columbia lottery ad employs a before-and-after scenario, with the "before" guy unshaven,

sporting matted hair, and the "after" guy shaved and
newly washed in a tux with a theater program in his
hand. The tag line: "Just One Ticket ... And It Could
Happen to You."[43]

+ The West Virginia lottery puts it this way: "Sooner or
later, you're gonna win!" a promise seconded by a
New York spot: "We won't stop until everyone's a mil-
lionaire."[44]

+ A spot for the Illinois lottery shows a player mocking
savings bonds; a commercial in New York shows a
mom suggesting that her daughter can lay off the
schoolwork because the mom is playing the lottery;
and a poster in the New York City subway reads, in
Spanish, "The New York lottery helped me realize the
American dream."[45]

+ An Ohio lottery advertising plan recommended that
"promotional pushes" take place at the beginning of
the month to correspond to the release of government
benefits, payroll, and Social Security payments on the
first Tuesday of each calendar month.[46]

+ Perhaps the most egregious example is a billboard
erected in a Chicago slum that told it like it wasn't—it
featured a picture of a lottery ticket and this caption:
"This could be your ticket out."[47]

Clearly these ads are selling a false and unrealizable hope
to people whose economic plight would be better faced by
hard work and perseverance. Writes Michael J. Sandel, a Harvard professor of government: "With states hooked on [lot-
tery] money, they have no choice but to continue to bombard
their citizens, especially the most vulnerable ones, with a message at odds with the ethic of work, sacrifice, and moral
responsibility that sustains democratic life. This civic corruption is the gravest harm that lotteries bring. It degrades the

public realm by casting the government as the purveyor of a perverse civic education. To keep the money flowing, state governments across America must now use their authority and influence not to cultivate civic virtue but to peddle false hope. They must persuade their citizens that with a little luck they can escape the world of work to which only misfortune consigns them."[48]

Ad campaigns that do not peddle such vacuous hope hawk a very strange kind of social responsibility. Because state lotteries frequently received their initial approval by selling themselves to their electorates as a source of revenue for all manner of worthy causes, they often advertise that each dollar gambled away is tantamount to supporting social programs. Thus, playing the lottery becomes a *civic duty*. In Colorado this duty is proclaimed this way: "When Colorado plays, everybody wins." In Missouri it goes like this: "The Missouri lottery: It makes life a little richer for all of us."[49]

Earmarking lottery proceeds for education is a very popular appeal, used by eighteen states. But this is, in many cases, a mere bait-and-switch tactic, an accounting gimmick. While players may think lottery proceeds go to state schools (or to parks, another popular funding project), the money itself becomes quite interchangeable once in government hands. Education funding does not grow in direct proportion with money made from the lottery; the money budgeted for education remains constant and the lottery funds are shuffled around. Says David Gale, executive director of the North American Association of State and Provincial Lotteries: "What happens is, the legislature budgets this much for education. They see the lottery will contribute this much. So they take the money they would have spent on education and put it to other uses."[50] Summarizes the NGISC report: "In the cases where revenue distribution was specified, no state could prove that program funding would not exist in the absence of lotteries. To the contrary, several states experienced reductions in actual general funding for programs for which lottery revenue was earmarked."[51]

In fact, a *Money* magazine study showed that states without lotteries actually spend a greater percentage of their budget on education than those with. In addition, since 1990, spending devoted to education has actually decreased in lottery states, while an increase has occurred in non-lottery states during the same period.[52]

Another unscrupulous advertising technique used by the states is fudging—or eliminating any mention of—the odds. One study in the mid-1990s found that a meager 20 percent of all lottery ads—12 percent of radio and TV ads—reported the odds accurately.[53] Many advertise the top prize but give odds for any prize at all, which is usually another lottery ticket.[54] A Connecticut TV ad put the "overall chance of winning" at 1 in 30, which was technically correct, but the odds for winning the big prize were more along the lines of 1 in 13,000,000.[55]

In actuality, lotteries can pretty much advertise anything they want to, any way they want to. After all, do you expect the state government to come down on the deceitful advertising practices of the state lottery, which is run by the state government, the result of which would curtail the flow of monies into the state government? The *federal* government theoretically could do something, but lotteries are conveniently exempt from Federal Trade Commission truth-in-advertising laws.[56]

In 1997 states spent over $400 million trying to entice their citizens to gamble on their lotteries, about 1 percent of total lottery sales.[57] These healthy advertising budgets, coupled with new generation after new generation of innovative games with which to snare easily-bored players and bring new "consumers" into its fold, make the lottery a thriving—and dangerous—player on our national gambling scene.

PARI-MUTUEL PARALYSIS

If any one sector of America's thriving gambling industry must long for the good old days when casinos were both rare and inaccessible, it would have to be pari-mutuel betting. So called because it throws all wagers into a common pool, from which winners are paid according to odds, pari-mutuel gambling includes dog racing (representing 14 percent of the pari-mutuel handle per year) and jai alai (accounting for less than 2 percent), but its main attraction is betting the horses.[58]

The ride horse racing has taken over the past few centuries has been interesting and colorful, to say the least, but since 1970 it has found itself traversing rocky terrain. It has traveled from an aristocratic pastime favored by the moneyed gentry, who stood genteelly by admiring the shanks and sinews of beautiful, powerful animals while simultaneously laying a quid or two on their horse, to an ecumenical activity peopled by quintessential bookies and handicappers and cigar-chewing aficionados. It went from the "sport of kings"—literally, in the persons of James I and Charles II of Stuart England—to a corruption-rife gambit controlled by the Mob. And now it appears to be riding off into irrelevancy.

It has retained some glamour, true, in its prestige races and star "athletes." The Kentucky Derby (and to a lesser extent, other legs of the Triple Crown) still commands great national attention, and at least one horse, Secretariat, made ESPN's top fifty athletes of the twentieth century. But its fortunes have dropped in the last thirty years from the nation's most popular and widespread form of legalized gambling to a mere blip on the gambling radar screen. Between 1982 and 1996 the handle (total amount bet) from on- and off-track horse betting increased by only 28 percent, compared to lotteries' 950 percent and casino gambling's 395 percent increases.[59]

The reason for racing's decline will come as no surprise—

it is the proliferation of casino gambling and the attendant instant gratification it supplies. Not many gamblers are willing—or able—to interpret the subtleties and vagaries of tout sheets, nor do many want to wait for the delayed satisfaction inherent in racetrack betting. It's much easier to simply drop the coins into a slot or push the chips across the felt at a nearby casino and almost immediately receive the fulfillment wagering offers.

Relatively recent innovations and generous breaks proffered by state governments insistent on propping up a faltering industry have kept horse racing from falling off the gambling map altogether. Off-track betting, first instituted in New York State in 1970, and simulcast interstate wagering, sanctioned by Congress in 1978, have allowed the industry to extend the wagering pool beyond the originating track. Simulcast interstate wagering is now employed by thirty-eight states.[60] It is largely a zero-sum game, however, as the revenue from simulcasting only replaces that lost from the decline in on-track betting at most venues.[61] Telephone account wagering, a system whereby gamblers can bet horses from locations away from a track, is now in place in eight states. Industry efforts are under way to expand the broadcast of live races directly into the home, replete with account wagering, outside of Kentucky—the only state that now allows it.[62]

But the pari-mutuel industry has also opened a we'd-rather-switch-than-fight front in their struggle for survival, petitioning states to permit entry of slots and other casino games onto their formerly horse-only premises. The introduction of 1,100 slots to Prairie Meadows Rack Track in Iowa in 1995 turned that troubled venue around to where now revenues from the machines overshadow those from the horses. Even the venerable Churchill Downs wants to install video gambling in order to stave off the raid nearby riverboats have mounted on its patrons.[63]

Some state governments have taken an even greater role in ensuring their tracks' survival. Iowa, New Jersey, Texas, Illinois, South Dakota, Nebraska, Wisconsin, and Massachusetts have all offered breaks of various kinds to its racetracks, ranging from tax rebates to loan guarantees to slashing their "take-out" rate on gambling revenues (tantamount to state taxes) to direct subsidies taken from other gambling sectors in order to bolster their racetrack businesses.[64]

Thus has the mighty "sport of kings" fallen. No longer can it even dangle before us the pretense that it is a noble undertaking centered on the admiration and welfare of sleek, magnificent beasts. It's all about gambling now.[65]

BEATING THE SPREAD

Permitted in only two states, betting on sports carves off only the tiniest wedge from the legalized gambling profits pie. Indeed, Nevada sports books accepted $2.3 billion in legal wagers in fiscal 1999, keeping nearly $99 million of it,[66] chump change when compared to the revenues casinos reap from slots and table games. Oregon, the other state where sports betting is legal, allows wagering on pro football only through "Sports Action," a game associated with its lottery.[67]

Its influence, however, extends countrywide. In fact, it is the relatively minuscule legal sports betting take that creates—and fuels—the rampant *illegal* sports betting business in this country. States the NGISC report: "Legal sports wagering—especially the publication in the media of Las Vegas and off-shore-generated point spreads—fuels a much larger amount of illegal sports wagering. Although illegal in 48 states, office betting is flourishing."[68]

Although for good reason notoriously slippery—bookies don't issue financial statements—estimates on the scope of illegal sports betting in the United States range from $80 billion to $380 billion a year,[69] putting it in the financial territory claimed only by lotteries and casinos. The Super Bowl alone prompts wagerers to plop down between $4 billion and $5 billion per year,[70] and in recent years "March Madness," the NCAA basketball tournament, may have eclipsed even that.[71]

Unlike casinos and lotteries, sports betting can claim no upside apart from giving the bettor a vested interest in the outcome of contests. Thanks to the invention of the point spread, even blowout games command his attention right down to the final gun. Only the bookie and the gambler himself stand to benefit from sports wagering.

Everybody else loses. For one thing, sports betting puts athletes in a vulnerable position and threatens the integrity of sport. Many have been the rigged athletic contests down through the years, fixed by bookies intent on covering their money or making a buck. The "Black Sox" scandal of 1919— in which eight members of the Chicago White Sox baseball team threw the World Series to the Cincinnati Reds—is only the most famous. Boxing has lived under the stigma of fixed fights for much of its history, and college basketball has also been compromised down through the years by point-shaving scandals, wherein players are persuaded not to play so poorly as to lose a game but to play poorly enough to win but not cover the spread.[72]

This ignominious practice continues to this day—indeed, is worse than ever. Said Senator Sam Brownback of Kansas, who coauthored legislation to ban betting on college sports in January 2000: "There have been more point-shaving scandals at our colleges and universities in the 1990s than in every other decade before it, combined. These scandals are a direct result of an increase in gambling on college sports."[73]

Some examples since 1992: Nineteen members of the University of Maine's basketball and football teams were suspended for their involvement in a $10,000-a-week gambling scheme. At Boston College, thirteen football players were suspended from the team for gambling on college sports, three of whom reportedly put money on BC's opponents.[74]

Highbrow Northwestern lived through gambling scandals involving both basketball and football players in 1994–95. Two former basketball players tried to fix three games and were convicted; four footballers lied to grand juries investigating sports betting at the Evanston, Illinois, university; and the school's leading career rusher ensured that the Wildcats would not beat the point spread by intentionally fumbling the ball on the goal line in one game.[75]

Perhaps the most illustrative example of the destructive web of sports gambling comes from Arizona State, in the story of all-American basketball guard Steven "Hedake" Smith. An almost-certain early-round NBA pick, Smith forfeited his NBA career by being at the center of the most lucrative point-shaving scandal in the history of college sports. It started "innocently" enough—with a $100 bet on a pro football game. He lost that bet, and trying to get even, went $10,000 in debt to a bookie in the course of a month.

The bookie promised to even the ledger—and throw in an extra ten grand—if Smith saw to it that his Sun Devils failed to cover the spread in a game against Oregon State. Because the bookie didn't believe one player could throw a game by himself, he convinced Smith to persuade a teammate to cooperate in the shaving scam. The two players shaved points in a number of games during the 1993–94 season, and a couple years later, pled guilty to conspiracy to commit sports bribery.

Says Smith: "Having been there, I can tell you how easily players can be drawn into fixing games. Poor, naive teenagers plus rich, greedy gamblers equal disaster. As simple as it was for me, it can only be that simple elsewhere."[76]

Even when not taking a dive, college athletes have become very active in the betting scene, laying money on sporting contests even though it is explicitly prohibited by NCAA rules. A University of Michigan study released in January 1999 surveyed about 750 college athletes and found that almost half the males (45 percent) had bet on sports.[77]

Indeed, college campuses themselves are hotbeds of illegal sports gambling. The NCAA's executive director, Cedric Dempsey, says "every campus has student bookies. We are also seeing an increase in the involvement of organized crime on sports wagering."[78] Another NCAA official, Bill Saum, has called campus sports betting "the Number One thing in the 90s in college."[79] *Sports Illustrated,* in a 1995 series on the subject, called sports betting on college campuses "rampant and prospering."[80]

Sports wagering also serves as one of the premier portals through which youngsters enter the gambling world, some of whom develop gambling problems. Arnie Wexler, who conducts workshops and seminars on the dangers of gambling addiction, says most kids get initiated to gambling through either sports betting or card games. Another expert, Dr. Valerie Lorenz, director of the Compulsive Gambling Center in Baltimore, estimates that about 90 percent of the teens she counsels have sports-betting problems.[81]

WWW.GAMBLING.COM

First reaching a mass audience in 1995, the World Wide Web has shot up to become the world's new wonder tool. It is everything to everybody, anything to anybody. It has no borders, no rules, no regulation, no limits of any kind attached to it. And while this can be cause for good—one can do research on it and read nearly any newspaper in the world, shop, or trade stocks from the comfort of one's home—it also promotes harm, in the form of limitless and always accessible pornography, for example.

And it has changed the face of gambling, for it is but a point-click away. Like Las Vegas, it never closes, and it's a whole lot closer than "Sin City." From the comfort of the gambler's den or home office, he can gamble for as long as he wants and wager as much as he wants in total and untraceable anonymity.

Although data on Web gambling are notoriously slippery (but no more so than any other Internet data), all indications are that its growth is stratospheric. Myriad Web sites offer online wagering: One periodical states that the number of Web sites offering real-time betting has jumped from 40 in 1997 to at least 850 by the year 2000.[82] Dollars bet online hit $1.67 billion in 1999, up more than 80 percent from 1998, according to Christiansen Capital Advisers, which monitors the industry,[83] with the end nowhere in sight. So great is the growth of online gambling revenue—expected to top $3 billion by 2002[84]—that the super casinos are vying for their places in cyberspace should online gambling ever receive governmental sanction.[85]

Whatever a gambler seeks is available on the Web: blackjack, craps, slot machines, roulette wheels. Even the casino ambience, the sounds and the sights (via graphics) of the casino floor, is being replicated online. "The [Internet] companies recognize," O'Brien writes, "as casinos did long before them, that a pleasant environment is the surest path to a bettor's wallet."[86] Even themed cyber-casinos, aping their *terra firma* counterparts, are beginning to appear, offering everything from virtual excursions to Africa and Australia to social experiences for singles.[87]

But the dynamics of the Internet curtail the market for gamblers somewhat. The Web is a tool of the young, and as such, is likely to draw primarily young gamblers. Sue Schneider, of the Interactive Gaming Council, a trade group in Maryland, expects Internet gamblers to comprise largely young, high-income, technologically astute men.[88]

The type of gambling that figures to benefit most from the Web is also the type that will appeal to this demographic, however. Sports betting, an activity illegal almost everywhere in the United States, figures to be a "killer app," as computer geeks say.[89] And sports betting is rampant on today's college campuses. By accessing a website located in a country that permits Internet gambling, college kids will be able to get action on all the games they want while avoiding illegal bookmakers or flying to Nevada. Youth as well, who bow to no age group when it comes to computer expertise, appear also to be vulnerable to Internet gambling.

Be it always new, increasingly "exciting" lottery games, the horses and the dogs, illegal bookmaking, or the World Wide Web, every sector of the gambling business is rushing for the communal feed bowl to get its "fair" share of the ever burgeoning American gambling dollar.

But they are still mere puppies in this national fight over resources. Synonymous with gambling in many American minds, steeped with folklore and illicit association, remains the casino industry. This is the big dog at the gambling feed bowl, and it is to the gambling halls of America that we now direct our attention.

THIRTEEN

Teaching an Old Dog
New Tricks

When Americans think of gambling, they think of casinos. Perhaps they harbor visions of the glitz and glamour associated with the casinos of lore and film—of beautiful people in tuxes and evening gowns pushing chips across the immaculate green felt, of "Deano" or Elvis or Wayne, or even the Chairman of the Board whizzing past on his way to croon his way into his fans' hearts. Maybe even of James Bond wagering bankrolls on a single turn of the card and always winning—how *does* he do it?—at the baccarat table. Perhaps they have a less sanguine view of these houses of chance—they have seen the slums contiguous to the Atlantic City gambling temples; they are aware of that dark underbelly of crime and social malaise masked by Las Vegas's overbearing tinsel and glitter; it disturbs them that so many of the players in Midwestern casinos are elderly.

Whatever comes to mind when they hear the word "casino,"

they are right in assuming that casinos represent the heart and soul of the luck business. They accounted for $32.3 billion (including Indian casinos) out of the total gambling take of $58.4 billion in 1999, over half of all gambling dollars lost that year.[1] And now that they've spread out from their former "exile" within the borders of Nevada, to New Jersey, Mississippi, countless interior riverbanks, and hundreds of Indian reservations, nearly every American is within a couple hours' drive of one of them. This expansion of casino gambling has been labeled the "most significant development" of the gambling industry in the 1990s.[2]

THE "NEW" LAS VEGAS

And when Americans think of casinos, they think of Las Vegas, Nevada. Nevada has consorted with legalized gambling off and on during its brief history, prohibiting it from 1864 to 1869 and once more from 1911 to 1931. It is a state with very libertarian views, however—even today, twelve of the state's seventeen counties permit legal prostitution—and even though gambling was officially outlawed in the past, citizens did it anyway.[3]

It took the austerity of the Depression to prompt the Silver State to break ranks with the other states, and in 1931 Nevada legalized casino gambling. Because of a clampdown on gambling in other states, many of those wanting to continue in the business fled to sunny Las Vegas, which began to thrive in the decades following legalization. The repeal of Prohibition in 1933 effectively eliminated booze from the Mafia's inventory, and the Mob turned its sights on this new, lucrative market instead. From organized crime's entrance onto the Vegas scene in the early thirties until its supposed eradication in the late seventies or early eighties, Mob money was instrumental in building many of the lavish resorts on the

Strip. In fact, modern Las Vegas would never have happened without the enormous sums the Mob poured into the Nevada city.[4]

This "modern" Las Vegas began with the construction of a new sort of resort on the Strip in 1966, Caesar's Palace, thus beginning the transformation of what had been a nondescript but well-lighted desert haven into the world's foremost monument to over-the-top kitsch. Writes O'Brien: "Caesar's paved the way for Las Vegas to become America's adult fantasyland, a place where a country's obsession with riches intersected with its inhabitants' desires to find themselves anywhere other than where they were. Caesar's was the first casino to anesthetize gamblers in a bath of flamboyant, baroque unreality."[5]

The next significant event in Vegas's history came a few years later in the form of Circus Circus, a Strip casino eventually catering not to the high rollers Caesar's attracted, but to the common man. By the mid-seventies the pink-and-white circus tent on the Strip offered a gambling experience very different from its uppity colleague—its interior lights were bright, its stakes were low, its games were unintimidating to the unschooled, its meals were ridiculously low-priced (an all-you-can-eat breakfast for $0.89; dinner for $1.90),[6] and its rooms were cheap and always full. The fertile lowbrow and middlebrow market had been tapped, and what's more, by offering these families all sorts of circus acts, carnival games, and sideshow entertainment cordoned off in another part of the casino, they could bring their kids. Circus Circus became known as "Nevada's baby-sitter."[7] By the mid-eighties the parent company owned five casinos, and while the rest of Vegas suffered through an economic slump, attendance at Circus Circus boomed.[8]

Circus Circus discovered low rollers and families but swerved into something else as well—the gold mine of slot machines. Slots had always been part of the casino scene, but were usually considered an inferior moneymaker and shunted off to the corners and back aisles to make way for the more profitable table games. Various enterprises did specialize in slots, but they were called "grind joints," tacky places that reaped only small rewards from players they ground down over time. On the upside, though, in this way they insulated themselves from any potential major hits incurred by high rollers.[9]

Slot machines are the perfect employees. They work for free, after all; are on the job 24/7/365; need very little or no maintenance; and never take maternity leave or call in sick.[10] "A Las Vegas casino can buy a slot machine for less than $6,000," wrote Gary Provost in 1994, "and if the casino markets its business correctly, that slot machine will turn over to it $50,000 a year without a peep or a whine."[11] In the mid-1970s Circus Circus set its machines to pay back an outrageous 97.4 percent of the money inserted,[12] and devoted 70 percent of its floor space to them (as opposed to the 30 percent of other Strip casinos at that time).[13]

So profitable were these one-armed bandits that soon all of the Strip was awash in them. The profit breakout of a casino in the 1950s and 1960s was 75 percent from table games and a mere 25 percent from the slots; in 1995 Nevada, though, slots constituted 62 percent of the state's winnings—even Caesar's, former bastion of the high roller, now generates over 65 percent of its take from the electronic devices. The number of slots in the state has skyrocketed in the past fifteen years, from 90,612 to 213,022.[14]

It is on the backs of these slot machines—and the players who play them—that the latest reinvention of the city that is constantly reinventing itself has been borne. "Slot machines," O'Brien writes, "performing like the effective little cash registers they were, reeled in low rollers in such vast numbers that Las Vegas built some of the most mammoth facilities in the world to accommodate them."[15]

This "new" Las Vegas, the city of exploding volcanoes, massive fairyland castles, huge Egyptian pyramids, South Sea islands, tropical jungles, staged open-sea buccaneer battles, and miniaturized New York Cities and Venices and Romes— called "super casinos"—is considered the brainchild of "Mr. Las Vegas," Steve Wynn, who kicked things off by opening the Mirage in 1989. This new Las Vegas is, in short, one huge, garish theme park, a destination resort city suitable, says the industry, for families and children who come for the food, the shopping, the amusement rides, the shows, the "happy feeling of it all."[16] "The Mirage and its competitors peddle the illusion that a trip to Las Vegas is primarily about spectacle," writes O'Brien.[17]

And, oh yes, in addition to the spectacle, one does have the opportunity to test one's luck as well. No matter how colossal the castles, how over-the-top the sights, how megalomaniacal the architecture, how gaudy and tawdry and dime-store the feel of it all, this new "Desert Disneyland," this "Orlando West," is still the city of "Lost Wages." Despite all the diversions, casinos still remain the polestar of modern Las Vegas.[18] Gambling revenues hit $5.7 billion in 1999, up $700 million from 1998, and revenues in Clark County, home to Vegas, hit $7.2 billion that same year, up from $6.3 billion in 1998.[19]

Whatever Las Vegas is peddling, Americans in great numbers seem to be buying it—so many so, in fact, that the city now boasts twelve of the thirteen largest hotels in the world.[20] Visitors to the city numbered almost 34 million in 1999, twice what Vegas drew in 1986.[21] A lot of those adult visitors have kids in tow. Terry Jicinsky, research coordinator for the Las Vegas Convention and Visitors Authority, says, according to profile crowds, that more visitors are bringing their kids with them these days. "It's basically due to the additions of the MGM Grand Hotel, Treasure Island, and the Luxor."[22]

Bringing in more kids is tantamount to recruiting those kids to gambling. Says Tom Grey of the National Coalition against Legalized Gambling: "By enticing families with a 'theme park' atmosphere, [gambling promoters] have found a way that they can target the very young. They're reaching the next generation."[23]

Some of these visitors like it so much they stay. Las Vegas led the nation in growth in the 1990s, according to the 2000 census, springing from a population of 852,646 in 1990 to an estimated 1,381,086 in 1999, a 62 percent hike.[24]

But turn off the 15,000 miles of neon that garlands this desert oasis, and a different picture emerges. The "feather shows" and bawdy, adult-only entertainment are still there, as are prostitutes plying their wares. The city's Yellow Pages offers over 130 pages of ads for "entertainers" working for companies like Hot Nasty College Girls and Wife by Day, Mistress by Night.[25] Handbills can be found in racks on the Strip luring visitors to "Totally Nude Adult Entertainment Lesbian Shows."[26] Clearly, sexual sin has not departed "Sin City."

Sex aside, the social conditions in this booming city offer vivid testimony to the decay that follows a community's unambiguous surrender of an economy—nay, a culture—to Lady Luck. Building a boomtown on greed and the frailty of human nature reaps severe consequences. Las Vegas is by far Nevada's largest city, and the state's ranking among the other forty-nine is very high in all the wrong places: first in suicides,[27] divorce,[28] high school dropouts,[29] child death by abuse or neglect (during the eighties),[30] and smoking-related deaths;[31] second in per capita alcohol consumption[32] (fourth in alcohol-related deaths);[33] third in abortions[34] and bankruptcies (one of every forty-six Nevada households filed for bankruptcy in 1997);[35] fourth in out-of-wedlock births,[36] rape,[37] and crime;[38] sixth in the number of prisoners incarcerated;[39] and dead last in percentage of citizens voting in the 1996 presidential election.[40]

Two findings are particularly troubling. A Kansas research firm, basing its analysis on data from the FBI's Uniform Crime Report, ranked Nevada the most dangerous state in the Union in 1996 and 1997,[41] and while most crimes have decreased nationally of late, homicide[42] and juvenile offenses[43] have soared in Las Vegas and Nevada. Second, as could be expected, Nevada is way out in front of other states in people with gambling problems, according to preliminary studies.[44]

In addition, Vegas schools are congested—not to mention the roads—and police say a hundred gangs with four thousand members are afoot around town. Locals worry about the water supply—all those golf courses and garish fountains out in the middle of a desert, you know—and some anticipate problems early in this century.[45]

And then there's the politics. Nevada is essentially a one-party state, and "it's not the Democrats or Republicans but the 'Gaming Party,'" says State Senator Joe Neal of Las Vegas.[46] Las Vegas is a one-industry town with, according to former city council member Steve Miller, "government for the casinos, of the casinos, and by the casinos—and the citizens be damned." Adds Chuck Gardner, former deputy attorney general: "I don't know if there has ever been a situation with so much power concentrated in one industry. It is government gone berserk."[47]

THE SOUTH BRONX MEETS LAS VEGAS BY THE SEA[48]

Made famous by Bert Parks's crooning and a bevy of all-American girls treading a runway vying to be the most American of all; offering the opportunity to stroll on the beach on wooden boards and see actual street names that are just like those in a Monopoly game—ever since it was built as a seaside escape for sweltering Philadelphians some 150 years ago, Atlantic City has always been a bit on the schlocky side.

Oh, it boomed all right, with population—and tourists—streaming in during the latter nineteenth and early twentieth centuries. But the city had a carny feel about it; it was a place of honky-tonk excess and political graft. It has been home to con artists, hoodwinkers, scammers, and must-see attractions like horses diving off sixty-foot platforms into the sea,[49] not to mention bootleggers and gamblers and prostitutes.

It thrived as a lower- and middle-class getaway for many decades, but after World War II things went south. Bypassed by the new interstate highway system, Atlantic City became one of those places you had to go to to get to—you never went through it on the way to someplace else. And residents of the big Eastern markets—Baltimore, Philadelphia, and New York—decided that if they had to go somewhere to get there, there were many nicer places to go to to get to than Atlantic City. The development of air travel also contributed to the city's declining fortunes.[50]

With the vacation business drying up, hoteliers let their properties go to seed, residents headed out, and urban decay headed in. So precipitous was the city's decline that, in 1976, the most popular bumper sticker in town read, "Will the last person to leave Atlantic City please turn off the lights."[51] By early 1977, unemployment stood at a staggering 23 percent.[52]

Riding to the city's rescue was—you guessed it—casino gambling. Although a similar referendum lost a statewide ballot in 1974—New Jerseyans were impressed with the success of their state lottery but didn't want casino gambling—a 1976 measure, limiting casinos to Atlantic City, got the citizenry's nod of approval. Casino gambling was sold as "a unique tool of urban redevelopment for Atlantic City" that would "facilitate the redevelopment of existing blighted areas, and the refurbishing and expansion of existing hotel, convention, tourist, and entertainment facilities."[53] Casinos were to create jobs for unemployed locals and bring new consumers to

Atlantic City's business establishments.[54] A tax of 8 percent on the casinos' winnings was also to be directed toward senior citizens[55]—this latter promise sending the irony meter well into the red zone, as seniors these days account for 65 percent of Atlantic City's gambling revenue.[56]

So great was the desire of the Eastern Seaboard to lose its money without flying all the way out to Vegas that, when the first casino, Resorts International, opened in 1978, the line to get in stretched a mile down the Boardwalk. Reports say that once players obtained seats at a blackjack or roulette table, some wet their pants rather than give up their chairs.[57] Atlantic City became a very hot place. Indeed, the city began to call itself the foremost tourist destination in the country during these post-legalization years, a description it could no longer use once other casinos opened on the East Coast in the 1990s, boasting over 30 million tourists a year.[58] But the figure is misleading, as these are not 30 million *different* tourists, but 5 million tourists making the trek over and over again[59]—many from just minutes away.

The more Atlantic City changed, the more it ... well ... the more it got worse. Even though $6 billion of private money was pumped into gambling-related enterprises,[60] the city became less Las Vegas by the Sea—as other cities would soon discover, the economic success of Las Vegas gambling is nearly impossible to replicate—and more the South Bronx. Atlantic City in essence became two Atlantic Cities—one comprised of swanky casinos rising from the sand, the other of boarded-up slums in the shadow of those showy gambling palaces. Unemployment actually *rose* in the aftermath of legalization, as the casinos opted to pull their labor force from the more affluent suburbs, allowing the largely black inner city to remain jobless. In 1977 unemployment in the city stood 30 percent higher than the state average; in 1987 the number was 50 percent.[61]

Other quality-of-life indicators have either stayed low or tumbled even further.

* *Crime.* Atlantic City went from fiftieth in the nation in per capita crime to first three years after casinos arrived.[62] In the nine years following legalization, the total number of crimes within a thirty-mile radius of the city skyrocketed by 107 percent.[63]
* *Family health.* The city had the third-highest rate of child abuse among New Jersey cities in 1993,[64] and Atlantic County ranked first in the state in juvenile arrests.[65] A 1993 series of *Hackensack (N.J.) Record* stories revealed that approximately five in eight Atlantic City kids live in families that are on welfare; half the city's children are raised by single parents; the city has the highest infant mortality and teen pregnancy rates in the state, and the second-highest AIDS infection rate; it also has the highest percentage of government-subsidized rent in the nation.[66]
* *Homelessness.* The Atlantic City Rescue Mission went from 28 beds before gambling to 240 after. The mission's caseload increases by roughly 10 percent with the opening of each new casino.[67] Twenty-two percent of mission clients admit to being homeless because of gambling addiction.[68]
* *Bankruptcy.* Atlantic County has by far the highest bankruptcy rate in the state, 71 percent higher than the New Jersey average, according to SMR Research Corporation, which conducted a major national study on bankruptcies.[69]

As for the economic vitamin E shot casino gambling was supposed to inject into the local business climate, it never took effect. Because Atlantic City is a day-trippers' paradise—in

1990, 98 percent of its gamblers came by car or bus and stayed for an average of six hours before heading home—the wealth gamblers were projected to spread around to local business stayed in the casinos right along with them.[70] During the first ten years of casino gambling, according to a 1993 article in the *Record*, "159 small businesses shut down, mostly within a short walk from casinos. But in the last two years alone, the rate of business failures has doubled, with 67 stores closing down." As of 1993, the city had no supermarkets or movie theaters.[71]

To cite one particular sector of the local economy, independent restaurants found they could not compete with casino prices, where food and drink was often free, or at the least, extremely cheap. Revenue in these Atlantic City eateries declined by 40 percent in one decade, during which time the number of actual restaurants plummeted as well, from 243 to 146.[72] Of the 46 restaurants offering "fine dining" that existed when the casinos arrived, only 16 remain (6 were closed in 1996 alone). At least one sector of the local business community did thrive, however. The number of pawn shops increased twelve-fold, from three to roughly three dozen, after the casinos arrived. Most of these are right out back from the casinos, and thus quite handy for compulsive gamblers, the rate of which also rose following the casinos' arrival.[73]

Further, even though casinos put new employees on their payrolls by the tens of thousands, other businesses in town didn't. When a new industry of similar scope enters a market, one could expect collateral development in other sectors, but Atlantic City has enjoyed virtually no private economic expansion in the wake of casino gambling. Two Rutgers University professors wrote, in the 1980s, that "there has been amazingly little spillover growth into non-casino employment within Atlantic City."[74]

One thing that has grown is taxes on existing businesses—

somebody has to pay the social costs of casino gambling. The *Philadelphia Inquirer* reported in 1996: "The idea that the casinos would lead to lower taxes has fallen hard. In the last six years, taxes have risen 48 cents per $100 of assessed property to a rate of $1.72."[75]

Bottom line: A city that recruits gambling as its economic savior may be worse off after the gambling arrives than before. In 1988 *Money* magazine declared Atlantic City the least livable community in the country.[76] In 1997, readers of *Conde Nast Traveler* magazine voted the jewel on the Jersey shore the worst destination resort in the world.[77]

THE NEW BUFFALO OR A SPIRITUAL CANCER?

One of the events most responsible for putting casinos cheek by jowl across this land of ours occurred not in a Las Vegas corner office or a New Jersey voting booth, however. It happened in a Washington, D.C., courtroom, where the U.S. Supreme Court ruled in 1987, in *California* v. *Cabazon Band of Mission Indians*, that states had no right to ban or even regulate activities on Indian reservations that it permitted elsewhere within its borders.

It began in 1980 as a dispute over whether this tiny band of Native Americans could legally run a card room from a small trailer on Indian land near Palm Springs, California. The Cabazons argued that, since California allowed card rooms around the state, they too should be permitted these enterprises on their land. The case worked its way through the courts until, seven years later, the Supreme Court radically altered the lay of the legalized gambling land in this country. As a result of this ruling, Indian tribes located in states that permitted casino gambling were allowed to open their own casinos. Indeed, many tribes attempt to open casinos in states that do not allow casino gambling—with some success—because of the confusing Indian Gaming Regulation Act (IGRA) passed by Congress in 1988 to oversee Indian gambling.

Many have been the tribes attempting to harvest this "new buffalo." While more than two-thirds of the 554 recognized Indian tribes in the United States engage in no legal gambling activity whatsoever, those 146 tribes that do have casinos operate 260 facilities in thirty-one states.[78] In large part because a few casinos opened in densely populated areas where no other opportunities for legalized gambling existed, Indian casinos have become the fastest-growing segment of the American gambling industry. In the decade from 1988 to 1997, revenues from tribal gambling burgeoned more than thirty-fold, from $212 million to $6.7 billion (1999 figure: $7.4 billion), while the take from the commercial casino sector only doubled.[79]

A few tribes are successful—some spectacularly so. Profitable Indian casinos dot Minnesota, Wisconsin, and Michigan, to name three states, but the Foxwoods Resort Casino, near Ledyard, Connecticut, outshines not only its fellow Indian casinos but all "rug joints" in the land with a $1-billion-a-year take.

Set on 2,300 acres on the Mashantucket Pequot Indian reservation in the wooded hills of eastern Connecticut, Foxwoods's 250,000 square feet of gambling space exceeds even the mammoth MGM Grand in Las Vegas by 75,000 square feet; it boasts nearly 4,500 slot machines and over 300 table games, and employs over 12,000.[80] Its patrons—the 550 Mashantucket Pequots—are among the most generously compensated people in the world (casino revenues are distributed amongst members of the tribe). Indeed, Foxwoods's success has sent thousands of Americans poring through their genealogical records looking for even a drop of Pequot blood in their family trees. As it currently stands, no tribal members can boast more than one-eighth Pequot blood.[81]

In a country whose native inhabitants continue to

encounter numbing socioeconomic problems—unemployment, alcoholism, suicide, crime, impoverishment, lack of
essential services, and apathy are all rife on reservations—a
majority of Americans favor Indian gambling (70 percent in a
recent Harris poll).[82] Part of this is no doubt attributable to
the guilt we as a nation feel over nearly two centuries of con-
quered land and broken treaties. Another part is no doubt
practical, as more self-generated economic activities on the
reservations, it is believed, will alleviate the citizenry's tax bur-
den. Indeed, the IGRA stipulated that gambling revenue be
used to promote the economic development and welfare of the
tribes, and selected tribes have seen tangible improvement in
living conditions on their reservations.

The Oneida of Wisconsin, for example, built a multimil-
lion-dollar hotel, a convention center, and an elementary
school on their reservation with gambling monies, and have
also subsidized a Head Start program. The Mille Lacs Band of
the Ojibwa in northern Minnesota and the Morongo Band of
Mission Indians in California have also dramatically improved
their living conditions.[83] Other tribes also claim impressive
decreases in their rates of reservation unemployment, rates
that were left unchanged by previous federal policies.[84]

But for the majority of tribes—especially those distant
from major population centers—the story does not end so
happily. An Associated Press (AP) computer analysis conducted in 2000 found that most American Indians have
gained little from gambling revenues. Unemployment rates on
reservations with casinos remained steady, at around 54 percent, from 1991 to 1997, and on some reservations have actually risen substantially, as non-Indians take many of the casino
jobs. As for lifting reservations out of poverty, the rates of
poverty in counties that include reservations with casinos
declined only 2.2 percent between 1989 and 1995, from 17.7
to 15.5 percent. The AP summarized: "Among the 130 tribes

with casinos, a few near major population centers have thrived while most others make just enough to cover the bills."[85] An analysis by the *Boston Globe* found "that just 2 percent of the country's Native Americans earn 50 percent of the country's $10 billion in Indian gaming revenues, and two-thirds of Indians get nothing at all."[86]

Thus is shot down one of the reigning myths of Indian gambling—that all tribes profit financially from it. The fact is, 50.5 percent of Indian gambling revenue is reaped by a mere twenty casinos, with the next eighty-five casinos accounting for 41.2 percent. Some casinos even operate at a loss, while others have been forced to shut their doors.[87]

Along with gambling have come other problems as well. Intertribal rivalry—and even violence—has broken out in some areas. In Michigan's Upper Peninsula, for example, what the *Detroit News* calls "the new Indian wars" have "featured stripped memberships, embezzlement charges, overthrown tribe governments, federal intervention, police standoffs, sliced auto brakes and homemade bombs," all in the struggle over how casino loot is to be distributed.[88] Also, the flood of tribal applicants has swamped the federal bureaucracy and made oversight very difficult. Which is not to mention the avalanche of wannabe Native Americans descending on tribal leaders—all wanting their cuts from this cash cow, some with very dubious, and often totally imaginary, Indian ancestry.[89]

Many Native Americans themselves oppose making this vice nice on their reservations, regardless of the pot of riches to be gained. Some argue that gambling, a notorious industry with historic links to organized crime, is not the best arena for them to test their rights of sovereignty. Others fear compromise or even nullification of Indian sovereign powers by entering into state compacts—as required by the IGRA—and thus permitting bureaucrats, police, and judges from outside the reservations to involve themselves in tribal affairs.[90] Indian leaders are also concerned that the "bingo chiefs," as the politically and economically independent gambling operatives are pejoratively called, are seeking financial self-aggrandizement to the detriment of overall tribal improvement.[91]

This is not to mention the ethical, and even spiritual, concerns many Native Americans have with the notion of basing economic rejuvenation on such traditionally unsavory activity. Despite the situational irony reveled in by some—that a "people defeated by imported alcohol and disease ... now find themselves, through a legal loophole, able to erect institutions to corrupt their oppressors," in the words of Thomas Dolan[92] —some Native Americans, according to Jon Magnuson, see "the proliferation of gaming [as] a spiritual cancer eating away at what is left of the soul of Native American communities."[93]

Others worry that traditional Indian values may be lost. Gerald Thompson, an Oneida who fought against casinos for his tribe, cites the increase of family breakdown, domestic violence, and child abuse that has been proven to follow in the wake of gambling, and asks: "Is the money worth the devastation that could happen to our people?"[94] Indeed, when tribal members are allowed to register their preferences, some have defeated casino gambling. In 1994 both the Seneca tribe of New York and the Navajo Nation of New Mexico and Arizona voted down propositions allowing casino gambling on their reservations.[95]

Other objections to Indian gambling have also been registered. For example, despite the rationale undergirding it—that it will allow tribal self-sufficiency—even tribes that have hit pay dirt continue to draw hefty federal subsidies. The Pequots, sitting on their billion-dollar-a-year treasure, took $1.5 million in low-income housing assistance in 1996. A tribe in Washington State, the Tulalips, built $300,000 luxury homes for tribal members with federal low-income housing grants.[96]

And a tribe in Minnesota chose to wait several years for governmental monies to fix a school with leaky roofs and insulation bulging out of its walls rather than tap its $30-million casino-generated bank account.[97]

Other tribes become mere fronts for Las Vegas interests who, ever vigilant for new markets, enter into "management contracts" with Indian tribes and pocket up to 40 percent of the proceeds.[98] One Illinois city hired a Nevada company not to run an existing gambling hall, but to recruit an Indian tribe in order to *open* one.[99]

It is possible, however, that the "new buffalo" may someday go the way of the old one, for with the proliferation of gambling opportunities around the country come increased competition for the Indian gambling dollar and the possibility that the market—and the profits—will stabilize. Even proponents of Indian gambling recognize as much. Already in 1994, the executive director of the National Indian Gaming Association, Timothy Wapato, hoped that, once revenues from Indian gambling tapered off, "other economic opportunities can be explored, so a broader base for [the tribes'] economy can be set up."[100]

TAKE ME TO THE RIVER

The modern reincarnation of riverboat gambling began in an unlikely place—Iowa. Home of bedrock middle American values, land of verdant fields and hardy men of the soil, of county "ag" buildings and 4-H Clubs, this Corn Belt state has historically been as removed from the gambling vice as Las Vegas is from Lynchburg, a state where even church bingo games were sometimes raided.[101] But bad economic times—in this case the recession of the late seventies and early eighties that hit especially hard the "Detroit of the Farm Belt," the Quad Cities, home to John Deere, International Harvester, and

Caterpillar—require inventive solutions. Iowa's lawmakers deigned not to adopt innovative countermeasures to deal with a new global economy, but to push through legislation that would allow legalized gambling.

Beginning in the mid-eighties, a lottery and horse- and dog-racing tracks were sanctioned in the state, followed in 1989 by a bill that would permit limited-stakes casino gambling on riverboats. This was a legislative act that the chairman of Iowa's Racing and Gaming Commission proudly hailed as possibly "as important to Davenport as the Bill of Rights and the Magna Carta."[102]

The hard sell employed by the pro-gambling forces was a foretaste of what was to come in other economically battered cities in the country—that is, they promised economic development and tourism dollars. Additionally, the Iowa cities traded on the image of the river itself, that the boats would offer harmless, recreational gambling imbued with the "lore of Mark Twain," according to one gambling promoter.[103] It was a more laid-back, less hedonistic form of gambling—$5 limits on individual bets, a $200 limit per day, a mere 30 percent of the ship's area for gambling, with an entire deck cordoned off for non-gambling purposes (and for gamblers' kids). Here throngs of eager players descended on April Fool's Day 1991 in Bettendorf and Davenport to break the figurative champagne bottle against the era of legal riverboat gambling in the United States.

It was successful too—until other states got wind of it. Within twelve months of the Quad Cities experiment, Illinois and Mississippi, jealous of the Hawkeye State's gambling profits, dropped their historic interdiction against legalized gambling, and going Iowa one step better, also canned many of the kinder, gentler stipulations of their Corn Belt rival. A casino opened in Joliet, Illinois, keeping Chicagoland monies closer to home. And then, lo and behold, two of the very boats that had launched Iowa's economic "miracle" showed up eight hundred miles to the south, having floated down Old Man River to find more profitable portage on the Gulf Coast and to latch onto what was hailed as the "Mississippi Miracle." Iowa, no doubt feeling like Professor Harold Hill had made a return trip to River City, dropped its kindness and gentleness—that is, its gambling limits—and rebounded into financial solvency.

What riverboat gambling has become in the decade since its inception is a mere interstate competition for tax dollars. And it has had a ripple effect throughout the Midwest. Here's how it works: Iowa gleans tax dollars from Illinois tourists (40 percent of the patrons visiting the *President*, Davenport's first boat, hailed from Chicago ZIP codes during its first year).[104] Illinois legalizes some boats at Joliet, to keep its tax money at home, and Iowa puts some boats on its other "coast," the Missouri River, to tap Nebraska. Indiana, to feed on Chicago money, opens a casino in Gary, and Illinois plops some boats hard by Alton and East St. Louis, enticing Missourians (and their money) across the Big Muddy. Missouri sticks some boats in a different river over by Kansas City, real close to all those gambling-deprived Kansans.

Most of the host cities in this old-fashioned shell game have in common one thing: hard times. Writes Marc Cooper: "To look at the clumps of casinos now clogging the heartland is to look at a map of every place that once had a booming industry—or had none at all."[105] In the Quad Cities the boats compensated for losses in the farm implement and heavy machinery business; in Joliet they compensated for U.S. Steel's vacation; and in Gary gambling revenues replaced those of flagging steel foundries. East St. Louis and Tunica, Mississippi, have long suffered severe economic troubles.

All told, by 1998 there were over forty floating gambling halls in Illinois, Indiana, Missouri, and Iowa, and nearly fifty in Louisiana and Mississippi. Revenues from these boats came in at $8.3 billion in 1999, up a billion from the previous year.[106] Add to these "boats" forty-five land-based casinos in three Colorado mining towns, which pocketed a tidy $595 million in revenues in fiscal year 1999–2000,[107] and the Deadwood, South Dakota, casino mecca, with dozens of gambling halls—both states instituting gambling to prop up dying mountain towns—and one can grasp the effectiveness of the progambling sales pitch.

Which brings us to the pertinent question: Are the gambling proponents right? Do these riverboats and land-based casinos deliver on their pledges of economic revival and tourist bonanzas? Do the casinos keep their promises?

Casino interests will point to isolated "success" stories. Places like East St. Louis, a town mired in great poverty and disrepair, with half its forty thousand residents qualifying for public assistance, has seen something of a renaissance, according to its mayor. Revenues from a casino berthed in the river west of town have doubled the town's budget and allowed it to slash its property taxes by 30 percent, cut its debt, and put twice as many police and patrol cars on the streets.[108] And in Tunica, whose ten "riverboats" are, if nothing else, a slander on the name—nothing out of *Life on the Mississippi* here—state law stipulates that the casinos must float, and they all do, as barges in shallow moats dredged in channels jutting off the river. The Big Muddy can actually be seen from all of *one* of the ten.[109] Per capita income in the county had almost doubled by 1994.[110]

Often hailed as an economic success is the Gulfport/Biloxi region, where commercial construction boomed nearly fortyfold in the years following the introduction of dockside casinos—big garish barges floating a few feet offshore. Thirteen hundred new jobs were added by the construction industry alone from 1990 to 1995, and retail sales growth rates jumped from 3 percent before the casinos to 13 percent after.[111] As for Joliet, its boats are the city's single biggest employer.[112]

Such are the cheery tidings trotted forth by mayors and chamber of commerce types. Countervailing evidence tends to cloud this sunny prospect, however. In Tunica, for example, although the casinos can claim improved telecommunications and roads in the county, crime rates have soared; the better roads have become congested and more dangerous, with drunken drivers returning home from casinos that ply them with free alcohol;[113] unemployment figures have vacillated wildly; and compulsive gamblers have been showing up in numbers,[114] this latter phenomenon being endemic to gambling towns in general. The boats themselves are heading north—to be closer to Memphis—thus leaving the actual town of Tunica the sleepy backwater it always has been. Writes O'Brien: "Caught in the shell game of riverboat casino development, the county is hostage to the possibility that its neighbor to the north, De Soto County, will legalize gambling and cut off Tunica's access to Memphis."[115]

And that's the story only at Tunica, one new gambling mecca among many. Similar problems, of varying scope and intensity, seem to appear wherever these riverboats park their faux paddle wheels and open their decks to casino games.

Crime, for one thing, seems to follow inevitably in their wake. The downside of dockside is a 43 percent increase in crime in the four years after the casinos' arrival. Harrison County, where most of the Gulf Coast gambling halls are located, reported a 58 percent jump in total crimes between 1993 and 1996.[116] As for the land-based casinos, in Lawrence County, South Dakota, home to Deadwood, the annual number of felony cases filed has soared by about 69 percent since the casino boom took hold.[117] In Colorado's casino towns, "crime is a growth industry," according to a newspaper report. Court filings in Gilpin County, home to Central City and

Black Hawk, rose from 718 in 1990 to 2,387 in 1999;[118] serious crime increased a whopping 287 percent in Cripple Creek, Colorado, in the first three years after its casinos opened.[119]

Other social problems, from high rates of bankruptcy to divorce to domestic abuse to child abuse to all the ills attendant to compulsive and problem gambling, also seem to rise after the entrance of casinos into a community.

But what of the economic boost these gambling halls supposedly produce? Because gambling does not operate in a vacuum but as a single industry in a dynamic economy, figuring out a clear cause-and-effect between casino gambling and economic development is difficult.[120] One Illinois study did discern measurable growth in non-gambling commercial enterprises in riverboat towns but concluded that "in most locations the improvement was more likely due to an upturn in the general economy than to the riverboats." A different study in the same state proclaims that "any city fortunate enough to be selected as a site for a riverboat casino is guaranteed a windfall," but wonders what happens to commerce in the neighboring towns.[121] Indeed, it is possible the riverboats may be detrimental to their economic health.

Even the benefit to the gambling town itself is suspect, due to what is called "cannibalization" or the "substitution theory." This hypothesis states that the ostensible increased economic activity generated by the casino is in reality dollars drained from the town's nongambling businesses. Restaurants are usually introduced as exhibit A—Atlantic City being a prime example, for the reasons mentioned above—but in Iowa, Colorado, Mississippi, and Illinois the general business climate in gambling towns seems to have suffered as well.[122]

As for establishing a tourism industry—the other prong of the progambling sales pitch—it seems that those towns that drew visitors even before the introduction of riverboat casinos, like Galena, Illinois, are the only success stories. The other towns fall victim to day-trippers, people living in the host community itself or excursionists who blow into town expressly to gamble and rarely if ever carry their money outside the casino's doors before they drive home later the same day.[123]

None of which bodes well for community well-being, according to William Thompson, a professor at the University of Nevada–Las Vegas. Casinos, he says, "have a negative impact on the community unless 50 percent of the gamblers come from out of state."[124] First, much of the profit often goes to out-of-state owners, and the tax intake is not distributed in the community per se but is spread around the state. And second, because casinos are often located in impoverished areas, for the express purpose of breathing new economic life into those areas—see Tunica, East St. Louis—a preponderance of local gamblers, most likely poor and ill educated, tends to exacerbate the very problems the casinos were imported to solve.[125]

At least a few states have noticed the flattening profit lines—and ancillary problems—these floating casinos have generated and have taken a step back to ponder their options. Iowa has legislated a five-year moratorium on gambling expansion during which they will assess gambling's future in the state, and Indiana has formed a commission to examine its experience with gambling.[126]

Sporting a face-lift and a new public image, legalized gambling has raced through our society since its modern reincarnation kicked off with the 1964 New Hampshire lottery. Some form of gambling is legal in all but three of our states, and so common has it become that the gambling business had been bestowed with legitimacy, sanctified—and often encouraged—by the very governments charged with the responsibility of our public welfare.

Gambling is here—in a big, big way—and it is legal.

But a problem described is not a problem solved. In the last chapter we will marshal the main arguments against a further proliferation of this vice-made-nice in our society, and will also tell the stories of Christians who have fought successful battles to turn back legalized gambling in their states.

FOURTEEN

The Case Against Gambling

Very rarely in our TV-saturated and immediate gratification culture do the thoughts of an important philosopher intrude into the national consciousness, but George Santayana's dictum, "Those who cannot remember the past are condemned to repeat it," is one exception. World history verifies the veracity of Santayana's epithet with myriad examples, but alas, he only got it half right, for it seems that those who *can* remember the past are doomed to repeat it as well.

Take our country's history with gambling, for example. The United States has had three up-close and personal encounters with this vice during our 225 years' existence, each having a negative effect on our nation's well-being, whether in the form of massive and widespread corruption or as a general erosion of the commonweal. Gambling, in whatever form it takes, using whatever technology is available, writes Rex M.

Rogers, "creates its own morality and gradually debilitates the people it touches."[1]

But all is not without hope, for two of the three waves of gambling were ultimately turned back, with the fate of the third wave, the one we are living through, still in the balance. What that means is that concerted and unrelenting effort *can* stop gambling in its tracks. It's been done before; it can be done again.

To mount such effort, we concerned citizens must be apprised of the battleground, of the arguments used to promote gambling and their rebuttals.

AT WHAT PRICE ECONOMIC REJUVENATION?

The package gambling promoters proclaim to targeted communities is almost invariably the same wherever they go: increased local revenue, decreased unemployment, and a general economic recovery and all the benefits associated with it. The sales pitch for lotteries is slightly different, focusing on the taxation that is thereby avoided and the governmental programs, like education and the environment, that are subsequently advanced. (For rebuttals to lottery expansion, see chapter 12.)

Indeed, in some depressed communities newly legalized casinos seem to spike certain economic indicators. Former senator Paul Simon mentions East St. Louis and Metropolis, Illinois, and Bridgeport, Connecticut, as examples of communities "who are desperate for revenue and feel they have no alternative" being helped by legalizing casino gambling.[2] Local officials from Elgin and Alton, Illinois; Tunica, Biloxi, Gulfport, and Bay St. Louis, Mississippi; Gary, Indiana; and Bettendorf, Iowa, all support gambling and claim increased revenues for their cities. An Indiana state senator says Gary, for example, after unsuccessfully courting major businesses to fill the void left by a downturn in the northeastern Indiana steel industry, is starting to turn around in the aftermath of legalizing casino gambling.[3]

Native Americans can claim similar successes on selected reservations. Casino gambling seems to have done what no federal program was heretofore able to do: It has created jobs and allowed some tribes to repair decrepit infrastructure, diversify their holdings, and provide critical health and educational structures for their members.

Casinos also produce jobs, some of which are full-time with attendant benefits. Add to this the growth of the hotel industry in some cities, an increase in revenue to the local government wherever casinos are established, a jump in construction activity and related job growth, a rise in property values in selected towns, and an increase in business to some retail establishments,[4] and gambling proponents paint a rather rosy portrait for any down-and-out municipality desperate for an economic sugar high.

Using the Wrong Model

The template for such robust projections happens to be a certain well-lighted gasoline stop between Los Angeles and Salt Lake City—Las Vegas, Nevada. Vegas, an isolated desert city that for decades enjoyed a monopoly on the casino business, was able to build its infrastructure on tourist dollars that were spread to the local commercial enterprises.[5] Today the city boasts minuscule unemployment figures (2.8 percent at the end of 1998; Nevada's rate was a comparable 3.1 percent)[6] and an economy strong enough to have weathered the recession of the early 1990s better than most cities. Taxable sales and homes sales were also up in 1998, to cite just one year.[7] Las Vegas, warts and all, serves as the poster city of gambling expansion.

But it is an erroneous model. The Vegas gambling mecca—indeed, the state of Nevada itself—prospers under singular conditions. With no industry other than gambling to speak of, the gambling industry cannot possibly displace other sectors of the economy or "cannibalize" existing businesses—almost all of the economy is gambling-related to begin with. Also, because 85 percent of Nevada's gambling revenues emanate from out-of-state visitors, these monies carry no concomitant negative costs. Gamblers roll into town, deposit their money in the casinos, and spread what they have left around town, but when they leave they take their problems home with them—be they those produced by compulsive and problem gambling or otherwise—to be solved by cities and states far from the scene of the "crime."

The problem is, there is only one Vegas, and only one Nevada—no other gambling venue, even Atlantic City, can replicate what the Silver State has wrought. Says the NGISC report: "Every other gambling venue in the United States [apart from those in Nevada] is far more reliant on spending by citizens in a far more concentrated geographic area. In many cases, gambling operations are overwhelmingly dependent on spending by local citizens."[8] Writes Robert Goodman: "Cities and towns entering the gambling market now face a fiercely competitive field, and they will be hard-pressed to draw patrons from outside their region. As a result, most of the people pouring money into their slot machines will be local residents."[9] The result of this is the "cannibalization" spoken of in chapter 12, the phenomenon whereby dollars that would normally be spent in surrounding businesses are gobbled up by the gambling venture, thus harming and, in some cases, debilitating the local economy. Atlantic City, of course, is exhibit A.

Remarkably, even gambling advocates admit that new gambling enterprises profit only casino owners, not the surrounding communities. "What we're doing," one casino consultant, Clifton Henry, told a group of urban planners and business leaders who were considering riverboat casinos in Pittsburgh, "is we're rearranging dollars.... And the people who usually win, quite frankly, are the casino operations. The people who lose are the cultural activities in the city, the eating and drinking establishments in other parts of the city, even automobile dealers, retail stores, etc.... There's absolutely no net gain in terms of the economic impact from gamblers who are located within the immediate trade area of fifty miles." Henry Gluck, CEO of Caesar's World casino firm, told a New York State Senate subcommittee in 1994 that expanding casinos into local communities would probably do little more than "simply circulate the local money." Steve Wynn, "Mr. Las Vegas," when speaking to local businessmen bent on revitalizing decaying downtown Bridgeport, Connecticut, with a casino, said, "It is illogical to expect that people who won't come to Bridgeport and go to your restaurants or your stores today will go to your restaurants and stores just because we happen to build this building here."[10] And even so high-profile a gambling impresario as Donald Trump agrees: "People will spend a tremendous amount of money at the casinos, money that they would normally spend on buying a refrigerator or a new car. Local business will suffer because they'll lose customer dollars to the casino."[11]

Sadly, in many cases this local patronage will comprise the poor. It is axiomatic that the poor spend more on gambling than the middle class, three times more, according to statistics.[12] Indeed, they often consider gambling the only investment they can afford. This applies to lotteries, as has been proved by numerous statewide studies over the past decade, but it is also true of casinos. To cite some examples, poor Mississippians living in counties with casinos lost a far greater percentage of their income in the casinos than did more well-to-do gamblers: those earning less than $10,000 per year lost about 10 percent of their family income to casinos while those earning over $40,000 spent only about 1 percent.[13] Half the gamblers in a 1994 Wisconsin casino survey reported an annual income over $5,000 less than the median state average that year,[14] and 52 percent of 1,800 Minnesotans in state-run gambling treatment programs had incomes of less than $20,000.[15]

Once the bloom is off a new casino, once the novelty wears thin and out-of-towners stop shining around, it will be locals, the very poor that the casino was to help lift out of poverty, who will put the dollars in casino management pockets. This, writes John Warren Kindt, a gambling policy analyst who is a professor of commerce and legal policy at the University of Illinois, "result[s] in dramatic increased costs to social programs, increased unemployment for minorities, and more proportional unemployment for minorities than for whites."[16]

Besides which, any economic boom promised by gambling promoters is in most cases short-lived and ethereal. Kindt says start-up gambling ventures will earn a profit for five years—the period of time before the local compulsive gambling "community" bottoms out—even without a single tourist showing up to pull a handle or lose a chip. These profit margins can be quite high—indeed, Kindt asserts that they "generally constitute the major revenue years for most legalized gambling organizations." But after five years' time, the gambling organizations "must find new markets and/or new marketing gimmicks to attract gamblers."[17]

The promised buildup of supportive facilities is also frequently abandoned long before it is complete. When some of the Iowa riverboats weighed anchor for more lucrative Mississippi waters shortly after they opened in 1991, they left behind 600 unemployed workers and an unfulfilled $2.6 million tax-money investment in a municipal dock in one river town, and "exactly *none* of the land-based tourist developments they'd promised in the lobbying campaign," according to one writer.[18] The city manager of Joliet, Illinois, whose city center was supposed to boom because of its proximity to the Chicago market, envisioned a rush of tourists and a revitalized downtown area, complete with a new hotel, once the boats got up and running in 1992. Predictably, the day-trippers didn't spread their money around town, and the only new business to start up was a small takeout coffee shop.[19]

New Orleans residents who put their trust in gambling-interest promises found themselves quickly disillusioned. In 1995, amid rumors that Harrah's New Orleans casino was flirting with bankruptcy lawyers, casino moguls placed a large ad in a New Orleans daily assuring readers that a temporary casino, a stopgap gambling hall to sate their hunger for revenues until a promised 100,000-square-foot permanent facility was complete, would remain open. Headlined in giant type on the ad was this: "Harrah's New Orleans Is Here to Stay. Bet on It." Those who did were no doubt surprised when, ten days later, casino authorities padlocked the facility, placed the casino project in Chapter 11, and threw 3,300 casino and construction workers out of their jobs.

The permanent casino, open only a year, is now threatened with closure, leaving the city to cope with unfulfilled dreams of massive revenue—upwards of $1 billion in annual gambling revenue was predicted—and an ugly white elephant on its riverfront.[20]

These are only a few chapters in what is a continuing saga of unfulfilled promises in towns that embraced casinos.

"Economically speaking," Kindt writes, "legalized gambling is a sucker bet."[21] For one thing, it can sustain itself only through massive migration of new gamblers, the constant infusion of out-of-town money. Failing that, the economic benefits promised by the gambling impresarios will dry up, for the gambling city's gains will be largely at the expense of the neighboring, supplier communities. Nor will new businesses be anxious to relocate in a gambling city, for the business environment is tainted with the ill effects of gambling, both economical and social.[22] Writes Kindt: "The less there is of legalized gambling, the more vibrant the economy will be."[23]

The Foot-in-the-Door Approach

When they pitch a new market, advocates of gambling frequently play down their intentions to local politicos and residents. The gambling they want to install is not the seedy, rapacious sort that marks a Vegas or an Atlantic City, they say, and they will even accept various limits to ensure that it doesn't become so—betting and loss limits, restricted hours of operation, riverboats that will actually push out into the current for a few hours every day.

Once they gain their toehold, however, the gambling interests sing a different tune. They want expansions and accommodations until they get the virtually unlimited gambling they privately sought in the first place. And—surprise!—the governments so intent on reining them in initially are now ever so willing to slacken their grip if for no other reason than that they have grown dependent on the revenue the gambling brings in and must mollify the constituency—the casino owners and workers—the gambling has spawned.

What happens is tantamount to a mutual admiration society between gambling interests and the government. Writes Goodman: "Once the novelty of a new casino or a new game wears off, as it inevitably does, revenues tend to fall or flatten, forcing legislators to look for new gambling ventures and gimmicks to keep their budgets afloat. And as enterprises suffer lower revenues from increased competition or fading consumer interest, they naturally turn to government for regulatory relief and sometimes direct subsidies."[24]

This nose-under-the-tent phenomenon has happened in

so many places that it looks suspiciously noncoincidental. In Illinois, for example, gambling was first legalized with a 1974 lottery. In 1990 and 1991 the number of off-track betting parlors was increased dramatically.[25] The state legislature gave the thumbs-up to riverboats in 1990, with the proviso of a $500 loss limit, a stipulation that was "accidentally" dropped at the eleventh hour, unbeknownst to the legislators themselves.[26] Video machine gambling was proposed in 1991–92, and the mayor of Chicago pushed a multibillion-dollar land-based casino complex in 1992.[27] Gambling in South Dakota has run a similar course: a state lottery in 1987; land-based casinos in Deadwood in 1989; Indian gambling in 1990; video-machine gambling throughout the state in 1991.[28]

In Louisiana the floating casinos were initially supposed to cruise the river, but now the riverboats ignore regulations requiring them to cruise, effectively giving the state dockside gambling.[29] In 1992 Missouri voters approved card games only on riverboats that were required to devote 50 percent of their floor space to nongambling, family-oriented pursuits, and that had to cruise up and down the Missouri and Mississippi Rivers. A couple years later these boats had slot machines, had been released from their floor-space limitations, did not ever actually cruise the rivers, and were not even required to be located *on* rivers. Doing away with the betting limits is the next hurdle the gambling industry wants to clear.[30]

In Atlantic City, all sorts of restrictions were written into the initial agreements in the late 1970s: no twenty-four-hour gambling; limited floor space devoted to slots; no electronic keno, poker, or sports betting; and limits to jackpots and prizes so players wouldn't lose too much. The only restriction to make it to 1994 was the one on sports betting.[31]

When Coloradans voted 57 to 43 percent to allow limited-stakes gambling in three dying mountain towns, they thought they would be getting "slot machines, blackjack and poker tucked into corners of existing businesses, with bets limited to $5."[32] Tax rates on gambling revenue, purposely set at 40 percent to discourage full-scale casino operations, were attacked almost immediately by casino interests, who moved in and virtually remade the towns into gambling-dependent economies. Within two years they were targeting the betting limits.[33]

Of the effect casino gambling had on these three towns and Deadwood, South Dakota, Katherine Jensen and Audie Blevins write: "Soon retailers from car dealers to ladies' ready-to-wear would sell out or convert to casino operations. The citizens who had voted for gambling with the vision that restaurants and bars, maybe even the bakery, might each have a few slot machines in the fronts of their businesses ... would soon find that businesses necessarily accommodated slot machines first, and only services that supported the playing of slot machines would survive."[34]

Iowa, the progenitor of the riverboat gambling fray, a state that merely dipped its toe into these troubled waters for a little local relief to a depressed Quad Cities, is now tantamount to Vegas with silos. Finding itself dependent on gambling monies, with a constituency of casino owners and workers to satisfy, the state "felt itself forced into a position where it had to promote much more hard-core forms of gambling in order to provide financial help to its remaining riverboats and encourage new ones to come to Iowa," Goodman writes.[35] Three years after the first boats launched from Davenport and Bettendorf under severe betting and loss limits, the state had lifted those limits, approved new games, reduced mandatory cruising hours, and dumped restrictions on gambling boat space. Also, because the riverboats were adversely affecting the racing industry, the state helped that out as well, lowering taxes, among other concessions, and even taking over a declining track in Des Moines.

The racing business, alas, needed more breaks, so it successfully petitioned the state for slots at the tracks. The door thus opened for Native Americans, Indian casinos came on line shortly thereafter.[36]

Legalized gambling, as Methodist minister and opponent of gambling expansion Rev. Tom Grey says, is a predator. Once it gains entry to a community, its appetite is voracious, a sentiment the authors of the NGISC report corroborate, albeit more discreetly: "Once gambling enters a small community, the community undergoes many changes. Local government becomes 'a dependent partner in the business of gambling.'"[37]

Unintended Consequences

Hand in hand with legalized gambling come consequences no one sought or even anticipated. Lotteries, of course, as detailed earlier in this book, serve as a gateway for youth and problem and pathological gamblers and also target those most susceptible to false hope. Casinos play a similar role in depressed communities, seducing those least likely to withstand the financial losses that are sure to follow multiple trips to the machines or the tables.

Very few of the other social results that accompany new gambling ventures positively affect the host community. The recent rise in bankruptcy rates, for one thing, can be linked to gambling. SMR Research Corporation, in a lengthy 1997 study, concluded: "It now appears that gambling may be the single fastest-growing driver of bankruptcy." A good 10 to 20 percent of the filings in areas around major casinos are gambling related.[38]

Dramatic increases in crime also plague casino towns. Countrywide, a *U.S. News and World Report* study found crime rates in casino communities to be 84 percent higher than the national average.[39] Reports from Minnesota, Mississippi,

Wisconsin, Connecticut, and Colorado indicate that local crime also shot up following the arrival of casinos.[40]

Much of this crime can be attributed to one thing: a concomitant rise in problem gambling behavior. As we noted in chapter 1, where there is gambling there will be problem gambling behavior. Iowa again serves as a prototypical case. In 1989, prior to the docking of riverboat casinos in selected Mississippi River towns, a mere 1.7 percent of the state's adults had gambling problems; by 1995, with legalized gambling in full swing in the state, the rate had skyrocketed to 5.4 percent.[41]

Gambling problems produce extreme and often demanding crises in the lives of those who succumb and the ones they love, problems that include suicide, spousal and child abuse and neglect, divorce, and many others. Many of these compulsives wander astray of the law, stealing, embezzling, writing bad checks, and so forth, to keep themselves flush in gambling money. All of which is very costly to the host community as well, in social costs, arrest and imprisonment costs, treatment, and lost work production, to mention just a few measures.

Crime of a very different sort—the organized type—despite ardent denials by gambling moguls, also flexes its muscles around some gambling venues. Some examples: Within ten years' time, an Indian casino near San Diego was twice targeted by organized crime figures.[42] In Louisiana, twenty-five people were convicted of participating in a scheme designed to skim video poker profits for Louisiana and New York crime families.[43] According to federal court documents and South Carolina corporate records, there was a link between that state's now-defunct video gambling industry and organized crime in Pittsburgh.[44] A 1994 *Minneapolis Star Tribune* story reported that "Companies and individuals with links to East Coast Mafia families have made millions of dollars doing business with five northern Minnesota casinos."[45] And Detroit Mafia figures stood trial in 1998 for trying to get a secret interest in three Nevada casinos, among other charges.[46]

Additionally, the idea that legalizing gambling would diminish the illegal variety—popular among gambling advocates—has been proven false as well. One former Chicagoland gambling director for the Mob contends that the opposite is true. William Jahoda testified before Congress in 1995 that "any new form or expansion of existing state-controlled licensed gambling always increased our market share. Simply put, the political dupes or stooges who approved riverboat gambling houses, lotteries, off-track horse betting sites, Las Vegas nights, etc., became our unwitting—and at least to my knowledge—unpaid pimps and frontmen."[47] The statement of American Gaming Association president Frank J. Fahrenkopf, Jr., that "The only place where organized crime can be linked to today's (casino) industry is in the movies,"[48] appears to be mere wishful thinking.

Speaking of politicians—Fahrenkopf formerly served as head of the Republican National Committee—who would have thought, forty years ago, that the gambling industry would be pumping money into election coffers at a rate to rival even major Washington players like the UAW and the NRA? And that it would be doing it *legally?* The money is big, and it is troubling, as both major parties vie for which can become gambling's most ardent public suitor. How big? More than $27 million has been contributed to political campaigns in recent years, $13.7 million to Republicans and $13.5 million to Democrats.[49] Many major national politicos of both parties have climbed into bed with the industry, including such household names as Bob Dole, Newt Gingrich, Trent Lott, Mitch McConnell, Tom DeLay, and Bill Frist on one side, and Al Gore, Tom Daschle, Richard Gephardt, Richard Bryan, Harry Reid, and Robert Torricelli on the other.[50]

The ironies on either side are ripe and ready to be plucked:

a party championing family values taking the money—and doing the bidding—of an industry that destroys families; a different party, ever embracing the plight of the underdog and downtrodden, cozying up to an industry that fleeces those very underdogs and downtrodden in lotteries and convenience casinos.[51] We are shocked—*shocked!*—that Congress deigns to rarely turn its collective thumb down on any gambling-related measure to come before it.

And that's only on the national scene. Gambling interests are even more active locally. According to *Mother Jones,* between 1992 and 1996 the industry gave state legislators more than $100 million in donations and lobbying fees.[52] When it can't sway votes in the legislature, it goes the referendum route, an increasingly popular way for special-interest groups to end-run their elected representatives. The money gambling interests spend to push their proposals into law is staggering, and almost always dwarfs that ponied up by their antigambling counterparts.

In Ohio they spent $8.5 million (in contrast to the $1.1 million spent by their opponents) on an ultimately failed campaign to put eight dockside casinos around the state.[53] In Arkansas the antigambling forces were outspent $9.2 million to $500,000 in an effort to bring in casinos, a state lottery, video lottery terminals, and charitable gambling.[54] Louisiana gambling proponents outfinanced their opponents by 200 to 1, $10.5 million to $53,000, to decide the fate of riverboat casinos, the New Orleans land-based casino, and video poker machines.[55] In other fights, the checks with the most zeros were invariably written by the progambling side.[56]

In terms of per-vote expense, however, gambling interests in West Virginia broke all the records in 2000, popping an extraordinary $232 for each of the 5,109 yes votes received in a ballot initiative to install a casino in Greenbrier Country. The total amount ponied up by gambling interests was

$1,200,000, versus a mere $21,888 doled out by gambling opponents (who won, incidentally, 58-42 percent).[57]

Woe to the intrepid elected official who stands up to this juggernaut. As much as $30 million of progambling money was used to oust South Carolina governor David Beasley, who had the temerity to label gambling a "cancer" eating away at families and communities in his state.[58] Fob James, former governor of Alabama, also was ushered unwillingly into his exit interview because of his courageous antigambling position.[59]

In addition to making it exceedingly difficult to counter the gambling industry's prodigious influence on the political scene, the huge contributions also present another unflattering possibility. Writes Simon: "Whenever there is easy money floating around, the temptation for corruption is present."[60] Politicians down through the years have too-frequently embraced an Oscar Wilde–type approach to this danger— "The only way to get rid of a temptation is to yield to it"[61]— and there is no reason to believe they will not continue down this path, what with the profligate sums being tossed at their feet by gambling interests.

Unintended Victims

In a country where children are rightfully treasured—and lamentably, also used as political pawns—does it not seem passing strange that our nation's leaders would not consider more fully these young people's emotional and spiritual health when deciding whether to legalize gambling? Living amid drastic changes in all aspects of their beings, bodily, psychologically, emotionally, kids are eager to explore what the world has to offer, and are particularly susceptible to the "forbidden fruits" of society.

Gambling is one of these, and it is highly intoxicating. As detailed in chapter 9, adolescents succumb to gambling problems at a rate from two to three times that for adults, and gambling has been called the fastest-growing teenage addiction by researchers.

Clearly, the widespread nature of legalized gambling in our country exacerbates this problem, but this phenomenon has another, less tangible effect as well: it's sending very bad signals to our kids. Outside of their family units and churches, children in our age will probably not be taught that gambling is intrinsically wrong or extrinsically counterproductive. They won't be raised in a secular atmosphere that has either condemned this activity or at least strongly discouraged it. What they're told by the gambling industry is that their only problem is their age—soon, when they're old enough, this wonderful world of chance and excitement will be open to them.

Such destructive indoctrination is bound to reap ill rewards over time. Kids are being subversively taught that luck, instead of education and industrious labor, holds the key to success in life. Because gambling produces no actual wealth in our society—in reality, it merely recycles money—our kids get the idea that productivity is not all their parents say it is. Moreover, they will get the message that success is tied to taking not prudent risks, but wild, improbable chances. In the words of the National Coalition against Legalized Gambling, "Gambling sets up artificial risks and glorifies individuals who take the biggest, most foolish risks."[62]

A House of Cards

Lost in the heat and fever that surround campaigns for legalized gambling is the light of rational, farsighted thought. It's far too easy for us as citizens to be caught up in the promises of increased educational or environmental spending, in the case of lottery legalization, and revitalization of sluggish local economies, as is promised when casinos enter town, and lose sight of the substantial downside any legalized gambling ventures bring with them.

The fact is, legalized gambling is *not* just like any other industry. In addition to taking over the town or community it enters, a casino, for example, produces no actual product, as does manufacturing, and thus no real sense of accomplishment for the producer. Writes Rex M. Rogers: "Work has intrinsic value, and the value of money is tied to the value of work. Gambling diverts people from useful labor. Money changes hands but with no exchange of material goods or services. Business, however, rests on the principle of fair exchange, value for value."[63]

As for wealth, gambling doesn't produce that either. A document produced by the Michigan Interfaith Council on Alcohol Problems presents this illustration: "Put 100 people together, legalize gambling, and let the action begin. When you return a week, a month, a year later, there will be no products created, no source of new wealth, only a redistribution of currency on an inequitable basis."[64] Rev. John Landrum, chaplain to Mississippi Beach, compares gambling to a shoe store that has no shoes. You, the customer, *bring* your shoes, and hope to leave with both your shoes and those of others. "Gambling is the only business that I know of that starts off with an empty store," Landrum says. "You bring in the product, and hope to leave with your product and somebody else's product."[65]

Contrast this with a traditional business transaction in which both parties win—the buyer gains the services of the product, the seller the money the buyer offers for such services —and the community in which the transaction takes place benefits as well. In gambling, though, "the gambler loses, and the community is forced to absorb social costs," Rogers writes. "Only the game owner wins."[66]

Nobel Prize–winning economist Paul Samuelson puts it more abstractly: "There is a substantial economic case to be made against gambling. It involves simply sterile transfers of money or goods between individuals, creating no new money or goods. Although it creates no output, gambling does nevertheless absorb time and resources. When pursued beyond the limits of recreation,...gambling subtracts from the national income."[67]

Also lost in the rush toward legalizing gambling is a larger philosophical issue, the very real possibility that gambling is sapping the national soul. A state that authorizes a lottery, a town that opens its arms to casinos—are they in actuality doing anything other than throwing in the towel, embracing a "magic-bullet" fix that may give them a quick economic high but will thrust upon them a dire socioeconomic low in the long run? The foundation of our country was built on principles that are diametrically opposed to those gambling promotes: perseverance; a trust in Providence; the belief that honest, hard work is its own reward; and prudent risk, to name a few. To look to gambling as a solution to any sort of problem, great or small, is a sign of national spiritual weakness. Grey blames our leaders for this. "I think the national character is often determined by the type of story that our leaders tell: political leaders, business leaders, religious leaders," he says. "I think our leadership has given up on us.... The American people are fine. They just need a leadership that says to them, 'you're better than this. You're better than bringing gambling in for economic development.'"[68]

What was unthinkable a mere four decades ago is now commonplace in our land: local communities, and even state governments, dependent upon and in most cases encouraging an economic enterprise built on shifting sand. It is an economy that promotes and then feasts on the human weaknesses inherent in us all; it further depreciates the character of people and debilitates the self-respect of the community that sponsors it; and it subverts the very values of hard work and enterprise that have made this country the greatest nation in the world.

A gambling economy is indeed a house of cards, a fragile creation that has really produced long-standing economic results—with many attendant social problems—in only one state in our nation: Nevada.

FIGHTING THE GOOD FIGHT

Given the current climate—what with gambling's massive money-dump on Washington and statehouses around the country, and the complicity of the governments themselves in extolling the "benefits" of legalized gambling—the odds would seem very definitely against those wishing to forestall this vice's inevitable spread across our land.

But the fight has been joined, and the resulting coalition has allowed Christians from both the right and the left—antagonists on such social issues as abortion and homosexuality—to find common ground in fighting the advance of gambling. Marvin Olasky, University of Texas professor, suggests that the gambling issue affords members of various denominations, all with differing theologies, the rare chance of uniting behind a cause without compromising doctrinal standards.[69]

One very visible group in the gambling wars comprises just such ecumenical membership, the National Coalition Against Legalized Gambling (NCALG), begun in 1994 and now headed by Rev. Tom Grey. When Grey, as a Methodist pastor in Galena, Illinois, saw the local county board green-light a riverboat casino in the big river that flowed west of town in 1991, despite overwhelming opposition—the local populace had nixed the project in an advisory referendum by 81 percent—he decided to take action. He educated himself on the issue and subsequently took his antigambling gospel to the country.[70]

He formed NCALG after a successful repulsion of an

Oklahoma lottery referendum, and built on that success by mustering a mere 1,261-vote defeat of a measure that would have expanded Missouri's riverboat industry. "We had no money; we generated a movement," Grey says. "The Right already had phone banks and was already working on this. The mainline churches hadn't really done a thing. So what happened was that God gave us this incredible victory."[71]

Antigambling forces have had mixed success in last decade's battles, however. In the mid-1990s, the NCALG scored a 90 percent victory rate over progambling forces in twenty-three referenda contests, one source said.[72] Four of seven statewide gambling initiatives were beaten back by gambling opponents in November 1994, the biggest plum coming in Florida, where voters soundly rejected casinos, despite a $16 million promotional blitz.[73] Also in that year, only one of seventy-one proposals dealing with casinos in state legislatures gained enough votes to pass. A year later, in 1995, citizens groups came up with "Casi*NO*" and "*NO* DICE" campaigns, and of nine states voting on progambling initiatives, only two sanctioned them.[74] In 1996 antigambling forces slam-dunked Vegas, scoring victories in twenty-three major battles over gambling legislation while suffering but one defeat.[75] But in the year 2000 the tally was less positive—five to five.[76]

Some of the more notable triumphs in recent years have been spearheaded by local coalitions led by churches, their pastors, and their parishioners. In one October week of 1999, called by one gambling expert "the biggest anti-gambling week in American history," both a lottery proposal in Alabama and South Carolina's rampant video-poker business took fatal hits from the electorate and the judiciary, respectively. In Alabama a newly elected governor's hobby horse, the institution of a lottery that he trumpeted with evangelistic zeal, was defeated by a 54 percent count with fully half the registered voters casting ballots—an unprecedented turnout for an off-year election. A little to the east in the Palmetto State, the supreme court banned that state's 36,000 video poker machines, thus obviating a blowout defeat by the state's voters scheduled three weeks thereafter (an infinitesimal 16 percent, according to one poll, supported the machines—this in a nation where 84 percent of the people wouldn't even agree that Elvis is dead).[77]

Both defeats were largely fashioned by energized churches and their pastors. Alabama pastors by the hundreds, and maybe the thousands, preached against gambling from their pulpits in the weeks leading up to the lottery vote. Churches conducted prayer vigils, registered voters, and even put their money where their mouths were, offering up major monetary contributions to the cause. Five days prior to the election, 460 preachers from various denominations took their opposition to the statehouse steps. "I knew we had a lot to do, and we needed to have a game plan," said Gary Palmer, president of the Alabama Family Alliance. "But I knew if the churches got involved, and if people would pray, it would be defeated."

The story from South Carolina was much the same. There the opposition was more ecumenical but equally militant. "The energy coming from the churches in South Carolina on this issue was completely unprecedented," said Gary Stanton, president of the Palmetto Family Council. "It was not just one type of church. It was liberal and conservative, evangelical and mainline churches all coming together." Kathy Bigham, a restaurateur, formed a coalition of business, community, and political leaders and then took her message to forums in more than thirty counties in the state, drawing upwards of 3,500 at some of them. "In every county our church leaders stepped up and took a leadership role in this effort," she said. One county leadership team included a Greek Orthodox priest, a Catholic lay leader, a Southern Baptist minister, an AME Zion bishop, and a Methodist minister.[78]

These two victories aside, not everything is so positive.

Key losses in South Carolina and South Dakota in November 2000, coupled with other advances by the gambling interests elsewhere in the country, make this an ongoing war, the outcome of which is still in doubt.

If the flood of gambling is to be turned back, it will be churches, their leaders, and their parishioners who will be at the vanguard of the movement, taking their rightful positions on the levees. Unless the American population is apprised of the dangers of this insidious activity, of the false promises of economic utopia that precede new ballot initiatives, and of the catastrophic addiction that descends on many who succumb to it, and the cost those addicts will inflict on their communities, there is little hope of stopping this contagion.

We Christians have our own reasons for entering this fray: gambling violates many of our precepts concerning work and stewardship, not to mention comprising, or at least setting up shop uncomfortably close to, the sins of greed, covetousness, and idolatry. But we can also take up arms on the secular level, for gambling wreaks havoc with the national polity. Its economic effects, as stated above, are injurious to cities and states that capitulate to its quick-fix nostrums; the crime that attends it is often overwhelming; it threatens our national quality of life, the legacy we will leave to our children and their children. These are concerns all Americans, not just Christians, can rally behind.

But most of all, gambling destroys lives and ruins families. The millions of adults who turn their lives over to Lady Luck leave behind them desolated and tattered spouses and emotionally and spiritually abandoned children. So great is their hunger for games of chance that they often destroy even themselves. The millions of teens who succumb to gambling addiction—at least twice as many as adults—fare no better, and may even face a more arduous climb out of addiction due to their youth and lack of responsibility. The family remains the basic political and social unit even in secular twenty-first-century America, and an activity that so seriously threatens the health and welfare of the family deserves our most sincere and sustained rebuke.

If we who want to preserve the probity, or honor, of this integral social unit will not venture forth into the battle, showing our collective might in the public square and at the ballot box, who will?

Notes

INTRODUCTION

1. Timothy L. O'Brien, *Bad Bet: The Inside Story of the Glamour, Glitz, and Danger of America's Gambling Industry* (New York: Random House, Times Books, 1998), p. 4.
2. O'Brien, p. 4.
3. The total amount wagered nationally is not available past 1998, but in that year Americans wagered $677.4 billion in all forms of legal gambling, according to *International Gaming and Wagering Business*, August 1999, as reported in the *Press of Atlantic City*, August 15, 1999; this number has certainly exceeded $700 billion in the subsequent years. The gross gambling revenues for 1999 totaled $58.4 billion, according to *International Gaming and Wagering Business*, August 2000, p. 15, and have certainly eclipsed the $60 billion mark subsequently.
4. O'Brien, p. 4.
5. Rex M. Rogers, *Seducing America: Is Gambling a Good Bet?* (Grand Rapids: Baker, 1997), p. 19.
6. Dave Shiflett, "Gambling and Its Discontents," *American Spectator*, March 1999, p. 42.
7. National Coalition against Legalized Gambling, "Gambling Addicts Say Revenues Are Not Worth the Suffering," October 14, 2000, available at coalition's website, www.ncalg.org.
8. Ronald A. Reno, "Gambler's Suicide Reveals Casino's Bottom Line," *Citizen Link*, n.d.

CHAPTER 1

1. Edward J. Federman, Charles E. Drebing, and Christopher Krebs, *Don't Leave It to Chance: A Guide for Families of Problem Gamblers* (Oakland: New Harbinger, 2000), p. 5.

2. Andy Hjelmeland, *Legalized Gambling: Solution or Illusion?* (Minneapolis: Lerner Publications, 1998), p. 8.

3. Hjelmeland, pp. 9-10.

4. Federman, Drebing, and Krebs, p. 5.

5. Rex M. Rogers, *Seducing America: Is Gambling a Good Bet?* (Grand Rapids: Baker, 1997), p. 108.

6. Hjelmeland, p. 13.

7. Ron Reno, "The Dirty Little Secret behind March Madness," *Citizen*, 1999.

8. Mark Cowan, "Gambling Losses Spark Mich. Deaths," *Family News in Focus Stories*, n.d.

9. National Gambling Impact Study Commission Report, June 1999, p. 4-9; hereafter cited as NGISC.

10. National Coalition against Legalized Gambling, "Gambling Addicts Say Revenues Are Not Worth the Suffering," October 14, 2000, available at the coalition's Web site, www.ncalg.org.

11. NGISC, p. 4-9.

12. Christopher W. Anderson, telephone interview with author, August 28, 2000.

13. Federman, Drebing, and Krebs, p. 33.

14. Paul Pringle, "Sin City Can Be a Tough Place to Live for Those Addicted to the Action," *San Diego Union-Tribune*, April 20, 1997.

15. Rob Bhatt, "Assigning Responsibility for Responsible Gambling," *Las Vegas Business Press*, June 22, 1998, p. 8; "Gaming Industry 'Amazed' over Neighborhood Slots Debate," *Las Vegas Sun*, February 20, 1998; Rex Buntain, "There's a Problem in the House," *International Gaming and Wagering Business* (July 1996): 40; Paul Pringle, "Dealing with Addiction; Las Vegas' Gaming Industry a Backdrop for High Rate of Compulsive Gamblers," *Dallas Morning News*, May 30, 1997, p. 1A.

16. Buntain, p. 40.

17. NGISC, p. 4-4.

18. Cited in NGISC, p. 4-4.

19. Rachel A. Volberg, "Gambling and Problem Gambling in Iowa: A Replication Survey," Iowa Department of Human Services, July 28, 1995.

20. Louise Taylor, "'People Leave with Tears in Their Eyes': Casino Industry Organizing to Help Those Who Bet More Than They Should," *Lexington (Ky.) Herald-Leader*, September 12, 1999.

21. Jeff Mapes, "Gambling on Addiction," *Oregonian*, March 9, 1997, p. 1A.

22. Robert Imrie, Associated Press, "Wisconsin Sees Rise in Gambling Addicts Since Casinos Opened," *Chicago Tribune*, August 2, 1999.

23. Ed Bierschenk, "Gamblers Anonymous Meetings Growing in Area," Copley News Service, September 22, 2000.

24. Robert Goodman, *The Luck Business: The Devastating Consequences and Broken Promises of America's Gambling Explosion* (New York: Free Press, Martin Kessler Books, 1995), p. 55.

25. NGISC, p. 4-19.

26. NGISC, p. 4-2.

27. Robert Custer and Harry Milt, *When Luck Runs Out: Help for Compulsive Gamblers and Their Families* (New York: Facts on File, 1985), p. 22.

28. This and other quotes from Dr. Linda Chamberlain in this chapter are from her conversation with author, Denver, Colo., August 15, 2000.

29. This and other quotes from Eileen Fox in this chapter are from her conversation with author, Colorado Springs, Colo., August 9, 2000.

30. Federman, Drebing, and Krebs, p. 13.

31. Dr. John M. Eades, telephone interview with author, August 23, 2000.

32. Hjelmeland, p. 83.

33. Stanton Peele, *Diseasing of America: Addiction Treatment Out of Control* (Boston: Houghton Mifflin, 1989), pp. 43-46.

34. National Research Council, "Pathological Gambling: A Critical Review," April 1, 1999, p. 4-9; hereafter cited as NRC.

35. Linda Berman and Mary-Ellen Siegel, *Behind the 8-Ball: A Guide for Families of Gamblers*, rev. ed. (San Jose: toExcel Press, 1998), pp. 43-44.

36. Of the $3.2 million poured into gambling research from 1996 to 1999 by the National Center for Responsible Gaming, a pro-gambling group, about $1.3 million went to projects designed to explore biological factors. See National Center for Responsible Gaming, "1998 Annual Report" and "Grant Awards: NCRG Funds New Research in 1999."

37. Richard E. Vatz and Lee S. Weinberg, "Heavy Gambling Is Not a Disease," in *Legalized Gambling: For and Against*, ed. Rod L. Evans and Mark Hance (Chicago and La Salle, Ill.: Open Court, 1998), pp. 54-63.

38. Vatz and Weinberg, pp. 61-62.

39. Peele, p. 3, emphasis Peele's.

40. Peele, p. 28.

41. Charles J. Sykes, *A Nation of Victims: The Decay of the American Character* (New York: St. Martin's Press, 1992), p. 136, emphasis Sykes's.

42. Wendy Kaminer, *I'm Dysfunctional, You're Dysfunctional: The Recovery Movement and Other Self-Help Fashions* (Reading, Mass.: Addison-Wesley, 1992).

43. Rogers, p. 115.

44. Rev. John Landrum, telephone interview with author, August 30, 2000.

45. Eades, interview.

46. Anderson, interview.

47. Quoted in Hjelmeland, p. 87.

48. John M. Eades, *Gambling Addiction: The Problem, the Pain, and the Pathway to Recovery* (privately published, 1999), p. 25.

49. Custer and Milt, p. 48.

50. Custer and Milt, p. 48.

51. Berman and Siegel, p. 31.

52. Federman, Drebing, and Krebs, p. 9; Richard J. Rosenthal, "Pathological Gambling," *Psychiatric Annals* 22, no. 2 (February 1992); NRC, p. 4-6.

53. NGISC, p. 4-11.

54. National Opinion Research Center, "Gambling Impact and Behavior Study, Report to the National Gambling Impact Study Commission," April 1, 1999, p. ix.

55. NRC, p. 3-15.

56. NGISC, p. 4-11.

57. Federman, Drebing, and Krebs, p. 35.

58. Federman, Drebing, and Krebs, p. 35.

59. Hjelmeland, p. 85; Rosenthal, "Pathological Gambling."

60. Ken Estes and Mike Brubaker, *Deadly Odds: Recovery from Compulsive Gambling* (New York: Simon & Schuster, A Fireside/Parkside Book, 1994), p. 34.

61. Rosenthal, "Pathological Gambling."

62. Dave Palermo, "Survey: Casino Workers More Prone to Addictions," *Gulfport (Miss.) Sun Herald*, September 24, 1998.

CHAPTER 2

1. Quoted in Henry R. Lesieur, *The Chase: Career of the Compulsive Gambler* (Rochester, Vt.: Schenkman Books, 1984), p. 44.

2. Lesieur, p. 44.

3. Timothy L. O'Brien, *Bad Bet: The Inside Story of the Glamour, Glitz, and Danger of America's Gambling Industry* (New York: Random House, Times Books, 1998), p. 173.

4. This and other quotes from Dr. Linda Chamberlain in this chapter are from her conversation with author, Denver, Colo., August 15, 2000.

5. Richard J. Rosenthal, "Pathological Gambling," Psychiatric Annals 22, no. 2 (February 1992).

6. Frederick Barthelme and Steven Barthelme, *Double Down: Reflections on Gambling and Loss* (Boston: Houghton Mifflin, 1999), pp. 119, 121.

7. To protect their anonymity, references to compulsive gamblers in this book will not include their names.

8. Lesieur, p. 47.

9. Don Hulen and Paula Burns, "Differences in Pathological Gamblers in Arizona," Arizona Council on Compulsive Gambling, February 2000, p. 2, available at the council's Web site, www.azccg.org.

10. Hulen and Burns, pp. 6-7.

11. Hulen and Burns, pp. 8-9.

12. Peter O'Connell, "Woman Going to Prison for Embezzlement," *Las Vegas Review-Journal,* September 18, 1999.

13. Rosenthal, "Pathological Gambling."

14. Robert Goodman, *The Luck Business: The Devastating Consequences and Broken Promises of America's Gambling Explosion* (New York: Free Press, Martin Kessler Books, 1995), p. 124.

15. Arizona Council on Compulsive Gambling, "Predisposing Factors of Escape Gamblers" and "1998 and 1999 Hotline Summary," both available at the council's Web site, www.azccg.org.

16. Quoted in Pete Earley, *Super Casino: Inside the "New" Las Vegas* (New York: Bantam Books, 2000), p. 316.

17. Ken Estes and Mike Brubaker, *Deadly Odds: Recovery from Compulsive Gambling* (New York: Simon & Schuster, A Fireside/Parkside Book, 1994), p. 73.

18. Earley, p. 315.

19. Dr. John M. Eades, telephone interview with author, August 23, 2000.

20. This and other citations from Tom Coates in this chapter come from his telephone interview with author, August 24, 2000.

21. Charles T. Clotfelter and Philip J. Cook, *Selling Hope: State Lotteries in America* (Cambridge: Harvard University Press, 1989), p. 105.

22. Charles T. Clotfelter, Philip J. Cook, Julie A. Edell, and Marian Moore, "State Lotteries at the Turn of the Century: Report to the National Gambling Impact Study Commission," April 23, 1999, p. 5.

23. Quoted in Peter Keating, "Lotto Fever: We All Lose!" in *Crapped Out: How Gambling Ruins the Economy and Destroys Lives*, ed. Jennifer Vogel (Monroe, Maine: Common Courage Press, 1997), p. 65.
24. Clotfelter et al., p. 2.
25. Joshua Wolf Shenk, "Eveyone's a Loser: How Lottery Ads Entice the Wrong People to Gamble," in *Crapped Out*, pp. 144-45.
26. Daniel Golden and David M. Halbfinger, "Lottery Addiction Rises, and Lives Fall," *Boston Globe*, February 11, 1997, p. A1.
27. Cited in Iris Cohen Selinger, "The Big Lottery Gamble," in *Crapped Out*, p. 152.
28. Clotfelter et al., p. 12.
29. The Pennsylvania and Tri-State Megabucks examples come from Shenk, p. 141.
30. Clotfelter et al., p. 13.

CHAPTER 3

1. *Detroit News*, February 8, 2000, cited in Ronald A. Reno, comp., "Gambling Summary: For the Week Ended February 11, 2000," *Citizen Link*.
2. National Gambling Impact Study Commission Report, June 1999, p. 4-10.
3. Associated Press, "Former New Bedford Principal Admits Stealing $20,000 in Student Funds," January 13, 2000.
4. Ronald A. Reno, "False Hope," *Citizen Link*, June 23, 1997.
5. Virginia Culver, "Parker Cleric Quits, Admits Taking $10,000," *Denver Post*, n.d.
6. NGISC, p. 7-25.
7. Testimony of Edward Looney, executive director, Council on Compulsive Gambling of New Jersey, before the NGISC, Atlantic City, N.J., January 22, 1998.
8. This and other quotes from Randall E. Smith in this chapter come from his conversation with author, Englewood, Colo., August 4, 2000.

9.   This and other quotes from Eileen Fox in this chapter are from her conversation with author, Colorado Springs, Colo., August 9, 2000.

10. Mary Heineman, *Losing Your Shirt: Recovery for Compulsive Gamblers and Their Families* (Center City, Minn.: Hazelden, 1992), p. xvi.

11. National Opinion Research Center, "Gambling Impact and Behavior Study, Report to the National Gambling Impact Study Commission," April 1, 1999, p. 46; hereafter cited as NORC.

12. This and other citations from Tom Coates in this chapter come from his telephone interview with author, August 24, 2000.

13. See Gary Ross, *No Limit: The Incredible Obsession of Brian Molony* (New York: Morrow, 1987).

14. National Research Council, "Pathological Gambling: A Critical Review," April 1, 1999, p. 5-4; hereafter cited as NRC.

15. John McCormick, "Many Iowans Going for Broke," *Des Moines Register*, June 15, 1997, p. 1. This applies to the years 1991–96.

16. SMR Research Corp., "The Personal Bankruptcy Crisis, 1997: Demographics, Causes, Implications and Solutions," 1997, p. 121. Study included counties with a minimum population of 25,000.

17. Ron French, "Gambling Bankruptcies Soar," *Detroit News*, December 3, 1995, p. A1.

18. SMR Research Corp., p. 116.

19. NORC, p. 44.

20. NORC, p. 48.

21. NORC, p. 49.

22. NORC, p. 48.

23. Martha Carr, "Suspect Tells All in Six Brutal Killings; Judge Asked to Toss Out Confession," *New Orleans Times-Picayune*, January 28, 1999.

24. Gretchen Schuldt, "Gambling Habit Leads to Prison: 64-Year-Old Manager of Credit Union Gets 4 Years for

Embezzling $275,000," *Milwaukee Journal-Sentinel,*
October 27, 2000.

25. Paula Christian, "Sentencing of Insurance Agent Delayed
Again," *Greensboro News and Record,* December 16, 1999.

26. Associated Press, "Former Bank President Admits Embezzling $1.9 Million," October 18, 2000.

27. John M. Eades, *Gambling Addiction: The Problem, the Pain,
and the Pathway to Recovery* (privately published, 1999), p. 22.

28. Both surveys cited at NRC, p. 5-2.

29. NORC, p. 50.

30. Rex M. Rodgers, *Seducing America: Is Gambling a Good
Bet?* (Grand Rapids: Baker, 1997), p. 110.

31. NORC, pp. 50-51.

32. NRC, p. 5-2.

33. NORC, p. 73.

34. Testimony of Rachel Caine, program director, Salvation
Army Domestic Violence Shelter, before the NGISC,
Biloxi, Miss., September 10, 1998.

35. See NGISC, p. 7-27.

36. NRC, p. 5-2.

37. Arnie Wexler, of Wexler Associates, testimony before the
NGISC, Atlantic City, N.J., January 22, 1998.

38. Joe Darby, "Sitter Indicted in Tot's Death," *New Orleans
Times-Picayune,* May 23, 1997, p. B1.

39. Quoted in Dave Shiflett, "Gambling and Its Discontents,"
American Spectator, March 1999, p. 45.

40. Stephanie Saul, "Tribe Bets on Growth; High Stakes Foxwoods Expansion Not Welcomed by All," *Newsday,* August
11, 1997.

CHAPTER 4

1. National Opinion Research Center, "Gambling Impact and
Behavior Study, Report to the National Gambling Impact
Study Commission," April 1, 1999, p. 6.

2. John M. Eades, *Gambling Addiction: The Problem, the Pain,
and the Pathway to Recovery* (privately published, 1999), p.
14, emphasis Eades's.

3. Linda Berman and Mary-Ellen Siegel, *Behind the 8-Ball: A Guide for Families of Gamblers*, rev. ed. (San Jose: toExcel Press, 1998), p. 39.

4. Robert Custer and Harry Milt, *When Luck Runs Out: Help for Compulsive Gamblers and Their Families* (New York: Facts on File, 1985), pp. 96-121.

5. Mary Heineman, *Losing Your Shirt: Recovery for Compulsive Gamblers and Their Families* (Center City, Minn.: Hazelden, 1992), pp. 1-13.

6. Eades, *Gambling Addiction*, pp. 18-23.

7. Richard J. Rosenthal, "Pathological Gambling," *Psychiatric Annals* 22, no. 2 (February 1992); Don Hulen and Paula Burns, "Differences in Pathological Gamblers in Arizona," Arizona Council on Compulsive Gambling, February 2000, pp. 2-5; Arizona Council on Compulsive Gambling, "The Four Phases of Escape Gambling," both available at the council's Web site, www.azccg.org.

8. Custer and Milt, p. 96.

9. This section is reliant upon the conclusions of compulsive gambling authorities, including Custer and Milt, *When Luck Runs Out;* Heineman, *Losing Your Shirt;* Henry R. Lesieur, *The Chase: Career of the Compulsive Gambler* (Rochester, Vt.: Schenkman Books, 1984); Edward J. Federman, Charles E. Drebing, and Christopher Krebs, *Don't Leave It to Chance: A Guide for Families of Problem Gamblers* (Oakland: New Harbinger, 2000); Berman and Siegel, *Behind the 8-Ball;* and Arizona Council on Compulsive Gambling (www.azccg.org), among others.

10. Heineman, p. 2.

11. The speaker of this quote and all others from compulsive gamblers will not be identified, in the interests of anonymity.

12. Eades, *Gambling Addiction*, p. 19.

13. Heineman, p. 3.

14. Custer and Milt, p. 103.

15. This and other citations from Tom Coates in this chapter come from his telephone interview with author, August 24, 2000.

16. Arizona Council, "Four Phases," p. 1; the information on escape gambling in what follows is from this document.
17. Quoted in Lesieur, p. 12.
18. This and other quotes from Dr. Linda Chamberlain in this chapter are from her conversation with author, Denver, Colo., August 15, 2000.
19. This and other quotes from Christopher W. Anderson in this chapter are from his telephone interview with author, August 28, 2000.
20. Berman and Siegel, p. 36, emphasis Berman and Siegel's.
21. Heineman, p. 9.
22. Rosenthal, "Pathological Gambling."
23. Arizona Council, "Four Phases," p. 2; Hulen and Burns, pp. 8-9; information for the section comes from the Arizona Council Web site.
24. Frederick Barthelme and Steven Barthelme, *Double Down: Reflections on Gambling and Loss* (Boston: Houghton Mifflin, 1999), p. 85.
25. Don Hulen and Paula Burns, "Differences in Pathological Gamblers in Arizona," Arizona Council on Compulsive Gambling, February 2000, p. 9.
26. Hulen and Burns, p. 9.
27. Gary Provost, *High Stakes: Inside the New Las Vegas* (New York: Dutton, Truman Talley Books, 1994), p. 124.
28. E. L. Grinols and J. D. Omorov, "Development or Dreamfield Delusions? Assessing Casino Gambling's Costs and Benefits," *Journal of Law and Commerce* (University of Pittsburgh School of Law) (fall 1996): 58-60.
29. WEFA Group, "A Study Concerning the Effects of Legalized Gambling on the Citizens of the State of Connecticut," prepared for state of Connecticut, Department of Revenue Services, Division of Special Revenue, June 1997, p. 8-3.
30. National Gambling Impact Study Commission Report, June 1999, pp. 4-5 and 4-9.
31. Dr. John M. Eades, telephone interview with author, August 23, 2000.

32. James Popkin, "Tricks of the Trade: The Many Modern Ways Casinos Try to Part Bettors from Their Cash," in *Crapped Out: How Gambling Ruins the Economy and Destroys Lives*, ed. Jennifer Vogel (Monroe, Maine: Common Courage Press, 1997), p. 166.

33. Pete Earley, *Super Casino: Inside the "New" Las Vegas* (New York: Bantam Books, 2000), p. 251.

34. Gary Ross, *No Limit: The Incredible Obsession of Brian Molony* (New York: Morrow, 1987), p. 165.

35. Popkin, pp. 161-62.

36. Popkin, p. 163.

37. Earley, p. 251.

38. This and other quotes from Randall E. Smith in this chapter are from his conversation with author, Englewood, Colo., August 4, 2000.

39. Eades, interview.

40. Ross, p. 89.

41. This and other quotes from Rev. John Landrum in this chapter come from his telephone interview with author, August 30, 2000.

42. Eades, interview.

43. Ross, pp. 100-101.

44. Custer and Milt, p. 117.

45. Heineman, p. 10.

46. Eades, *Gambling Addiction*, p. 22.

47. Associated Press, appearing in the *St. Louis Post-Dispatch*, January 6, 2000.

48. Norma Draper, "Mom's Gambling Habit Drove Her to Robbery," *Minneapolis Star Tribune*, July 10, 1995, cited in *Crapped Out*, pp. 85-88.

49. Rosenthal, "Pathological Gambling."

50. Quoted in Eades, *Gambling Addiction*, p. 23.

51. Hulen and Burns, p. 5.

CHAPTER 5

1. This and other quotes from Chaplain Trennis Killian in this chapter come from his telephone interview with author, August 21, 2000.

2. Robert Custer and Harry Milt, *When Luck Runs Out: Help for Compulsive Gamblers and Their Families* (New York: Facts on File, 1985), pp. 175-76.

3. Custer and Milt, p. 122.

4. Edward J. Federman, Charles E. Drebing, and Christopher Krebs, *Don't Leave It to Chance: A Guide for Families of Problem Gamblers* (Oakland: New Harbinger, 2000), p. 15.

5. These behaviors are from Federman, Drebing, and Krebs, pp. 16-17.

6. Federman, Drebing, and Krebs, p. 16.

7. Eileen Fox, conversation with author, Colorado Springs, Colo., August 9, 2000.

8. Linda Berman and Mary-Ellen Siegel, *Behind the 8-Ball: A Guide for Families of Gamblers*, rev. ed. (San Jose: toExcel Press, 1998), pp. 57-58.

9. Mary Heineman, *Losing Your Shirt: Recovery for Compulsive Gamblers and Their Families* (Center City, Minn.: Hazelden, 1992), pp. 175-76.

10. Berman and Siegel, p. 62, emphasis Berman and Siegel's.

11. Heineman, p. 26.

12. Berman and Siegel, p. 63.

13. The following section is derived from Berman and Siegel, pp. 61-70; Federman, Drebing, and Krebs, p. 69.

14. To protect the anonymity of compulsive gamblers and their spouses, references to them in this book will not include their names.

15. Tom Coates, telephone interview with author, August 24, 2000. This and other citations from Coates in this chapter come from this interview.

16. Custer and Milt, p. 177.

17. The following section is derived from Berman and Siegel, pp. 71-79; Custer and Milt, pp. 177-83.

18. Custer and Milt, p. 181.

19. Berman and Siegel, p. 75.

20. Berman and Siegel, pp. 86-89.

21. Berman and Siegel, pp. 84-89.

CHAPTER 6

1.   Robert Custer and Harry Milt, *When Luck Runs Out: Help for Compulsive Gamblers and Their Families* (New York: Facts on File, 1985), p. 123.

2.   This and other citations from Tom Coates in this chapter come from his telephone interview with author, August 24, 2000.

3.   Linda Berman and Mary-Ellen Siegel, *Behind the 8-Ball: A Guide for Families of Gamblers*, rev. ed. (San Jose: toExcel Press, 1998), pp. 96-97.

4.   Berman and Siegel, p. 97.

5.   Custer and Milt, p. 129.

6.   Edward J. Federman, Charles E. Drebing, and Christopher Krebs, *Don't Leave It to Chance: A Guide for Families of Problem Gamblers* (Oakland: New Harbinger, 2000), p. 54.

7.   Federman, Drebing, and Krebs, p. 90.

8.   Berman and Siegel, p. 103.

9.   Mary Heineman, *Losing Your Shirt: Recovery for Compulsive Gamblers and Their Families* (Center City, Minn.: Hazelden, 1992), p. 116.

10. This and other quotations from Dr. John M. Eades in this chapter come from his telephone interview with author, August 23, 2000.

11. Berman and Siegel, p. 103.

12. This and other quotations from Randall E. Smith in this chapter come from his conversation with author, Englewood, Colo., August 4, 2000.

13. Rev. John Landrum, telephone interview with author, August 30, 2000.

14. See Berman and Siegel, pp. 146-48, for other such difficult judgment calls.

15. Berman and Siegel, p. 149.

16. Berman and Siegel, p. 152.

17. Berman and Siegel, p. 152.

18. This and other quotes from Dr. Linda Chamberlain in this chapter are from her conversation with author, Denver, Colo., August 15, 2000.

19. Berman and Siegel, pp. 162-65. For more on finances, see Berman and Siegel, pp. 145-68; Federman, Drebing, and Krebs, pp. 151-75.

20. Berman and Siegel, p. 170.

21. See Custer and Milt, pp. 185-215; Berman and Siegel, pp. 169-90, for tips on such confrontations.

22. This and other quotes in this chapter from Chaplain Trennis Killian come from his telephone interview with author, August 21, 2000.

CHAPTER 7

1. Quoted in Ken Estes and Mike Brubaker, *Deadly Odds: Recovery from Compulsive Gambling* (New York: Simon & Schuster, A Fireside/Parkside Book, 1994), p. 138.

2. Dr. John M. Eades, telephone interview with author, August 23, 2000.

3. The names of compulsive gamblers and their spouses will not be used in this book, to protect their anonymity.

4. Robert Custer and Harry Milt, *When Luck Runs Out: Help for Compulsive Gamblers and Their Families* (New York: Facts on File, 1985), p. 29.

5. This and other quotations from Randall E. Smith in this chapter come from his conversation with author, Englewood, Colo., August 4, 2000.

6. Christopher W. Anderson, telephone interview with author, August 28, 2000.

7. Eades, interview.

8. Eileen Fox, conversation with author, Colorado Springs, Colo., August 9, 2000.

9. Christopher Anderson, interview.

10. Dr. Linda Chamberlain, conversation with author, Denver, Colo., August 15, 2000.

11. Christopher W. Anderson and Lia M. Nower, "Playing God: The Spiritual Bondage of Gambling Addiction" (paper privately sent to author).

12. Christopher Anderson, interview.

13. Christopher Anderson, interview.

14. Linda Berman and Mary-Ellen Siegel, *Behind the 8-Ball: A Guide for Families of Gamblers*, rev. ed. (San Jose: toExcel Press, 1998), p. 194.

15. The following comes from Edward J. Federman, Charles E. Drebing, and Christopher Krebs, *Don't Leave It to Chance: A Guide for Families of Problem Gamblers* (Oakland: New Harbinger, 2000), pp. 187-94.

16. Federman, Drebing, and Krebs, p. 194.

17. Federman, Drebing, and Krebs, p. 186.

18. Cited in Estes and Brubaker, p. 198.

19. Mary Heineman, *Losing Your Shirt: Recovery for Compulsive Gamblers and Their Families* (Center City, Minn.: Hazelden, 1992), p. 82.

20. Gamblers Anonymous, *"Combo Book,"* revised June 1997, p. 1.

21. Custer and Milt, p. 198.

22. Berman and Siegel, p. 196.

23. Gamblers Anonymous, p. 4.

24. Custer and Milt, p. 199.

25. Gamblers Anonymous, pp. 4-5.

26. Berman and Siegel, p. 197.

27. Berman and Siegel, p. 197.

28. These and other citations from Tom Coates in this chapter come from his telephone interview with author, August 24, 2000.

29. These and other quotes from Chaplain Trennis Killian in this chapter come from his telephone interview with author, August 21, 2000.

30. Custer and Milt, p. 232.

31. Custer and Milt, p. 223.

32. Custer and Milt, p. 199.

33. Heineman, p. 85.

34. Quoted in Estes and Brubaker, p. 201.

35. National Gambling Impact Study Commission Report, June 1999, p. 4-15.

36. Estes and Brubaker, p. 191.

37. Christopher Anderson, interview.

38. Anderson and Nower, "Playing God."
39. B. R. Browne, "The Selective Adaptation of the Alcoholics Anonymous Program by Gamblers Anonymous," *Journal of Gambling Studies* 7, no. 3 (1991): 1, cited by Anderson and Nower, "Playing God."
40. Christopher Anderson, interview.
41. Christopher Anderson, interview.
42. Anderson and Nower, "Playing God."
43. Anderson and Nower, "Playing God."
44. Eades, interview.
45. This and other citations of Rev. John Landrum in this chapter come from his telephone interview with author, August 30, 2000.
46. The chief work used by Landrum and others is Neil T. Anderson, *The Bondage Breaker* (Eugene, Ore.: Harvest House, 1990).
47. John M. Eades, *Gambling Addiction: The Problem, the Pain, and the Pathway to Recovery* (privately published, 1999), p. 85.
48. Eades, interview.
49. Eades, interview.
50. Christopher Anderson, interview.
51. Christopher Anderson, interview.
52. Eades, interview.
53. Eades, *Gambling Addiction*, p. 103.
54. Eades, interview.
55. Eades, interview.

CHAPTER 8

1. John M. Eades, *Gambling Addiction: The Problem, the Pain, and the Pathway to Recovery* (privately published, 1999), p. 32.
2. The names of compulsive gamblers and their spouses will not be used in his book, to protect their anonymity.
3. Linda Berman and Mary-Ellen Siegel, *Behind the 8-Ball: A Guide for Families of Gamblers*, rev. ed. (San Jose: toExcel Press, 1998), p. 200.
4. Dr. John M. Eades, telephone interview with author, August 23, 2000.

5. Ken Estes and Mike Brubaker, *Deadly Odds: Recovery from Compulsive Gambling* (New York: Simon & Schuster, A Fireside/Parkside Book, 1994), pp. 227-28.
6. Eades, interview.
7. Eades, *Gambling Addiction*, p. 97.
8. This and other citations in this chapter from Tom Coates come from his telephone interview with author, August 24, 2000.
9. This and other quotes in this chapter from Chaplain Trennis Killian come from his telephone interview with author, August 21, 2000.
10. Eades, interview.
11. Eades, interview.

CHAPTER 9

1. Quoted in Rex M. Rogers, *Seducing America: Is Gambling a Good Bet?* (Grand Rapids: Baker, 1997), p. 124.
2. National Research Council, "Pathological Gambling: A Critical Review," April 1, 1999, p. 4-21; hereafter cited as NRC.
3. NRC, p. 3-9.
4. NRC, p. 3-15.
5. Howard J. Shaffer and Matthew N. Hall, "Estimating the Prevalence of Adolescent Gambling Disorders: A Quantitative Synthesis and Guide toward Standard Gambling Nomenclature," *Journal of Gambling Studies* (summer 1996): 193.
6. Edward F. Dolan, *Teenagers and Compulsive Gambling* (New York: Franklin Watts, 1994), p. 22.
7. James Westphal, Jill Rush, and Lee Stevens, "Preliminary Report on the Statewide Baseline Survey for Pathological Gambling and Substance Abuse, Louisiana Adolescents (Sixth through Twelfth Grades) School Year 96-97," Department of Psychiatry, Louisiana State University Medical Center School of Medicine in Shreveport, June 30, 1997.

8. Ronald A. Reno, "You Bet Your Life," *Citizen Link*, October 1, 1998.

9. Alan F. Arcuri, David Lester, and Franklin O. Smith, "Shaping Adolescent Gambling Behavior," *Adolescence* (winter 1985): 936.

10. National Gambling Impact Study Commission Report, June 1999, p. 7-23, hereafter cited as NGISC; NRC, p. 3-24.

11. David Johnston, *Temples of Chance: How America Inc. Bought Out Murder Inc. to Win Control of the Casino Business* (New York: Doubleday, 1992), p. 183; all anecdotes in this and the preceding paragraph come from Johnston, pp. 178-85.

12. Robert Goodman, *The Luck Business: The Devastating Consequences and Broken Promises of America's Gambling Explosion* (New York: Free Press, Martin Kessler Books, 1995), p. 44.

13. "Groups Want Congress to Investigate 'Slots for Tots,' Gambling Industry," press release from *Citizen Link*, November 22, 1999.

14. Rogers, p. 35.

15. James Varney, "Class Conflict," *New Orleans Times-Picayune*, December 14, 1997, p. B1; Leslie Zganjar, "State, Industry Trying to Reach Agreement on Donation Restrictions," Associated Press, December 1, 1998.

16. Scott Harshbarger, attorney general, Commonwealth of Massachusetts, "Kids and Keno Are a Bad Bet: A Report on the Sale of Keno Tickets to Minors in Massachusetts," October 8, 1996.

17. A Massachusetts survey found that 80 percent of minors purchased lottery tickets (Scott Harshbarger, attorney general, Commonwealth of Massachusetts, "Report on the Sale of Lottery Tickets to Minors in Massachusetts," July 1994); another survey of Bay State teens showed that 30 percent of seventh-graders had purchased lottery tickets during one month (Goodman, p. 44); and the New York City Council discovered that "11 percent of the businesses that were investigated sold scratch-off lottery tickets to teens aged

fifteen to sixteen" (Edward J. Federman, Charles E. Drebing, and Christopher Krebs, *Don't Leave It to Chance: A Guide for Families of Problem Gamblers* [Oakland: New Harbinger, 2000], p. 93).

18. Cited in Ken Estes and Mike Brubaker, *Deadly Odds: Recovery from Compulsive Gambling* (New York: Simon & Schuster, A Fireside/Parkside Book, 1994), p. 90.

19. Family Research Council Washington Update, March 29, 2000.

20. Wexler quote and Lorenz citations from Ron Reno, "The Dirty Little Secret behind March Madness," *Citizen*, 1999.

21. Timothy L. O'Brien, *Bad Bet: The Inside Story of the Glamour, Glitz, and Danger of America's Gambling Industry* (New York: Random House, Times Books, 1998), p. 246.

22. Reno, "Dirty Little Secret."

23. Family Research Council Washington Update, March 10, 2000.

24. NGISC, p. 7-23.

25. Linda Berman and Mary-Ellen Siegel, *Behind the 8-Ball: A Guide for Families of Gamblers*, rev. ed. (San Jose: toExcel Press, 1998), p. 69.

26. Dolan, pp. 55-56.

27. *Gamblers Anonymous: Young Gamblers in Recovery*, a publication of Gamblers Anonymous (n.d.), pp. 1-2, quoted in Dolan, p. 116.

28. Dolan, p. 73.

29. Dolan, pp. 17, 73.

30. Some of these questions adapted from Berman and Siegel, pp. 69-70.

31. These points adapted from Berman and Siegel, pp. 78-79.

32. Federman, Drebing, and Krebs, p. 92.

33. This and other quotations from Dr. John M. Eades in this chapter come from his telephone interview with author, August 23, 2000.

34. Federman, Drebing, and Krebs, p. 92.

35. This and other citations from Tom Coates in this chapter come from his telephone interview with author, August 24, 2000.
36. Federman, Drebing, and Krebs, p. 155.
37. Federman, Drebing, and Krebs, pp. 92-96.

CHAPTER 10

1. Jeanne Sahadi, "Snake Eyes Sap Seniors," March 17, 2000, on the CNN Web site, http://cnnfn.cnn.com.
2. *Senior Times* 1, no. 1 (July 1998), available at www.800gambler.org.
3. Timothy L. O'Brien, *Bad Bet: The Inside Story of the Glamour, Glitz, and Danger of America's Gambling Industry* (New York: Random House, Times Books, 1998), p. 73.
4. *Senior Times* 1, no. 5 (April 2000), available at www.800gambler.org.
5. Chaplain Trennis Killian, telephone interview with author, August 21, 2000.
6. Sahadi, "Snake Eyes Sap Seniors."
7. Information for this paragraph from Arizona Council on Compulsive Gambling, "Seniors and Gambling: What Keeps Them Going Back," n.d., available at the council's Web site, www.azccg.org.
8. Rev. John Landrum, telephone interview with author, August 30, 2000.
9. Council on Compulsive Gambling of New Jersey, "Senior Gambling: A Growing National Concern," n.d.
10. *Senior Times* 1, no. 1 (July 1998).
11. Arizona Council on Compulsive Gambling, "Seniors and Gambling: Introduction," n.d., available at the council's Web site, www.azccg.org.
12. This and other quotes from Dr. Linda Chamberlain in this chapter are from her conversation with author, Denver, Colo., August 15, 2000.
13. Arizona Council on Compulsive Gambling, "Predisposing Factors of Escape Gamblers," n.d., available at the council's Web site, www.azccg.org.

14. Information for this list comes from the Arizona Council's Web site; Sahadi, "Snake Eyes Sap Seniors"; and the Web site of the North American Training Institute, www.nati.org.

15. Edward J. Federman, Charles E. Drebing, and Christopher Krebs, *Don't Leave It to Chance: A Guide for Families of Problem Gamblers* (Oakland: New Harbinger, 2000), pp. 96-98.

16. Federman, Drebing, and Krebs, p. 96.

17. This and other citations in this chapter from Tom Coates come from his telephone interview with author, August 24, 2000.

CHAPTER 11

1. Rex M. Rogers, *Seducing America: Is Gambling a Good Bet?* (Grand Rapids: Baker, 1997), p. 59.

2. Rogers, p. 55.

3. Rogers, p. 67.

4. Timothy L. O'Brien, *Bad Bet: The Inside Story of the Glamour, Glitz, and Danger of America's Gambling Industry* (New York: Random House, Times Books, 1998), p. 286.

5. Don Feeney, "Is Gambling Immoral?" *Beyond the Odds*, June 1999, available at www.miph.org/bto/jun99/1.html.

6. Rogers, p. 55.

7. Thomas B. Franzmann, "It Is a Complex Issue," *Northwestern Lutheran*, March 15, 1988, available at www.wels.org/sab/nl/9905-06.html.

8. Commission on Theology and Church Relations of the Lutheran Church–Missouri Synod, "Gambling," February 1996, p. 13; hereafter cited as CTCR.

9. CTCR, p. 13.

10. CTCR, p. 14.

11. Catholic Bishops of Florida, "Statement Opposing Casino Gambling," July 7, 1994, available at www.flacathconf.org/B5/C3/D4/B5c3d414.htm.

12. See Rogers, pp. 55-56.

13. O'Brien, p. 289.

14. Quoted in Rogers, p. 56.

15. O'Brien, p. 289.

16. Catholic Bishops of Florida, "Statement Opposing Casino Gambling."

17. Quoted in Rogers, p. 56.

18. Evangelical Lutheran Church in America Division for Church in Society, "Session 2: Gambling and the Godly Life," available at www.elca.org/dcs/session2.html.

19. Ronald A. Reno, "Gambling and the Bible," *Citizen Link*, November 17, 1999.

20. R. Albert Mohler, Jr., "When the Accounts Are Called: A Christian View of Gambling," *Fidelitas*, July 13, 1998, available at www.sbts.edu/mohler/fidelitas/gambling.html.

21. Norman L. Geisler, *Gambling: A Bad Bet* (Grand Rapids: Revell, 1993), available at www.ccf-ark.com/issues/gambling/bib-case.htm. Pages 111 through 119 of this book are reprinted at this Web site.

22. Geisler, *Gambling*.

23. *New Bible Dictionary*, 2nd ed. (Wheaton, Ill.: Tyndale House, 1982), s.v. "mammon."

24. "A Look at Gambling!" *Badger Lutheran*, December 4, 1975.

25. *Luther's Large Catechism: A Contemporary Translation with Study Questions*, trans. F. Samuel Janzow (St. Louis: Concordia, 1978), p. 14.

26. CTCR, p. 7.

27. Geisler, *Gambling*, emphasis Geisler's.

28. CTCR, p. 7.

29. Rogers, p. 63.

30. Geisler, *Gambling*.

CHAPTER 12

1. National Gambling Impact Study Commission Report, June 1999, executive summary, p. 2; hereafter cited as NGISC.

2. Andy Hjelmeland, *Legalized Gambling: Solution or Illusion?* (Minneapolis: Lerner Publications, 1998), p. 116.

3. Timothy L. O'Brien, *Bad Bet: The Inside Story of the Glamour, Glitz, and Danger of America's Gambling Industry* (New York: Random House, Times Books, 1998), p. 157.

4. O'Brien, p. 158.

5. Hjelmeland, p. 42.

6. Rex M. Rogers, *Seducing America: Is Gambling a Good Bet?* (Grand Rapids: Baker, 1997), p. 30.

7. David Johnston, *Temples of Chance: How America Inc. Bought Out Murder Inc. to Win Control of the Casino Business* (New York: Doubleday, 1992), p. 25.

8. Hjelmeland, pp. 43-44.

9. Johnston, p. 25.

10. Hjelmeland, pp. 46-47.

11. Hjelmeland, pp. 50-51.

12. Cited in Johnston, p. 26.

13. Johnston, p. 26; O'Brien, pp. 106-8.

14. NGISC, p. 3-4.

15. O'Brien, p. 156.

16. Johnston, p. 49.

17. Thomas Grey, interview for *Frontline* TV show, 1998, available at www.pbs.org/wgbh/pages/frontline/shows/gamble/procon/igrey.html.

18. Rogers, p. 43.

19. "American Attitudes toward Casino Entertainment," available at www.harrahs.com/survey/ce97/ce97_acceptance.html.

20. Joe Weinert, "Acceptance Declines for Casino Gambling," *Press of Atlantic City*, October 21, 2000.

21. O'Brien, p. 159.

22. Charles T. Clotfelter and Philip J. Cook, *Selling Hope: State Lotteries in America* (Cambridge: Harvard University Press, 1989), p. 35, quoted in O'Brien, p. 158.

23. O'Brien, p. 164.

24. O'Brien, pp. 167-69.

25. NGISC, p. 2-1.

26. David Warsh, "A Rising Gorge," *Boston Globe*, March 4, 1997, p. D1.

27. Robert Draper, "You Lose! The Sad Truth about the Texas Lottery," in *Crapped Out: How Gambling Ruins the Economy and Destroys Lives*, ed. Jennifer Vogel (Monroe, Maine: Common Courage Press, 1997), pp. 100-102.

28. NGISC, p. 3-4.

29. O'Brien, pp. 170-71.

30. O'Brien, p. 171.

31. Jeff Mapes, "Gambling on Addiction," *Oregonian*, March 9, 1997, p. 1A.

32. R. D. Carr, J. E. Buchkoski, L. Kofoed, and T. J. Morgan, "'Video Lottery' and Treatment for Pathological Gambling: A Natural Experiment in South Dakota," *South Dakota Journal of Medicine* (January 1996): 31.

33. O'Brien, p. 171.

34. Christopher W. Anderson, telephone interview with author, August 28, 2000.

35. NGISC, p. 7-10.

36. NGISC, p. 7-10.

37. Joshua Wolf Shenk, "Everyone's a Loser: How Lottery Ads Entice the Wrong People to Gamble," in *Crapped Out*, pp. 139-40.

38. David M. Halbfinger and Daniel Golden, "The Lottery's Poor Choice of Locations," *Boston Globe*, February 12, 1997, p. A1.

39. James C. Dobson, open letter of April 1999, available at Focus on the Family website, www.family.org.

40. "Lottery Preys on Vulnerable Poor," *Fort Lauderdale Sun-Sentinel*, September 22, 1993, p. 12A.

41. The poorest citizens in Texas, for example, earn only 2 percent of the state's total income but account for 10 percent of the state's lottery sales (Donald Deere and James Dyer, "Heads I Win, Tails You Lose: The Economic Impact of the Texas Lottery on Demographic Groups," Texas A&M University, February 18, 1994). In Colorado, the thirty-two counties with the highest per-capita lottery sales each have incomes below the state average (Genevieve Anton, "Money

Bet on a Miracle," *Colorado Springs Gazette Telegraph,*
August 25, 1996, p. A1), and in New Mexico, the three
poorest counties all rank among the state's top ten counties
in per capita lottery sales (Carla Crowder, "N.M. Lottery
Costs Rank High," *Albuquerque Journal,* April 27, 1997,
p. A13). Those living in the most impoverished areas of
New York State spend eight times more of their income on
lottery tickets than those living in the most affluent sections
(Ford Fessenden and John Riley, "And the Poor Get
Poorer ... ," *Newsday,* December 4, 1995, p. A7). A
Wisconsin survey revealed similar results: People living in
poor areas play the lottery more—four times more—than
those in richer areas ("Lottery Claims Bigger Slice of Poor's
Income," *Chicago Tribune,* May 26, 1995, sec. "News,"
p. 3).

42. Shenk, p. 138.
43. Shenk, p. 140.
44. Shenk, p. 143.
45. Iris Cohen Selinger, "The Big Lottery Gamble," in *Crapped Out,* p. 149.
46. Clotfelter and Cook, p. 203.
47. Robert Goodman, "The Lottery Mystique: Why Work at All?" *Newsday,* June 28, 1991, p. 59.
48. Michael J. Sandel, "The Hard Questions: Bad Bet," *New Republic,* March 10, 1997, p. 27.
49. Shenk, p. 143.
50. Quoted in Shenk, pp. 143-44.
51. NGISC, p. 7-10.
52. Peter Keating, "Lotto Fever: We All Lose!" *Money,* May 1996, pp. 144, 147.
53. Selinger, p. 149.
54. Robyn Gearey, "The Numbers Game," *New Republic,* May 19, 1997, p. 20.
55. Selinger, p. 149.
56. Ellen Perlman, "Lotto's Little Luxuries," *Governing Magazine,* December 1996, p. 18.
57. NGISC, p. 3-15.

58. NGISC, pp. 2-11 and 2-12.
59. O'Brien, p. 188.
60. NGISC, p. 2-13.
61. O'Brien, p. 206.
62. NGISC, pp. 2-13 and 2-14.
63. O'Brien, p. 207.
64. Robert Goodman, *The Luck Business: The Devastating Consequences and Broken Promises of America's Gambling Explosion* (New York: Free Press, Martin Kessler Books, 1995), pp. 90-92.
65. Rogers, p. 48.
66. Laurence Arnold, Associated Press, "Colleges, Casinos Gear Up for Congressional Fight over Sports Betting," *Las Vegas Sun*, January 13, 2000.
67. NGISC, p. 2-14.
68. NGISC, p. 3-9.
69. NGISC, p. 2-14.
70. O'Brien, p. 214.
71. Ron Reno, "The Dirty Little Secret behind March Madness," *Citizen*, 1999.
72. A major scandal between 1947 and 1950 implicated thirty-three players from seven schools who, combined, fixed eighty-six games (O'Brien, p. 242). Other point-shaving scandals rocked college basketball in 1961, 1981, and 1985 (O'Brien, pp. 242-43).
73. Arnold, "Colleges, Casinos Gear Up."
74. Donald L. Barlett and James B. Steele, "Throwing the Game," *Time*, September 25, 2000, p. 54.
75. Barlett and Steele, p. 54; Matt O'Connor, "Sentence Closes Book on NU Betting Scandal," *Chicago Tribune*, March 15, 2000.
76. Steven (Hedake) Smith, as told to Don Yaeger, "Confessions of a Point Shaver," *Sports Illustrated*, November 9, 1998.
77. Reno, "Dirty Little Secret."
78. Quoted in Gary Lundy, "NCAA Says Lady Vols Not Safe from Gamblers," *Knoxville News-Sentinel*, August 6, 1998, p. C1.

79. Quoted in Susan Yerkes, "Gambling Most Critical Issue for NCAA," *San Antonio Express News,* March 30, 1998, p. C1.

80. Tim Layden, "Bettor Education," *Sports Illustrated,* April 3, 1995, p. 68.

81. Reno, "Dirty Little Secret."

82. Marci McDonald, "Betting the House: Online Gambling Proves Addictive—Even to the Big Casinos," *U.S. News and World Report,* October 16, 2000, p. 44.

83. Dave Palermo, "Industry Observers: Question Is When, Not If, Internet Gambling Will Be Legal," *Gulfport (Miss.) Sun Herald,* October 24, 2000; Reuters, "Web Gambling Grows at Torrid Rate Worldwide," May 31, 2000.

84. Reuters, "Web Gambling Grows."

85. McDonald, p. 44.

86. O'Brien, p. 16.

87. Reuters, "Web Gambling Grows."

88. O'Brien, p. 12.

89. O'Brien, p. 13.

CHAPTER 13

1. "Preliminary 1999 Gross Gambling Revenues by Industry and Change from 1998," *International Gaming and Wagering Business* (August 2000): 15.

2. National Gambling Impact Study Commission Report, June 1999, p. 2-6.

3. Timothy L. O'Brien, *Bad Bet: The Inside Story of the Glamour, Glitz, and Danger of America's Gambling Industry* (New York: Random House, Times Books, 1998), p. 24.

4. O'Brien, pp. 24-26.

5. O'Brien, p. 34.

6. Pete Earley, *Super Casino: Inside the "New" Las Vegas* (New York: Bantam Books, 2000), p. 87.

7. Earley, p. 83.

8. O'Brien, pp. 37-39.

9. O'Brien, p. 40.

10. Gary Provost, *High Stakes: Inside the New Las Vegas* (New York: Dutton, Truman Talley Books, 1994), p. 114.

11. Provost, p. 114.
12. Earley, p. 86.
13. Earley, p. 84.
14. The first figure, for 1985, comes from O'Brien, p. 41; the second, for 2000, comes from the Nevada Gaming Control Board, telephone communication, January 31, 2001.
15. O'Brien, p. 40.
16. O'Brien, p. 50.
17. O'Brien, p. 54.
18. O'Brien, p. 54.
19. "Frequently Asked Research Questions," made available by the Las Vegas Convention and Visitors Authority, at www.vegasfreedom.com/gen_resfaq.html.
20. O'Brien, p. 47.
21. "Visitor Statistics: 1970 to Present," a chart made available by the Las Vegas Convention and Visitors Authority, at www.vegasfreedom.com/gen_vstat.html.
22. Scott DeNicola, "Sin City Repackaged—Family-Style," *Citizen Link*, February 20, 1998.
23. Quoted in DeNicola, "Sin City Repackaged."
24. "The Nation's Fastest Growing Cities," *Denver Rocky Mountain News*, October 20, 2000, p. 34A.
25. Barry M. Horstman, "New Vegas: Original Sin City Tries Family Values," *Cincinnati Post*, September 16, 1997.
26. O'Brien, p. 52.
27. Bureau of the Census, *Statistical Abstract of the United States, 1997*, 117th ed. (Washington, D.C., 1997), p. 99.
28. Bureau of the Census, p. 108.
29. Bureau of the Census, p. 161.
30. Philip W. McClain et al., "Geographic Patterns of Fatal Abuse or Neglect in Children Younger Than 5 Years Old, United States, 1979 to 1988," *Archives of Pediatrics and Adolescent Medicine* (January 1994): 82.
31. "Nevada Leads U.S. in Female Lung Disease Deaths," *Las Vegas Sun*, May 14, 1996.
32. G. Williams, F. Stinson, L. Sanchez, and M. Dufour, "Surveillance Report #43: Apparent Per Capita Alcohol Consumption:

National, State, and Regional Trends, 1977-95," National Institute of Alcohol Abuse and Alcoholism, December 1997.

33. "County Alcohol Problem Indicators 1986-1990," U.S. Alcohol Epidemiologic Data Reference Manual, Volume 3, National Institute on Alcohol Abuse and Alcoholism, July 1994.

34. Bureau of the Census, p. 87.

35. Mana Zarinejad, public affairs coordinator, American Bankruptcy Institute, personal communication with Focus on the Family, October 13, 1998.

36. Bureau of the Census, p. 79.

37. Bureau of the Census, p. 202.

38. Bureau of the Census, p. 202.

39. Darrell K. Gilliard and Allen J. Beck, "Prisoners in 1997," Bureau of Justice Statistics Bulletin, August 1998, p. 5.

40. Bureau of the Census, p. 290.

41. Ed Koch, "Nevada: Most Dangerous?" *Las Vegas Sun,* July 16, 1997.

42. "Crime Down Nationally, Vegas Homicides Up 36 Percent," *Las Vegas Sun,* June 2, 1997.

43. Associated Press, "State Sees Crime Boom by Juveniles," *Las Vegas Review-Journal,* June 30, 1997.

44. Rob Bhatt, "Assigning Responsibility for Responsible Gambling," *Las Vegas Business Press,* June 22, 1998, p. 8; "Gaming Industry 'Amazed' over Neighborhood Slots Debate," *Las Vegas Sun,* February 20, 1998; Rex Buntain, "There's a Problem in the House," *International Gaming and Wagering Business* (July 1996): 40; Paul Pringle, "Dealing with Addiction: Las Vegas' Gaming Industry a Backdrop for High Rate of Compulsive Gamblers," *Dallas Morning News,* May 30, 1997, p. 1A.

45. O'Brien, p. 53.

46. Lou Cannon, "Trying to Beat the Odds in Nevada," *Washington Post,* August 26, 1998, p. A3.

47. Craig Offman, "The 10 Most Corrupt Cities in America," *George,* March 1998.

48. David Johnston, *Temples of Chance: How America Inc.*

Bought Out Murder Inc. to Win Control of the Casino Business (New York: Doubleday, 1992), p. 53.

49. O'Brien, p. 65.
50. Johnston, p. 54.
51. Johnston, p. 54.
52. O'Brien, p. 68.
53. Quoted in Robert Goodman, *The Luck Business: The Devastating Consequences and Broken Promises of America's Gambling Explosion* (New York: Free Press, Martin Kessler Books, 1995), p. 19.
54. Goodman, *The Luck Business*, p. 19.
55. Johnston, pp. 45, 54.
56. *Senior Times* 1, no. 1 (July 1998), available at www.800gambler.org.
57. Johnston, p. 45.
58. Johnston, pp. 52-53.
59. Mike Kelly, "Gambling with Our Future," *Hackensack (N.J.) Record*, July 11, 1993.
60. Goodman, *The Luck Business*, p. 20.
61. Goodman, *The Luck Business*, p. 23.
62. Goodman, *The Luck Business*, p. 23.
63. Andrew J. Buck, Simon Hakim, and Uriel Spiegel, "Casinos, Crime and Real Estate Values: Do They Relate?" *Journal of Research in Crime and Delinquency* (August 1991): 295.
64. Mike Kelly, "A City and Its Legacy," *Hackensack (N.J.) Record*, July 18, 1993.
65. *1995 Kid's Count Data Book*, Association for Children of New Jersey, p. 6.
66. Mike Kelly, "Atlantic City Journal" (series), *Hackensack (N.J.) Record*, July 11-18, 1993.
67. Rev. Barry Durman, interview, September 17, 1997.
68. "Report to the National Gambling Impact Study Commission," Atlantic City Rescue Mission, January 21, 1998, p. 17.
69. SMR Research Corp., "The Personal Bankruptcy Crisis, 1997: Demographics, Causes, Implications and Solutions," 1997, p. 117.

70. Goodman, *The Luck Business*, p. 20.
71. Kelly, "Gambling with Our Future."
72. Goodman, *The Luck Business*, p. 22.
73. Frank Langfitt, "Marylanders Look for a Lesson," *Baltimore Sun*, October 7, 1995; "Summary of 1996 Statistics for 1-800-GAMBLERTM Helpline," released by Council on Compulsive Gambling of New Jersey, 1997.
74. George Sternlib and James W. Hughes, "Even Been Had? The Atlantic City Gamble: A Twentieth Century Fund Report," *Economist*, June 2, 1984.
75. Amy S. Rosenberg, "Progress Slow, but Atlantic City Begins to Fulfill Dream Deferred," *Philadelphia Inquirer*, October 20, 1996, p. B1.
76. John Warren Kindt, "Legalized Gambling Is Bad for Business," in *Legalized Gambling: For and Against*, ed. Rod L. Evans and Mark Hance (Chicago and La Salle, Ill.: Open Court, 1998), p. 145.
77. "Authority Tells Magazine: Atlantic City Not Destination Resort," *Atlantic City Press*, September 27, 1997.
78. NGISC, p. 6-2.
79. NGISC, pp. 6-1 and 6-2; "Preliminary 1999 Gross Gambling Revenues by Industry and Change from 1998," *International Gaming and Wagering Business* (August 2000): 15.
80. O'Brien, p. 139.
81. Gene Sloan, "Gamble Pays Off with New Pequot Museum," *USA Today*, August 7, 1998.
82. Rex M. Rodgers, *Seducing America: Is Gambling a Good Bet?* (Grand Rapids: Baker, 1997), p. 46.
83. Andy Hjelmeland, *Legalized Gambling: Solution or Illusion?* (Minneapolis: Lerner Publications, 1998), pp. 70-73.
84. NGISC, pp. 6-15 and 6-16; and p. 6-6.
85. David Pace, "Casino Boom Bypasses Indians," Associated Press, August 31, 2000.
86. Sean Murphy and Adam Piore, "A Big Roll at Mohegan Sun," *Boston Globe*, December 10, 2000.
87. NGISC, p. 6-3.

88. Francis X. Donnelly, "Tribes Squabble over the Profits," *Detroit News*, December 18, 2000.

89. Murphy and Piore, "Big Roll."

90. Goodman, *The Luck Business*, p. 118.

91. Paul Pasquaretta, "Modern Gambling Is Unlike Traditional Indian Games of Chance," in *Legalized Gambling: For and Against*, p. 353.

92. Quoted in Jon Magnuson, "White Unease about Indian Gambling May Reflect Nostalgic Imperialism," in *Legalized Gambling: For and Against*, p. 347.

93. Magnuson, p. 344.

94. Quoted in Goodman, *The Luck Business*, p. 119.

95. Goodman, *The Luck Business*, pp. 119-20.

96. James C. Dobson, open letter of April 1999, available at Focus on the Family Web site: www.family.org.

97. Sean Paige, "Gambling on the Future," *Insight*, December 22, 1997, p. 8; Pat Doyle, "The Casino Payoff: Tribal Spending Priorities Spark Debate," *Minneapolis Star Tribune*, November 3, 1998.

98. Tracey A. Reeves, "Gaming Companies Are Cozying Up to Tribes," *Philadelphia Inquirer*, March 16, 1997.

99. Alex Rodriguez, "Long Odds for Romeoville Casino Bid," *Chicago Sun-Times*, December 22, 1996.

100. Quoted in Goodman, *The Luck Business*, p. 120.

101. *How Gambling Ruins the Economy and Destroys Lives*, ed. Jennifer Vogel (Monroe, Maine: Common Courage Press, 1997), p. 32.

102. L. C. Pike, quoted in Goodman, *The Luck Business*, p. 95.

103. Robert Arnoud, an Iowa state representative, quoted in Goodman, *The Luck Business*, p. 97.

104. Cooper, p. 33.

105. Cooper, p. 30.

106. "Preliminary 1999 Gross Gambling Revenues by Industry and Change from 1998," *International Gaming and Wagering Business* (August 2000): 15.

107. Dick Foster, "Glitz vs. History," *Denver Rocky Mountain News*, November 12, 2000, p. 7A.

108. Hjelmeland, pp. 99-100.
109. Stephanie Saul, "Rural Renewal: But Poverty Persists as Casinos Thrive in Mississippi County," in *Crapped Out,* p. 50.
110. Hjelmeland, p. 100.
111. NGISC, p. 2-8.
112. Hjelmeland, p. 101.
113. John Gaskill, "Casino Road Living Up to Its Deadly Moniker," *Memphis Commercial Appeal,* December 18, 2000.
114. O'Brien, p. 113.
115. O'Brien, p. 113.
116. Robert Waterbury, "1996 Mississippi Coast Crime Statistics," Mississippi Coast Crime Commission, May 1997.
117. Information provided by the Eighth Circuit Court of South Dakota, November 12, 1997.
118. Joe Garner, "Influx of People and Money Spawns Crime," *Denver Rocky Mountain News,* November 12, 2000, p. 47A.
119. J. Joseph Curran, Jr., "The House Never Loses and Maryland Cannot Win: Why Casino Gaming Is a Bad Idea," Report of Attorney General J. Joesph Curran, Jr., on the Impact of Casino Gaming on Crime, October 16, 1995, p. 12.
120. NGISC, p. 2-7.
121. Both Illinois reports are documented in NGISC, pp. 2-7 and 2-8.
122. In Clinton, Iowa, 12 percent of the town's businesses witnessed an increase in trade following the mooring of a riverboat, while 29 percent reported a decrease and 60 percent no change (Cathy H. C. Hsu, "The Impact of Gambling on Iowa Tourism and Rural Businesses," Gambling and the Family Conference, Iowa State University, October 31, 1996). Gilpin County, Colo., home to the majority of the state's casinos, lost twenty retail businesses—from thirty-one down to eleven—within a couple years of the gambling halls' arrival (Patricia A. Stokowski, *Riches and Regrets: Betting on Gambling in Two Colorado Mountain*

Towns [Niwot: University of Colorado Press, 1996], p. 159). Over 70 percent of the Natchez, Miss., business community reported declining sales within a few months of that city's entry into the gambling market (Goodman, *The Luck Business*, p. 31). A mere 3 percent of business owners in Illinois riverboat casino towns were helped a great deal by the casinos, while more than half reported either a negative effect or none at all (J. Terrence Brunner, "Statement on Riverboat Gambling to the Metro Ethics Coalition Project," Better Government Association, October 1994).

123. Eighty-five percent of Illinois riverboat gamblers lived within fifty miles of the casino they patronized, according to one study (Ricardo C. Gazel, William N. Thompson, and J. Terrence Brunner, "Casino Gamblers in Illinois: Who Are They?" 1996, p. 7). Nearly 67 percent of the gamblers at a casino and racetrack near Des Moines were from the county, and 94 percent were from Iowa (Hsu, "The Impact of Gambling"). Two surveys of Kansas City casinos bore similar findings: in one, 88 percent of the gamblers at a casino lived forty-five minutes or less away (Rick Alm, "Taking a Chance on the Boats," *Kansas City Star Magazine*, June 30, 1996, p. 9); in the other, 94 percent of the cars in the lots bore Missouri or Kansas license plates (Anne Lamoy, "Kansans Leave Cash at Casinos," *Kansas City Star*, September 23, 1995, p. C1).

124. Quoted in Ray Parker, "Gambling Is Professor's Work," *Las Vegas Review-Journal*, February 19, 1997, p. 12A.

125. NGISC, p. 2-9.

126. NGISC, p. 2-7.

CHAPTER 14

1. Rex M. Rogers, *Seducing America: Is Gambling a Good Bet?* (Grand Rapids: Baker, 1997), p. 38.

2. Paul Simon, "Gambling Has High Social Costs and Should Be Restricted by the Government," in *Legalized Gambling: For and Against*, ed. Rod L. Evans and Mark Hance (Chicago and La Salle, Ill.: Open Court, 1998), p. 206.

3. Earline Rogers, testimony before the National Gambling Impact Study Commission, Chicago, Ill., May 30, 1998, cited in National Gambling Impact Study Commission Report, June 1999, p. 7-7; hereafter cited as NGISC.

4. NGISC, p. 7-5.

5. Robert Goodman, *The Luck Business: The Devastating Consequences and Broken Promises of America's Gambling Explosion* (New York: Free Press, Martin Kessler Books, 1995), pp. 6-7.

6. Associated Press, "Nevada Jobless Rate Falls to Lowest in History," February 3, 1999, cited in NGISC, p. 7-17.

7. Monica Caruso, "Economy Ends Year with Gains," *Las Vegas Review-Journal*, March 17, 1999, p. 1D, cited in NGISC, p. 7-17.

8. NGISC, p. 7-17.

9. Goodman, p. 7.

10. Above quotes are from Goodman, pp. 32-33.

11. Quoted in Dave Shiflett, "Gambling and Its Discontents," *American Spectator*, March 1999, p. 44.

12. Commission on the Review of the National Policy toward Gambling, "Gambling in America," 1976, p. 65.

13. William Rivenbark and Don Slabach, "Who Pays to Play? Voluntary Tax Incidence and Mississippi Gaming," Mississippi State University, John G. Stennis Institute of Government, July 1996, p. 33.

14. William Thompson, Ricardo Gazel, and Dan Rickman, "The Economic Impact of of Native American Gaming in Wisconsin," Wisconsin Policy Research Institute Report, April 1995, p. 23; U.S. Bureau of the Census, *Statistical Abstract of the United States: 1996*, 116th ed. (Washington, D.C., 1996), p. 465.

15. Pat Doyle, "Compulsive Gambling Hitting Poor Hardest, New State Study Says," *Minneapolis Star Tribune*, July 25, 1997, p. 1B.

16. John Warren Kindt, "Legalized Gambling Is Bad for Business," in *Legalized Gambling*, p. 136.

17. Kindt, p. 135.

18. Marc Cooper, "Casinos Destroy Industry and Rob the Poor," in *Legalized Gambling*, p. 91, emphasis Cooper's.

19. Goodman, pp. 28-29.

20. Peter Elkind, with Patty DeLlosa and Eileen P. Gunn, "The Big Easy's Bad Bet; How Does a Casino Become a Disaster? Mix Grandiose Dreams with Crazy Politics—and Set It All in Louisiana," *Fortune*, December 8, 1997; Alan Sayre, "Once Touted as an Economic Savior, State to Decide Whether to Kill Casino," Associated Press, December 5, 2000.

21. Kindt, p. 135.

22. Kindt, pp. 144-53.

23. Kindt, p. 152.

24. Goodman, p. 10.

25. Kindt, p. 132.

26. Kathy O'Malley and Hanke Gratteau, "Gamblin' Man: The Sky's the Limit," *Chicago Tribune*, January 15, 1990.

27. Kindt, p. 132.

28. Kindt, p. 132.

29. Associated Press, "Louisiana Boats Told: Get Moving," *Las Vegas Review-Journal*, August 11, 1997.

30. Keith Chrostowski and Rick Alm, "Betting Limit Hurts Riverboats, Commission Says," *Kansas City Star*, March 4, 1997, p. A1; Phil Linsalata and Fred W. Lindecke, "Gambling Bill Signed; Casinos May Roll on State Rivers as Early as This Fall," *St. Louis Post-Dispatch*, April 30, 1993, p. 1A; Ronald A. Reno, "False Hope," *Citizen*, June 23, 1997, pp. 10-13.

31. Goodman, p. 11.

32. Dick Foster, "Glitz vs. History," *Denver Rocky Mountain News*, November 12, 2000, p. 44A.

33. Patricia A. Stokowski, *Riches and Regrets: Betting on Gambling in Two Colorado Mountain Towns* (Niwot: University of Colorado Press, 1996), cited in Ronald A. Reno, "Gambling's 'Foot-in-the-Door' Approach to Growth," *Citizen Link*, February 23, 1998.

34. Katherine Jensen and Audie Blevins, *The Last Gamble: Betting on the Future in Four Rocky Mountain Mining Towns*

(Tucson: University of Arizona Press, 1998), p. 9, quoted in NGISC, pp. 7-17 and 7-18.

35. Goodman, p. 99.

36. Goodman, p. 99.

37. NGISC, p. 7-18, interior quote from Jensen and Blevins, p. 9.

38. SMR Research Corp., "The Personal Bankruptcy Crisis, 1997: Demographics, Causes, Implications & Solutions," 1997, p. 117.

39. Joseph P. Shapiro, "America's Gambling Fever," *U.S. News and World Report,* January 15, 1996, pp. 58, 60.

40. In the first six years of casino gambling in Minnesota, the crime rate in counties with casinos was more than twice that in those without (Dennis J. McGrath and Chris Ison, "Gambling Spawns a New Breed of Criminal," *Minneapolis Star Tribune,* December 4, 1995, p. A6). Crime shot up 43 percent on the Mississippi Gulf Coast in the four years after casinos' arrival (Robert Waterbury, "1996 Mississippi Coast Crime Statistics," Mississippi Coast Crime Commission, May 1997); up the big river a bit in Tunica County, the number of court cases vaulted from 689 in 1991, the year prior to the arrival of the casinos, to 11,100 in 1996 (Bartholomew Sullivan, "Once-Sleepy Tunica Awakens to Gambling-Inspired Crime," *Memphis Commercial Appeal,* October 20, 1997, p. A5). An average of over five thousand new Wisconsin crimes per year are attributed to the presence of casinos in that state (William N. Thompson, Ricardo Gazel, and Dan Rickman, "Casinos and Crime in Wisconsin: What's the Connection?" Wisconsin Policy Research Institute Report, November 1996); the average number of calls to the Ledyard, Conn., police department quadrupled, to 16,700 per annum, within five years of the opening of nearby Foxwoods casino (Mayor Wesley J. Johnson, Sr., "Fiscal Impacts of Foxwoods Casino on the Town of Ledyard, Connecticut," April 1997). Police in the Colorado mining towns that legalized casinos in the early 1990s have also been slapping cuffs on many more wrists

than they did before casinos came in—arrests shot up 275 percent in Central City in the year after the casinos arrived and 287 percent in Cripple Creek in the first three years (J. Joseph Curran, Jr., "The House Never Loses and Maryland Cannot Win: Why Casino Gaming Is a Bad Idea," Report of Attorney General J. Joseph Curran, Jr., on the Impact of Casino Gaming on Crime, October 16, 1995, pp. 9, 12).

41. Rachel A. Volberg, "Gambling and Problem Gambling in Iowa: A Replication Survey," Iowa Department of Human Services, July 28, 1995.

42. Matthew Fordahl, "Indictment Alleges Organized Crime Infiltration of Indian Casino," Associated Press, April 18, 1997.

43. Joe Gyan, Jr., "Book Closes on Mob Try to Infiltrate Louisiana Gambling," *Baton Rouge Advocate*, October 13, 1996, p. 1A.

44. Mike Soraghan, "Crime Ring Linked to Video Poker," *Charleston (S.C.) Post and Courier*, February 15, 1998, p. A1.

45. Chris Ison and Lou Kilzer, "Mafia Associates Had Ties to Five Casinos," *Minneapolis Star Tribune*, May 29, 1994, p. 1A.

46. Associated Press, "Skimming Scheme Overheard, FBI Agent Testifies at Detroit Trial," *Las Vegas Sun*, March 3, 1998, p. 6B; David Josar, "Defense Rests in Mob Trial," *Detroit News*, April 9, 1998, p. C2.

47. William Jahoda, statement before the House Judiciary Committee Hearing on the National Gambling Impact and Policy Commission Act, September 29, 1995.

48. Frank J. Fahrenkopf, Jr., letter to the editor, *Baton Rouge Advocate*, August 8, 1997, p. 8B.

49. "Casino/Gambling: Long-Term Contribution Trends," a chart available at www.opensecrets.org/industries/indus.asp?Ind=N07.

50. James C. Dobson, open letter of January 1999, available at Focus on the Family's website, www.family.org.

51. James C. Dobson, "The GOP—'Gambling's Own Party'?" *Citizen Link*, January 1999.

52. Shiflett, p. 43.

53. Office of the Secretary of State Ohio, Campaign Finance Department, cited in Ronald A. Reno, "Referenda Spending by the Gambling Industry," *Citizen Link*, February 23, 1998.

54. Rachel O'Neal, "Gambling Effort: $9.2 Million Bad Bet," *Arkansas Democrat-Gazette*, January 9, 1997, p. 1A.

55. Brad Cooper, "Gambling Interests Spend $10 Million on '96 Elections," *Shreveport Times*, January 21, 1997, p. 1B.

56. In referenda to either install casinos or broaden their purview, gambling interests easily outspent their opponents: by a tune of $1.7 million to $12,000 in Washington State (Rob Carson, "Voters Again Say No to Slot Machines," *Tacoma News Tribune,* November 6, 1996, p. B3); $16.5 million to $1.7 million in Florida (Michael Griffin, "Court Clears Way for Casino Vote in '96," *Orlando Sentinel Tribune*, June 9, 1995, p. C1); and $15.0 million to $395,000 in Missouri (Missouri Ethics Commission, "1994 Missouri Annual Campaign Finance Report").

57. Associated Press, "Greenbrier Spent Nearly $1.2 Million on Gambling Campaign," *Las Vegas Sun*, December 8, 2000.

58. Shiflett, p. 43; James C. Dobson, "Sounding the Alarm on Gambling," *Citizen Link,* June 1999.

59. Associated Press, "Election State-by-State," November 4, 1998.

60. Simon, p. 215.

61. Oscar Wilde, *The Picture of Dorian Gray* (1891), quoted in *The International Thesaurus of Quotations*, comp. Rhoda Thomas Tripp (New York: Thomas Y. Crowell, 1970), p. 633.

62. National Coalition against Legalized Gambling, "The Case against Legalized Gambling," last updated December 5, 2000, taken from the coalition's Web site, www.ncalg.org.

63. Rogers, p. 93.

64. *Casino Gambling: The Myth and the Reality* (Lansing, Mich.: Michigan Interfaith Council on Alcohol Problems, 1985), quoted in Rogers, p. 93.

65. Rev. John Landrum, telephone interview with author, August 30, 2000.
66. Rogers, p. 93.
67. Quoted in Simon, p. 209.
68. Thomas Grey, interview for *Frontline* TV show, 1998, available at www.pbs.org/wgbh/pages/frontline/shows/gamble/procon/igrey.html.
69. John Zipperer, "Christians Agree That Gambling Is a Sin," in *Legalized Gambling*, p. 23.
70. Ronald A. Reno, "Danger Ahead, Dad," *Citizen Link*, February 20, 1995.
71. Quoted in Zipperer, p. 24.
72. Marc Cooper, pp. 86-87.
73. Reno, "Danger Ahead, Dad."
74. Rogers, p. 84.
75. National Coalition against Legalized Gambling, "NCALG Crushes Gambling Advocates in 1996," November 6, 1996, available at www.ncalg.org/press-110696.htm.
76. National Coalition against Legalized Gambling, "Civil War against Slavery to Gambling Not Over, NCALG Director Warns," November 13, 2000, available at www.ncalg.org/new-11132000.htm.
77. Credit for this line goes to Michael Medved, who once said, on his radio talk show, that 80 percent of the nation couldn't agree that Elvis is dead.
78. Details and quotes from both the Alabama and South Carolina fights are from Ron Reno, "Guess Who Stopped the Gambling Juggernaut?" *Citizen*, n.d.

More Dicey Resources
From Focus on the Family ⊙

Victims of Gambling I-II

Gambling proponents have carefully camouflaged this dangerous activity as one that saves communities and helps the poor. Dr. James Dobson describes on this audiocassette the reality, which is completely different. You'll get a feel for this bitter reality by hearing guests describe their experiences as addicts, reaching the point of repentance and taking the road to recovery.

Gambling: You Can't Win I-II

The one sure bet about gambling is that you'll lose. It gradually deteriorates a player's attitude, spiritual well-being and quality of life—not to mention how it affects society as a whole. Dr. James Dobson discusses on this audiocassette the far-reaching implications of gambling and the addiction that accompanies it. Get ready to change lives by having biblically sound answers to this culturally driven force.

Gambling: Risky Business?

What's so bad about playing the slots? Or a little casino poker? More than meets the eye, if you'll look past the lure to the fallout. This 25-minute video exposes the game's explosive growth for what it really is. A Christian perspective, provided by host John Eldredge and guests including pastors and counselors, guides you to solid answers about this risky and addictive activity that's sweeping the nation.

• • •

Look for these tapes and video in your Christian bookstore or request a copy by calling 1-800-A-FAMILY (1-800-232-6459). Friends in Canada may write Focus on the Family, P.O. Box 9800, Stn. Terminal, Vancouver, B.C. V6B 4G3 or call 1-800-661-9800.

Visit our Web site (www.family.org) to learn more about the ministry or find out if there is a Focus on the Family office in your country.

Printed in the United States
84541LV00001B/94-399/A

3 4711 00179 9149